Performance, Monitoring and Evaluation in Leisure Management

Stephen Howell and Pat Badmin

PITMAN
PUBLISHING

in association with the Institute of Leisure and Amenity Management

PITMAN PUBLISHING
128 Long Acre, London WC2E 9AN

A division of Pearson Professional Limited

First published in Great Britain 1996

© Pearson Professional Limited 1996

British Library Cataloguing in Publication Data
A CIP catalogue record for this book can be obtained from the British Library.

ISBN 0 273 61624 2

10 9 8 7 6 5 4 3 2 1

Typeset by Phoenix Photosetting, Chatham, Kent
Printed and bound in Great Britain by Redwood Books, Trowbridge, Wiltshire.

The Publishers' policy is to use paper manufactured from sustainable forests.

Contents

Contents

Acknowledgements

The authors would like to acknowledge the generous assistance, advice and support they have received in writing this book.

Particular thanks are due to Pitman and the Institute of Leisure and Amenity Management, not only for their role in bringing this title to print but also for their collaborative efforts in the whole of their leisure management series.

We are indebted to Darlington Arts and Hambleton District Council who have provided a practical framework for the theories put forward.

We acknowledge the invaluable assistance of Joyce and Lynda in the compiling and editing of this text. To you all and many others, thank you. This book would not have been possible without you.

Crown copyright is reproduced with the permission of the Controller of HMSO.

Introduction

Back in 1978 before ILAM was formed and the ISRM was still the Institute of Baths Management a young gentleman by the name of Ted Blake spoke to the annual conference of the Association of Recreation Management. Ted can be classed as the 'grandfather' of recreational management and the question he put forward was,

> 'Why don't you devise an economic indicator as a measure of the public good you are doing'.

The provision of recreation was very much driven by the enthusiasm of local government reorganisation, joint provision, new leisure centres and social policy. There was much emphasis on equal access and positive discrimination towards the disadvantaged. At the time Ted's argument was that the balance of costs and subsidy against income and public social good was unknown. If recreation was to justify itself in the argument for resourses and for inclusion on political agendas then it would be necessary to clearly demonstrate the overall worth to the community; i.e. the 'good' needed quantifying in the form of what he called an 'economic indicator'.

This book is written for all those managers who did not listen then and those managers now who are required to respond to the pressures of Compulsory Competitive Tendering (CCT) and all that it has brought with it, i.e. objectivity, quantification, measurement, monitoring, analysis, evaluation, clients, contractors and specifications, etc. This book is about how to set up a performance, monitoring and evaluation system and the issues of implementing such a system.

The text is divided into three broad sections. Section 1 acts as a grounding in the performance, monitoring and evaluation (PME) culture. The reader is orientated to the world of performance monitoring. Its scope and limits are examined within a recreational context so as to leave the reader in no doubt as to what performance monitoring and evaluation encompass. Performance, monitoring and evaluation are shown to form an intergrated system and clear definitions regarding the process are given.

Within the same section the influences on the process are examined. Whilst these are ever changing the main influence of policy is examined in some detail and how to assimilate it into the process shown. Additionally the section also gives a basic introduction into the handling of data, the basic commodity of performance, monitoring and evaluation.

Armed with this information, the reader can more easily make use of Section 2, which deals with the more practical issues of 'How to measure it'. The section examines this under three further headings of financial, contract and usage monitoring, which echo the main concerns of performance in leisure enterprises today. All are present with the intention of providing managers with valid and reliable measures of the services they provide.

The final section concerns the implementation of such a performance, monitoring and evaluation system. It strongly implies that to implement the PME system is not only a technical issue but a human one. The problem is about people and organisations within which they work. To this end the final section provides a potted version of theories associated with the work contexts. It is essential that managers appreciate the ethos of their organisations so that they may decide on what's possible and impossible. It is only with such information that the manager can take a socio-political stance from which to implement change or in this case a PME system effectively. The section also provides a range of techniques which can be used to win over the employee to become involved and committed to the new system. The final part of the section examines the phases of implementation, viz:

- establishing a political stance
- analysis of the situation
- designing the change
- implementing the change
- evaluation.

The importance of involving employees in all the phases of the implementation process is emphasised, their participation and commitment is essential to any change if it is to be effective. The final chapter is strongly supported by further techniques to support situational analysis and the involvement of the employee in the project.

The text is liberally punctuated with diagrams, worked examples, illustrations, definitions and key points. The extensive Appendix further enriches the series of examples and techniques.

Section 1

This initial section of the text will introduce the reader to what performance, monitoring and evaluation aims to achieve. It will examine the role of PME in the leisure industry.

By locating the subject in a wider context the reader will be made aware of the issues which have made performance, monitoring and evaluation topical. The influences of the service sector, Citizen's Charter and compulsory competitive tendering will all be examined in relation to their part in the evolution of a performance culture.

A further chapter will examine the nature and collection of data. An ability to understand and handle data is a basic skill in the development of a PME system.

1

What is performance, monitoring and evaluation?

Introduction

The phrase 'performance, monitoring and evaluation' has been pushed to the front of leisure management thinking in recent years. It is the buzz phrase of current thinking particularly in local government leisure and recreation departments. In fact the process, of performance monitoring and evaluation has been around for a very long time and is a fundamental and essential part of managing any organisation.

This chapter has the purpose of introducing the reader to the idea of performance, monitoring and evaluation and more specifically provides an understanding of:

- the terminology and its definitions
- the basic ideas behind performance, monitoring and evaluation
- the inter-relatedness of the three aspects, and
- work examples.

Firstly it should be recognised that there are a number of technical words that need to be defined. If a particular territory of knowledge is to be fully understood it is necessary to be familiar with the jargon used. Computers and information technology are prime examples of this. From time to time in the text key definitions will be highlighted.

Definitions

Efficiency—the amount of useful work done in relationship to the total cost or energy expended.

Effective—to bring about or accomplish an objective or task.

Reliability of sound and consistent character—that is if something were to be tested under similar conditions results would be consistent i.e. the same.

Validity—that the test or measure adopted actually measures what it is supposed to measure.

It may be appropriate to expand on these raw definitions. Efficiency is a word that could be used to describe a head waiter in a restaurant because they always fuss about and keep the tables full with a quick turnaround of customers. This approach however may not be effective because the customers are always being fussed over and politely pressured to finish their meal. They want to have time to savour their food and have conversation. The headwaiter is failing to satisfy the customer who is unlikely to be a repeat visitor. If the business wishes to encourage repeat visits and build up a portfolio of clients the headwaiter is not being very effective.

Reliability and validity are two technical terms often associated with the undertaking of surveys in leisure centres. Ambiguous questions or ones that are difficult to understand may get different answers if they were asked of the same customers under similar conditions some time later. Validity refers to asking questions that will provide the information that is really wanted. For example the manager of a centre might want to know how effective his staff are. The manager might ask of customers 'do you like the member of staff that looks after your session of activities, yes or no'. Children might answer yes because the member of staff fools about with them, whilst adults might answer no because the staff member is always associated with noise and nuisance.

It is now possible to return to the main theme of the text to explain that performance, monitoring and evaluation form a process very often used to identify if an organisation is running efficiently and effectively. That process is required to be reliable and valid. It must ask the right questions about the running of the enterprise if it is to establish that it is efficient and effective in the way it is operated.

In its most simplistic form PME is based on the well established 'input, output' model. This was and still is used widely in the production sector of industry and is illustrated in Figure 1.1

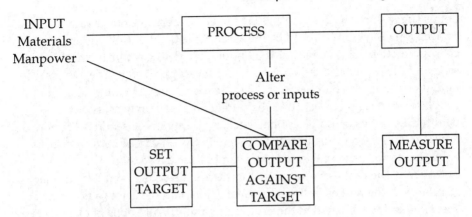

Figure 1.1 Simple input output model

The principle of the input output model, although it has its roots in the production of products is fully applicable to the service industry. Maybe the inputs are more complex and it might be that the outputs are less distinct but the principle is just the same. It should in addition be remembered that production processes can be much more complicated as well. Figure 1.2 illustrates how this might this be applied to a leisure enterprise.

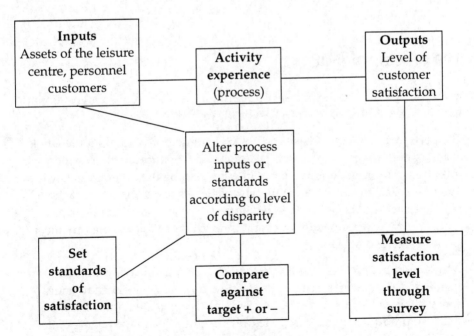

Figure 1.2 Input output model for leisure enterprise

Let us suggest that in this case it is customers' experience of a theatre production. The inputs would be the asset of the theatre itself and its condition; the personnel would be two fold. Firstly the actors themselves and secondly the front of house staff, technical and support staff. The customers would be those who had paid for tickets to see the performance. The standards that might be set could be purely on a take up of seats but qualitative ratings could be applied such as cleanliness of seating area and toilets and a scaled rating of satisfaction with the quality of performance. After the performance customers or a sample, are asked to measure their experience. The replies from the customers are then compared with the set standards. If the replies indicate dissatisfaction with the actors against what was expected it is likely that the performing group will not be booked again. If the feedback is such that there are indications that the auditorium was dirty then it would be wise for the management to investigate the cleaning schedules and identify who was responsible for the cleaning task. There may be a very good explanation as to why the auditorium was unclean. For example an early evening performance might have immediately followed a matinee which had over run its time. An oversight of the management and schedule adjustments will need to be made. Such difficulties are quite common in joint provision centres where community use takes over immediately after school use and special ad hoc cleaning arrangements are made.

The process of PME

In the above example the process of performance, monitoring and evaluation has been demonstrated and can best be illustrated in Figure 1.3.

The performance element has been not only the actors' output but the whole enabling of the experience for the customer. The monitoring has been the collection of information from customers concerning the experience they have purchased, and the evaluation reflects what levels of customer satisfaction have been achieved against expected or target satisfaction. Usually this process is cyclical; it operates over and through time which is the way most leisure experiences operate.

Why should the process of performance, monitoring and evaluation be installed? The answer is that all leisure industry enterprises need to know how well or badly their organisation is doing. Management must have the ability to produce a broad based picture of the health and well-being of the organisation they are managing. In the commercial sector this ultimately will

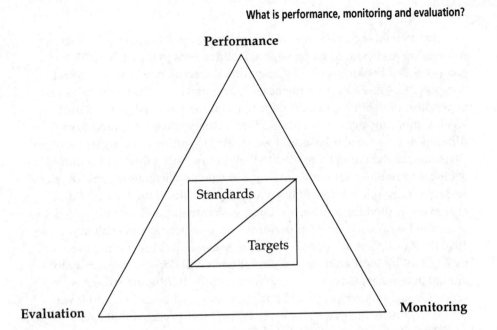

Figure 1.3 The process of performance, monitoring and evaluation

be reflected in the company accounts and the dividend that will be paid to shareholders. The voluntary sector club's account may show a surplus and members will give a sigh of relief as they recognise that subscriptions may not have to be increased for another year. In the local government sector matters are not so clear. Compulsory competitive tendering (CCT) has brought about two sets of clients. Clients or customers who come through the door of the leisure facility to enjoy the experience of taking part in an activity and the local government client/officer who sets the standards/targets to which the contractor/direct service organisation (DSO) is required to operate the leisure facility. Sometimes the two sets of client targets are compatible, at many centres they are divergent. The primary cause for divergence is the pressure on increasing income and decreasing costs so that the total subsidy paid by local government for leisure services is reduced. In the commercial sector there is a distinctive relationship between the customer and the resultant increased spend and frequency of visit, assuming good management. As suggested the output criteria of various stakeholders, i.e. managers, clients, customers shareholders or local government committee, can become complicated depending on the types of organisation. What is necessary is that a whole raft of performance, monitoring and evaluation processes underpin the final output measures so that managers fully understand the health of the organisation.

7

The commercial sector has had for a long time sophisticated performance, monitoring and evaluation processes. Holiday Inns in the early 1970s had a computerised booking and till system that linked all hotels into a central computer in America on a daily basis. Each hotel had a budget income and expenditure target by cost centre (bars, restaurant and beds) on a daily, weekly, monthly and annual basis. Hotel managers were required to explain differences on a regular basis and were party to setting new targets each year. Performance then directly related to their salary. Such target and standard setting was not just limited to finance and extended in considerable detail to such matters as cleanliness of linen, wattage of light bulbs, length of time customers waited for service, etc. Local government until recently was not as concerned with the process of performance, monitoring and evaluation. Pre-1990 the Audit Commission did produce some figures concerning the expenditure of local government departments. All departments produced annual budgets relative to past and future years. Furthermore there were ratios for such matters as subsidy per head per visit by facility and it was common knowledge that in the early 1980s it was expected that every swim in a pool was likely to be subsidised to the tune of a £1.

It can be concluded that the process of performance, monitoring and evaluation is not simple. Often the outputs are presented in simplistic terms such as shareholders' dividend as a single rate per pound, but such a figure hides a complicated raft of measurement and indicators which better reflect the organisation's health. It is too easy to take the measurement of numbers through the door as an index of success or failure. The component parts of the index or measure may be unfamiliar and new. How does one really quantify the quality of a service, what units of measurement should be adopted and will the process be valid and reliable?

Key point

Performance, monitoring and evaluation is usually an ongoing cyclical process which is designed to enable managers to understand the health of the organisation for which they are responsible.

Performance, monitoring and evaluation are buzz words which have now become common to those involved in the operating of contracts on behalf of a local authority. The jargon is familiar but not widely understood. The terms performance, monitoring and evaluation are loosely applied to various aspects of an organisation and often mistakenly used in an undistinguishable manner. These terms are not interchangeable. Each form part of a larger process and are individual specific tasks that may be associated with investigating the state of an organisation.

PME is an approach to investigating leisure organisations which underpins the type of management process shown in Figure 1.4.

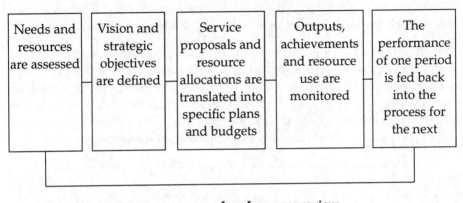

| Needs and resources are assessed | Vision and strategic objectives are defined | Service proposals and resource allocations are translated into specific plans and budgets | Outputs, achievements and resource use are monitored | The performance of one period is fed back into the process for the next |

Figure 1.4 The management process of performance review
Source: *Performance review in local government*, Audit Commission, HMSO 1988

In order to understand more exactly the nature of performance, monitoring and evaluation we need to examine each stage individually. In understanding the exact nature of these tasks we begin to appreciate the use of a logical, methodical approach to reviewing leisure organisations. In doing so we are more equipped to navigate the difficulties of making practical applications and reap the benefits of investigation from a solid footing. If only for reasons of clarifying the process it becomes essential to identify and define the specific elements of the approach.

Performance monitoring and evaluation defined

Performance

<u>Key point</u>
Performance is essentially the *doing* of the task.

If we refer to the earlier theatre visit example, performance relates to the front of house staff actually undertaking the tasks to prepare the auditorium and services for paying customers. The preparation of the auditorium would entail a number of tasks e.g. vacuuming carpets, emptying the ash trays, removal of litter, cleaning foyer, ensuring staff know their servicing tasks, ordering sufficient stocks of consumables, cleaning and organising the bar areas, cleaning the lines etc. All these tasks would have to be performed. You will notice that the emphasis is on the task being performed not on the manner in which it is being performed or at what quality it is being performed.

The identification of single aspects of performance is essential in the development of indicators and measures. The series of tasks or performances should be linked to objectives, targets or in a broader sense a purpose. A clear statement of purpose or objective helps the process. If there are to be no pieces of litter lying around it is clear what the objective is. If six pieces of litter are found it is clear that the task has been performed unsatisfactorily.

Definitions

Aims—the longer term more general purpose or direction of an organisation e.g. to provide leisure opportunities for disadvantaged members of the community at a subsidised rate.

Objectives—to achieve a specific target in a specific period of time e.g. to increase the number of children using the centre by ten per cent by 31 December 1996.

In a broader organisational sense, especially in local government departments it has been much more difficult to isolate clearly defined purposes or objectives which the organisation is attempting to achieve. Purposes are often hidden in generalities such as 'provide leisure opportunities for all members of the community'. The Audit Commission has concluded that matters are clearly unsatisfactory and has suggested that services should be assessed on their performance in the following areas:

- resources, both financial and human

- customers, how many and what type of customers use and do not use the service

- services provided, how many swimming pool, theatres etc. are provided, how long are they open, what activities do they run

- quality of service, subjective to many managers but it can be assessed satisfactorily

- ultimate results, the outcome or contribution to the quality of life. For leisure services, at least within local government, this is the primary reason or motive for the organisations existence and yet it remains the least addressed.

The indication from these suggestions is that the Audit Commission itself is having great difficulty in defining those tasks of performance that will make up a quality local government leisure service. It is at present going to be very much left to the leisure departments and managers of facilities to devise more definitive criteria which can be measured against task performance. The commercial sector to some extent are more fortunate because they are able to ditch the social and political purposes and measure their overall success by profit. Here there is a much closer link between customer satisfaction and the criteria of success.

Monitoring

Definition

Monitoring is the act of keeping regular surveillance, i.e. the regular collection of task performance indicators or measurements.

In the theatre visit example this might be the regular recording of numbers and types of seats sold for each performance. In the case of litter collection it would be the recording of found pieces of litter after cleaning. The position of the litter might be important if more than one cleaner was involved — as trivial as this might seem.

Commercial operators will regularly update records in what they determine as important, e.g. the number of people at each bingo session, the taking for the main events, secondary spend, levels of prize money, costs relative to income, etc.

This collection and recording of performance is often called data collection rather than the collection of information.

Definitions

Data is the collection and recording of raw scores or indices.

Information is that meaningful part of data which can be used for making managerial decisions.

This raises the importance of what is done with the data that is collected in the monitoring process. Prior to CCT, monthly budget statements always arrived on a manager's desk five weeks in arrears. Much too late to do anything with and therefore mainly useless data. Just note how that situation compares with the Holiday Inn approach mentioned earlier. The public sector has become much more realistic now. This raises the important issue of the form of the data and what is to be done with it. Within monitoring lies the debate on the type of data to be generated and how it is to be analysed, viz.:

- quantitative
- qualitative
- given to statistical calculation and analysis
- identification by exception
- the timing.

There are three broad areas of monitoring within the operation and management of leisure services:

- financial
- contractual
- usage.

Financial monitoring

Financial monitoring makes use of the techniques and methods that we may associate with management accounting. Such techniques are implemented to monitor the financial position of the organisation. This is essentially as a result of the need for accountability. Such accountability is a reality for both clients, who have a responsibility for the use of public money, and contractors whose operation and survival is dependent upon a financial return.

Contractual monitoring

Contractual monitoring is the process of ensuring that contractors are fulfilling their obligation to comply with the specifications of the contract. Such issues are unlikely to be of a financial nature. They are more likely to concern themselves with issues such as, is the pool water being kept at the temperature to which the contract specifies or is the required ratio of lifeguards to people in the pool being maintained at all times. Accountability is particularly important in the public sector because politicians need to be able to show that public monies are being spent in a proper manner and with a value for money ethic.

Usage monitoring

Usage is about monitoring the number of visitors that attend a particular facility or attraction. This might be reflected on a national scale for example with visits to National Trust properties or to an individual facility such as a hotel, cinema or leisure centre. The commercial sector will be more directly interested in income generated through primary and secondary spend. Local authority or contract run leisure centres will have similar agendas but there will in addition be qualitative and target market segments. For example, why has female or ethnic minority usage fallen or not reached its target? A good recent example of usage monitoring is that visits to swimming pools have fallen nationally by six per cent (ISRM Circular, January 1995). This is not necessarily linked to income but could have serious consequences for contracted out leisure facilities. Simplistically the blame is put down to the recession but it may be more complicated than that e.g. price increases and inelasticity, broader range of options, local management of schools, etc.

Usage monitoring can often be applied on a temporary basis and can be linked to policy changes. For example detailed monitoring could be initiated before and after a price change to measure the impact of that change; or specific monitoring could be targeted at the effectiveness of a promotional and advertising campaign.

Evaluation

Definition

Evaluation is the process by which the worth of a measure is judged or accessed.

This is the element of the performance, monitoring and evaluation process where it is decided if something is doing well or not. In order to do this there is a requirement to have a basis of comparison. There is a need to have targets or benchmarks against which comparisons might be made. It is important to note that if comparisons are to be made then it must be like with like. For example there is little to be gained by comparing attendance at a pool in the six months of summer with the six months of winter. Comparing summer with summer or winter with winter can only be meaningful providing all other factors are equal i.e. the pool was not shut for one month over Christmas in one case. The following might form a basis:

- over time, one year of performance against a previous year

- against a specific standard in a contract

- comparison with a target set by experience or judgement — particularly useful when starting with an initial programme of activities or an event for the first time.

The evaluation stage of the process reflects the operational or decision making functions of the organisation. At this stage managers are presented with the results of the monitoring process. This information may be in the form of an income and expenditure statement, a financial ratio, a level of cleanliness, number and type of users or any other form of information that has been deemed necessary. What the manager is required to do is make operational decisions based on this information which requires a basis of comparison.

Putting the process together

A simplistic approach to performance, monitoring and evaluation might look like the model shown in Figure 1.5.

Unfortunately it is rare to be able to take such a simplistic stance and each specific performance, monitoring and evaluation process is related to others which themselves are set in a conflicting range of social, political and economic policies and issues. It is therefore necessary to construct a more complex model as seen in Figure 1.6.

The model in Figure 1.6 shows the process of performance, monitoring and evaluation in more detail. To the left of the diagram the three stages of performance, monitoring and evaluation are indicated. To the right are shown the level of organisational functioning i.e. strategic, technical and operational.

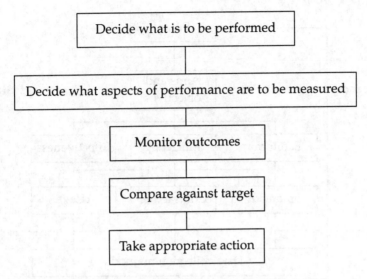

Figure 1.5 Simple performance, monitoring and evaluation model

The strategic plans of an organisation will develop policies from which aims and objectives derive. For example a local authority might make the strategic decision that leisure subsidies will only be targeted at the disadvantaged and that everyone else should pay a true cost for the leisure experience. Policies would have to evolve to classify the disadvantaged, their level of subsidy, the true cost of experiences and a pricing model. From this it would be possible to construct objectives and targets which would act as benchmarks for operational performance. It is probable that within the context of local government these benchmarks of performance would fall into financial, contractual and usage monitoring categories.

Having established the objectives the tricky stage arrives of deciding how levels of performance can be measured or indicated. This brings another distinction which is important to the PME process.

Definitions

Performance measures are units of a precise nature such as number of children viewing an event.

Performance indicators are less precise measurements. They are suggestive rather than precise, e.g. an index of variable satisfaction.

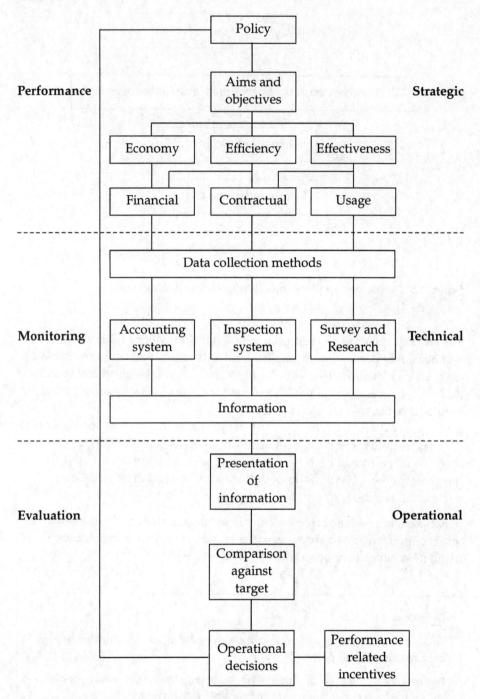

Figure 1.6 Complex performance, monitoring and evaluation process

Performance measures might best be illustrated by monetary measurement in a commercial organisation which will refer to its profits over the year or last quarter. Local government leisure facilities do use performance measures e.g. number of children swimming by day or week but facility management success or failure might be linked to political aims and objectives which are more difficult to measure. There might be some measures of customer satisfaction over time on a scale of 1 to 9. Varying circumstances such as weather, time of day or changes in staff would make the results of such a measure less reliable and would therefore be regarded as a performance indicator. Both types of measure would alert management to changes but the performance measure, the cash takings that day would be precise. The interpretation of the performance indicators may be more circumspect. For example a five-a-side soccer event might have been outside in the rain giving a low indicator rating, but there is a sensible reason beyond the control of the manager and it would be unlikely for a manager to get worried unless the trend of ratings remained low over time.

It is therefore important that leisure facility managers should be clear about whether they are constructing or dealing with performance indicators or performance measures. It relates back to what the operational objectives are and how and what data should be collected so that the level, success, or failure of the operation can be monitored. This will relate directly to the block marked accounting system, inspection system and survey and research in Figure 1.6.

Operations proceed and performance measures and indicators are collected. This monitoring process can collect huge amounts of data which can be in the form of a weighty computer print out of which 99 per cent is useless. In the past such volumes of material were dumped on the manager's desk for evaluation. It therefore becomes important as to how this data should be presented to management as information which is related to the decision making process. It is the presentation of this data relative to the basis of comparison that is the heart of evaluation. Material or information should only be presented on the basis of operational matters which might require decisions. Underlying evaluation is the concept of management by exception. Managers do not need or want to know about the 95 per cent of things going right; they want to know about the five per cent of operations going wrong. Computers can be programmed and personnel instructed only to react to performance which is within ten per cent of target. Management time and effort is then concentrated on matters of importance and decision rather than reading through volumes of computer print out.

It can be seen that PME is rather more than a simple input output model and Figure 1.6 has developed the level of integration and complication.

17

Activity

Consider your own organisation or one with which you are familiar and examine it within the following context.

- Does your organisation collect data?

- Is the information transformed into information?

- Is the data collected for particular reasons? If so what are the reasons?

- Is the data valid and reliable?

- Is the information in the form of performance indicators or measures?

- Would you say that the organisation that you are considering has a comprehensive performance, monitoring and evaluation process?

- What performance indicators and measures do you individually collect?

The role and scope of PME

The commercial sector has always had a strong interest in monitoring the success or failure of their businesses. They concentrate on performance measurement rather than indicators and often take drastic action if the health of the organisation is weak through rapid cost cutting exercises and shedding of staff. The local government leisure sector was less concerned with monitoring performance until the introduction of CCT. Even within this context the performance is often centred on the bottom line rather than the various activities that contribute to the bottom line. Certainly CCT has focused attention and some councils have written detailed specifications for activities that have been required in reaching the bottom line. In reality all professionally run businesses in both the commercial and private sector should have well run performance, monitoring and evaluation processes. It is now even more important that local government establish and operate comprehensive PME processes. There are five broad areas where performance monitoring in local government leisure departments can make a significant contribution:

■ Strategy and policy — in allowing an organisation to assess its arrangements for achieving strategic aims and enabling new policies to be formed

■ Equity — in giving managers the ability to ensure that services are fairly distributed amongst all segments of the community. A role which has gained increased importance since the introduction of CCT:

- Quality — the continual maintenance and improvement of standards

- Operational ownership — managers who possess a broader based picture of an organisation are better positioned to influence decision making and control over the organisation

- Planning — preparing for the future is a simpler process when there is good quality information about current operations and the recent past.

It is clear that having valid and reliable information in the areas above must be good management practice. It gives good general information which can support strategic, political and social developments. In addition many of the techniques that would be adopted are essential for the day to day operation of any facility e.g. takings by cost centre, number of visitors, complaints recording, safety reports and working hours of full and part-time staff, etc. It becomes possible to detect absentee rates and take necessary actions. It enables managers to ask the right questions. From such patterns of information and experience over time it allows managers to debate and set realistic targets for which they can be held responsible. There is the danger that poor PME systems are set up with insufficient thought, little reliability and validity in which case inaccuracies and confusion will arise.

The Audit Commission (*Performance Review in Local Government*, 1988) recognise four main arguments that were forwarded by managers not wishing to develop comprehensive monitoring systems. viz:

- out dated management attitudes i.e. managers unable to move with the times

- poor existing arrangements, organisation and procedures

- failure to introduce performance review systems on the basis of expense

- poor understanding of the measurement process.

The above have fundamentally been used as excuses for not introducing performance review systems into local government leisure departments. Such reasoning is weak and effort needs to be made to establish a knowledge base and adopt a structured logical approach to developing a performance, monitoring and evaluation process. In order to construct such a review system a manager needs to primarily draw on the skills from three study areas: management accounting, social science and statistics. It will be necessary to begin by establishing the purpose and direction of the organisation and developing policies upon which objectives and targets can be set. It will than be necessary to establish a web of performance measures and indicators that will provide reliable and valid data for presentation and evaluation relative to targets. Regular review of both the information and performance review mechanisms will provide the manager with a process by which the organisation can be moved towards greater effectiveness and efficiency. In the commercial sector this will mean increased profit, in the public sector the equation of better value for money should be achieved.

Conclusion

Readers should now have a reasonable knowledge and understanding of what performance, measurement and evaluation means and how it operates as an integrated process. There follows a series of statements with which the reader should now be familiar.

LEARNING POINTS

- Simplistically, PME is an input output model.
- PME is related to standards and targets and has a cyclical nature (Figure 1.3).
- The PME process is necessary to gauge the health of an organisation.
- The process of PME should apply to all types of organisation; voluntary clubs, commercial businesses and local government leisure departments.
- PME is usually an ongoing cyclical process which is designed to enable managers to understand the health of the organisation for which they are responsible.
- PME is not a new idea and has become more well known because of CCT and the requirement to reduce costs.
- It is relatively easy to measure performance in a commercial organisation by profit. It is more complex in leisure departments because of political and social elements that are difficult to quantify.
- Financial monitoring, contractual monitoring and usage monitoring are the three broad areas of concern in leisure enterprises.

■ Integrating PME into a more complicated process is shown in Figure 1.6.

■ The five broad areas where PME can make a significant contribution to the operation of a local government leisure department are strategy and policy, equity, quality, operational ownership and planning.

REFERENCES AND FURTHER READING

Audit Commission (1988) *Performance Review in Local Government,* A handbook for auditors and local authorities, HMSO

Department of the Environment Audit Inspectorate (1983) *Development and Operation of Leisure Centres,* selected case studies, HMSO

Jackson, P. and Palmer (1989) *First Steps in Measuring Performance in the Public Sector: a Manager's Guide,* Public Finance Foundation

Stabler, M. J. (1984) *The Use of Performance Indicators in the Management of Sports Centres, an economic view,* University of Reading

2

Influencing and shaping performance, monitoring and evaluation

Introduction

It has already been shown that performance, monitoring and evaluation *is* directly related to the aims and objectives of an organisation. Like most organisations, leisure has a number of influences which shape and throw emphasis upon what is important within the industry. These influences have a direct effect upon the PME process.

This brief chapter is intended to give to the reader an insight into the influences which act as the catalyst of the performance, monitoring and evaluation process.

Key point

Performance, monitoring and evaluation in a leisure enterprise should be a reflection of the intent and purpose of the organisation.

Figure 2.1 below shows some of the influences on leisure enterprises that effect the performance, monitoring and evaluation process. Not every leisure enterprises will be influenced by all those suggested. This will depend upon a combination of the organisation's public or private sector ownership and operational environment.

Highlighting these issues is not an academic exercise as they have practical implications regarding the development of a reliable and valid PME process.

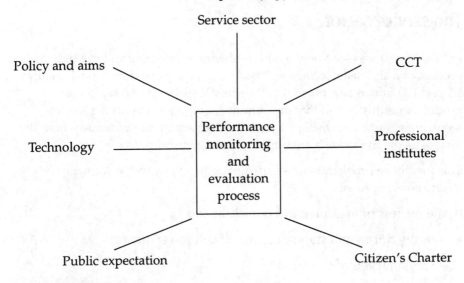

Figure 2.1 Influences on leisure enterprise PME

Familiarity with the issues will make the problems of implication more apparent. The main influences on performance, monitoring and evaluation in leisure enterprises include:

- being part of the service sector
- the influence of local government
- the influence of central government
- the economic environment
- technology
- the development of indicators and indices.

The above influences determine:

- what aspects of performance are measured, and
- how they are measured.

For example the priority given to disabled sport will be determined at a local level. Depending on the priority assigned a measure may or may not be devised to determine levels of participation. As such local policy determines what is included in the process. Conversely, the Audit Commission, as part of the Citizen's Charter for example, dictate not only what is to be measured but also how it is to be measured, setting out specific measures and how they are to be determined.

The service sector

In Chapter 1 it was seen how the performance, monitoring and evaluation process, in a simplistic form, was based upon an input output model (Figures 1.1 and 1.2). It was also noted that the roots of such a model lay in the production industry and that the outputs for organisations in the service sector were much less distinct. Leisure enterprises by nature reside within the service sector and as such are subject to intangible outputs.

This presents a problem to those attempting to review the performance of leisure enterprises as:

- the process of measurement is difficult and
- Industry norms and standards are difficult to set due to

  —varying levels of provision

  —varying management and political priorities.

To demonstrate these points consider the purpose of the following leisure enterprises. If performance review is to reflect these it requires:

- a basis of measurement
- a basis of evaluation.

The purposes given below are examples suggested by the Audit Commission (1990), they also help to highlight the nuances that may be associated with performance review in a number of different section of the leisure industry.

Sports centres and pools

Purpose

To contribute to the quality of life in the local area and to promote health and alleviate depravation through stimulating and responding to public demand for sport by

- ensuring that residents have access to sports centres and swimming pools
- ensuring that sports centres/swimming pools are targeted on the largest practical customer base
- targeting groups of users, perhaps through a 'passport' scheme
- maintaining health and safety standards
- ensuring that the service provided is cost effective and that revenues are optimised

---

Entertainment and tourism

Purpose

To enhance the quality of life for residents, and to increase the attraction of the area for visitors and potential business by:

- providing and supporting theatres, cinemas, special events, play schemes and shows, in accordance with council policy
- encouraging the development of attractions for visitors
- publicising entertainment to ensure that as many potential customers as possible are aware of the service
- co-ordinating the programme of entertainment's to support other council and local initiatives
- obtaining sponsorship for events
- supporting local providers of entertainment's

Parks and open spaces

Purpose

To contribute to the quality of life of residents and others through:

- ensuring that all residents and visitors are aware of park and open space amenities
- ensuring access of residents and visitors to parks and open spaces
- organising events and consider targeting on special need groups, for example younger or elderly people
- ensuring that the standards of maintenance of parks and open spaces are adequate
- ensuring that the service provided is cost effective

Key point

The less defined an organisation is in terms of its purpose the more difficult it will prove to monitor.

Whilst for some purposes, for example cost-effectiveness, it will be relatively easy to provide measures. Other concepts such as 'the quality of life' will require an element of judgement and creativity in the provision of a measurement instrument.

> **Key point**
>
> Being part of the service sector imposes a level of judgement as to what should be measured and how.

The local situation is highly influential in leisure organisations. As a result the purpose and aims will vary from situation to situation and the process of delineating them into observable entities will also have to take place at a local level.

The ability to undertake the transition from vague intangible aims and policies to reliable and valid measures requires a structured thought process if it is to succeed.

Thinking it through — from concept to indices

In order to bring about measures of service, it is necessary to first decide what is to be measured. What are the key elements of the service? The purpose of a number of types of leisure organisation have already been examined and it was stated that any performance, monitoring and evaluation process should be a reflection of the intent and purpose of the organisation.

The 'purpose' whether expressed as policy, aims or objectives is therefore what requires measuring. A brief examination of the purposes outlined in Figure 2.1 shows this to be no simple task. Many of the purposes are associated with intangible items or imagery. For example 'the quality of life' and 'deprivation'.

These intangible items need to be rendered observable if they are to form part of the performance, monitoring and evaluation process. Many ideals associated with the provision of leisure experiences, such as 'public good, 'recreational welfare', 'quality leisure experiences', etc. are difficult to pin down. Yet it is essential to do so if they are to be incorporated into the process.

It therefore becomes necessary to conceptualise these issues.

> **Definition**
>
> Concepts: categorisation on the basis of common properties or qualities, which help to simplify and contain the detail of an environment.

Key point

To be of use in the performance, monitoring and evaluation process, concepts associated with the organisation's purpose must have empirical indicators.

In the monitoring of leisure enterprises, concepts often require measurement via either questionnaire or observation methods. Both common features of the performance , monitoring and evaluation process.

The concepts which leisure enterprises will deal with are numerous and will depend upon many influences. What is required is a method or scheme which can be used fairly universally to translate concepts into observable items.

Lazarsfeld's scheme for measuring concepts allows this process to take place. The scheme suggests four steps as shown in Figure 2.2.

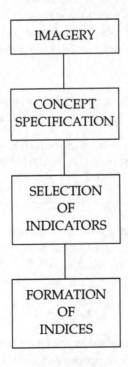

Figure 2.2 Lazarsfeld's concept measuring model

> **Key point**
>
> Lazarsfeld's approach to measuring concepts is equally as useful for establishing the validity of measures when used in reverse.

To demonstrate how the process works consider the following example regarding the development of indices to monitor a local government leisure service.

In the first instance a certain imagery will exist about a particular element or facet of the organisation. Let's say in this instance its notions of local government leisure services as portrayed by public good and recreational welfare. The next stage is to breakdown this imagery into some component parts, i.e. what concepts are contained within the image of local government leisure services? It is at this stage that an organisation's mission statement may be of assistance to the process. A mission statement can give a focused insight into the purpose of a leisure enterprise, what it's about, what it intends to do. Whilst often brief, the mission statement is usually the result of a long and informed discussion which provides a rich source of information as to why the organisation exists. The problem is essentially to take this kind of statement and produce indices which reflect the notions and concepts contained within them.

> **Key point**
>
> The task of producing indices from concepts is one of great responsibility. The success or failure of a service may be determined by the resulting indices.

The mission statement brings about concept formulation. Examination of any such statement allows for the identification of a number of concepts contained within. These can be both:

- implicit
- explicit.

For the large part these are explicit as the thought process involved in developing a mission statement produces a level of concept formulation. Examples in this instance may include:

- community

- opportunity

- excellence.

Other concepts may remain implicit or implied, i.e. the following statement, 'offering opportunity for participation to all sectors of the community' may be seen as implicit of the concept of equity. What is important is to identify a number of component 'concepts' which make up the initial imagery.

The third stage is central to the process, and involves identifying 'indicators' or signposts to the concepts under investigation. For example, the concept of 'opportunity' has been identified. The question to ask is what is a fair indicator of opportunity, i.e. what can be observed to assess if opportunity is present or not?

The fourth and final stage requires identifying scales or scoring mechanisms by which indices are then produced as demonstrated in Figure 2.3.

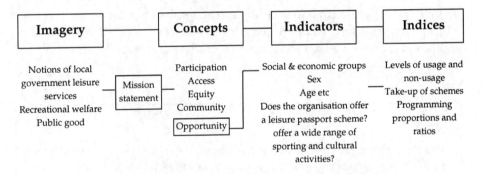

Figure 2.3 Lazarsfeld scheme for measuring concepts applied to a local government leisure department

The Citizen's Charter

The Citizen's Charter is a government initiative aimed at improving levels of public service. The Charter hopes to make public services respond better to the needs of their customers and improve the efficiency and effectiveness of those services.

The Charter has had two main effects on performance, monitoring and evaluation in the leisure sector:

- encouraged a performance culture

- stipulation of given measures.

The principles upon which the Citizen's Charter has based public service include:

- standards
- information and openness
- choice and consultation
- courtesy and helpfulness
- putting things right
- value for money.

At the same time the Charter is about empowering the citizenry. Giving the citizen a voice in the delivery of the services that they pay for. An integral part of that empowerment is the giving of information regarding the performance of services.

As part of this process the Charter requires all local authorities to publish information regarding the performance of its services. Leisure is no exception to this and the Charter indicates a number of areas on which information must be published.

Key point

The statutory requirement to publish information regarding levels of service makes a performance, monitoring and evaluation system mandatory for local government services.

Key point

The Citizen's Charter allows the citizenry to play an active part in the evaluation of leisure services.

Whist the Citizen's Charter has been criticised for producing indicators and measures which do not truly represent the work of leisure departments, the mandatory requirement to examine performance may be seen as increasing interest in the performance, monitoring and evaluation process in leisure provision (see Figure 2.4).

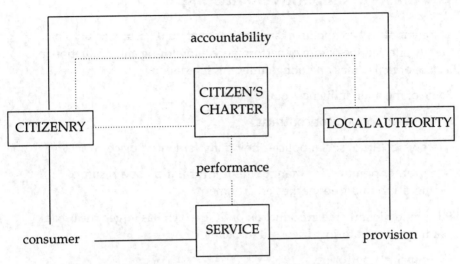

Figure 2.4 The Citizen's Charter as a mediator of performance

Increasing public expectations

The Citizen's Charter is part of a movement which is demanding high standards of public services and has encouraged the public to expect increasingly higher standards.

Key point

Public expectations regarding levels of leisure provision are on the increase.

The satisfaction of a customer is based upon expectation. Real satisfaction is attained when expectation is surpassed. Only through a comprehensive system of performance, monitoring and evaluation can leisure managers hope to stay ahead of the game regarding public expectation.

A performance, monitoring and evaluation system can give insights into:

- actual levels of service
- expected levels of service, i.e. what people want.

Compulsory competitive tendering

The compulsory competitive tendering of sport and leisure facilities has greatly affected the nature of performance, monitoring and evaluation in leisure organisations operating under this legislation.

Some of the main influences of CCT include:

- the need to monitor contracts
- stewardship of social policies being implemented by contractors
- a greater demand for management information as a result of operating in a free market environment.

It is predominantly the introduction of CCT which has forged the broad headings of monitoring discussed in Chapter 1 of:

- financial monitoring
- usage monitoring
- contractual monitoring.

CCT has assisted in developing the performance, monitoring and evaluation process by:

- giving justification to the allocation of resources to the performance, monitoring and evaluation task
- concentrating attention on a monitoring role
- clarifying aims and objectives.

Many leisure departments now have sections or officers assigned to the monitoring of sport and leisure management contracts. Whether they reside in a client or agency department they represent a huge increase in the resources allocated to this task.

The result of this is that officers are more capable of applying themselves to the task. The initial justification on legal grounds to monitor contracts, i.e. the stewardship of public funds, has in many cases been surpassed. The nurturing of a performance culture has broadened the role and scope of PME in leisure organisations.

The very nature of CCT has forced local authorities into defining in more detail their policies, aims and objectives concerning leisure. This proved an essential part of putting the service out to tender. Without clear guidelines as to the service's purpose, the writing of specifications becomes more difficult.

Whilst criticism is levied that such statements are still of a qualitative and subjective nature and written without the concern for the development of services, the focus of attention onto policy, aims and objectives and therefore clarification, has to be seen as a benefit to the performance, monitoring and evaluation process.

Key point

Policy, aims and objectives are the root of the performance, monitoring and evaluation process.

LEARNING POINTS

- Performance, monitoring and evaluation are related to the aims and objectives of an organisation.

- Performance, monitoring and evaluation should reflect the intent and purpose of an organisation.

- There are numerous influences on the process in leisure organisations (Figure 2.2).

- Industry norms and standards are difficult to set due to varying levels of provision.

- The less defined an organisation is in terms of its purpose the more difficult it will prove to monitor.

- Being part of the service sector imposes a level of judgement on what should be monitored and how.

- To be of use concepts must have imperial indicators.

- The requirement to publish indicators under the Citizen's Charter makes performance, monitoring and evaluation mandatory in local government leisure services.

- Public expectation regarding levels of service is on the increase.

- The need to monitor sport and leisure contracts has lifted the profile of performance, monitoring and evaluation in leisure organisations.

REFERENCES AND FURTHER READING

Audit Commission, 1990, *Leisure, Performance Review Supplement, Implementation Guide*, HMSO, pp 1–5

Benington, J. and White, J. (eds) (1988) *The Future of Leisure Services*, Longman

Bryman, A. (1989) *Quality and Quantity in Social Research*, contemporary social research series, Unwin and Hyman Ltd

HMSO (1992) *The Citizen's Charter*, First report, HMSO

Lazarsfeld, P. (1958) 'Evidence and inference in social research', *Daedalus*, vol 87, no. 4 pp 100–130 1958

3

Data and data analysis

Introduction

Today's leisure manager is heavily involved in the tasks of planning, controlling and undertaking performance review. Through this involvement leisure managers find themselves with masses of data from varying sources. They require a method of simplifying data with the least loss of meaning, so that it may be used in decision making. This chapter is intended to familiarise leisure managers with the structure of data to enable better use of data sets.

Definitions

Data: the raw scores or material as collected.

Information: data which has been translated, by some form of analysis, so as to be meaningful to the performance process.

Leisure managers responsible for the production of information need to give consideration to the quality of that information, whether it is for their own consumption or for distribution internally or externally to the organisation.

Key point

Data is the basic commodity of performance, monitoring and evaluation. It is the result of the monitoring process.

Whilst usually of a quantitative nature data may also be qualitative. What is essential, is that leisure managers understand that all data is not the same and can not be treated in a similar manner. A greater understanding of the form, nature and use of various types of data can only assist in aiding the validity of the management processs.

The need for leisure managers to understand the nature of data is important. Providing indicators and measures on not only financial but also contractual and usage issues, means dealing with many different forms and types of data. The possibility of making a wrong application is obviously increased when dealing with such a wide array of data forms.

In accepting the responsibility of performance review, leisure managers begin to broaden the scope of their work. As mentioned earlier the skills required of performance review are multi-disciplinary calling on the skills of the management accountant, the social scientist and the statistician.

Leisure managers are often familiar with figures in an accounting or monetary context, but they need to step into the realms of social science and statistics. However a basic understanding of how to handle various forms of data is all that is required to allow most leisure managers to tackle with confidence these areas of their work.

There is no great secret to handling data, only a few simple rules which must be observed. Such rules give consideration to how data is collected, the type of data obtained and how it is analysed once obtained. First consider what is meant by data.

Data

In the world of performance review data can take on many forms. It may come as a surprise to some that numerical or quantitative data is not all that may be classed as data. In the performance process, data may also be words or pictures as well as figures.

The use of numerical data in the process of performance review is common. Financial recording is a good example, but in monitoring contracts and examining usage a broader understanding of how to handle data is necessary. As a result of the intangible nature of the outputs often given by leisure organisations, descriptive data can assist in the process. Other media such as photographs can also play a part in demonstrating aspects of performance, such a levels of cleanliness, with more meaning than either numeric or discourse information is capable of achieving.

It is the handling of numerical data which is likely to present the leisure manager with the greatest challenge. This chapter will therefore examine the use of this data for performance review in leisure organisations. The use of qualitative data will not be omitted and will be discussed at the end of the chapter. In arranging the chapter in such a manner it is not the intention to lead the reader into underestimating the use of qualitative data by assigning it a footnote position. Essentially the techniques and rules of use are greater for quantitative data and will therefore require a longer explanation. As to the pragmatic application of quantitative and qualitative data, they should be treated on level terms.

Types of numerical data

It is helpful for a manager to understand the different types of data and how it can be analysed. There are essentially four types of data, which are arranged in a hierarchical order (see Figure 3.1).

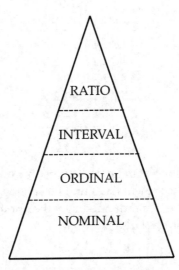

Figure 3.1 The data hierarchy

Nominal data

> **Definition**
>
> Nominal level data is that in which the values act merely as labels.

For example in a survey of usage at a golf course, the sex of the players may be obtained and assigned a code of 1 for Males and 2 for Females. With such data the size of the number is irrelevant, 2 is not greater than 1 and conversely neither is 1 greater than 2. In fact they have no relative value. Analysis of this lowest form must be given consideration before proceeding. For example three types of users at a leisure centre, dry sports, wet sports and non-sports, have been coded in a survey as 1, 2 and 3 respectively. In this instance even the simple technique of addition is not possible 1 + 2 does not equal 3. Whilst addition would be unlikely in this case, an oversimplified example serves to demonstrate the dangers faced when handling nominal level data.

For example, a leisure centre carries out a survey to find out where its users come from. The catchment area contains three towns A'ton, B'ton and C'ton. The surveyor selected a sample of users and asked them from which town they came and coded them 1, 2 and 3 respectively. The results concerning location were as follows using a sample of 100.

$$
\begin{array}{l}
1\,2\,3\,3\,1\,2\,1\,3\,1\,3 \\
1\,2\,1\,3\,3\,1\,2\,2\,1\,3 \\
1\,3\,2\,3\,1\,3\,1\,2\,1\,2 \\
3\,1\,2\,3\,1\,2\,1\,3\,1\,2 \\
3\,1\,2\,1\,2\,3\,2\,2\,3\,2 \\
1\,3\,1\,2\,2\,2\,1\,2\,3\,1 \\
2\,3\,2\,3\,1\,2\,3\,1\,2\,3 \\
3\,1\,2\,1\,2\,3\,1\,2\,3\,3 \\
1\,3\,2\,1\,2\,3\,2\,1\,1\,2 \\
1\,1\,3\,1\,2\,3\,1\,1\,2\,3
\end{array}
$$

Having carried out the survey and obtained the raw data set above the manager wished to analysis the data to find the average user. To do this he took the values added them and divided by n the number of values, hence attempting to convert the data into information by:

$$
\begin{aligned}
1 &= 41 \times 1 = 41 \\
2 &= 33 \times 2 = 66 \\
3 &= 26 \times 3 = 78
\end{aligned}
$$

$$\text{TOTAL} = 185$$

$$\frac{185}{n100} = 1.85$$

From the analysis the manager concluded that the average user must live close to or on the outskirts of B'ton as 1.85 was nearest to 2 the code for B'ton.

The above analysis is completely misleading. The manager has made the fundamental mistake of applying a technique that requires a higher level of data to operate. In the above example the manager has used the technique of averaging known as the mean when he should have used a technique known as the mode which highlights the most frequently occuring value — 1 which apears 41 times and shows A'ton to be the town from which the most users come.

This fairly frivolous example demonstrates how a simple well known technique can be misused. In isolation it would not be expected to make such an obvious mistake, but such data and analysis is often embodied in larger data sets and forms only part of a larger analysis not as unclouded as this distinct example. If however the results of such surveys are to form part of the policy development process and have budgetary and resource allocation consequences the lesson of this simple example could avoid a serious misjudgement.

Ordinal level data

The next level of data is that of ordinal or ranked scales.

Definition

Ordinal data: the relative magnitude of values can be demonstrated by ranking in ascending or descending order.

The main difference from nominal level data is that ordinal data gives some insight into the relative magnitude which the numbers represent. A good example of this is the positions of a race. For example the result of the 5000 metre Olympic final of 1956 reads as follows:

> 1st Vladimir Kuts USSR
> 2nd Gordon Pirie GB
> 3rd Derek Ibbotson GB

From such a results list we can establish that Kuts was faster than Pirie and Ibbotson, and that Pirie was quicker than Ibbotson. What we are unable to tell from the placing alone is how much better Kuts was than Pirie or how far behind Ibbotson was. The race could of been a photo finish between all three runners. In fact Kuts won by a substantial margin with Pirie and Ibbotson following close together.

The point is that with ordinal data it can be put it into some kind of order, yet no knowledge of the relative quantities is known. The consequences of this are similar to those associated with nominal level data in that it restricts the type of analysis which can be applied.

Interval and ratio level data

Interval level data is seen by many as the threshold of analysis in terms of data levels. It is the point at which analysis becomes easier regarding the methods of analysis and the risk of breaking the model assumptions of the techniques involved.

Definition

Interval data has the characteristic in which the figures or numbers actually represent the degree or magnitude of difference between them.

One of the more difficult aspects of this data continuum to explain is the difference between interval and ratio data. Simply put, ratio level data has a absolute or true zero point whereas interval scales do not.

For example consider the temperature of a swimming pool in which our unit of measurement is the Celsius temperature scale. Whilst a change in temperature from 10 degrees to 15 degrees involves the same amount of movement along the scale as a change from 15 degrees to 20 degrees, it would not be true to say that the water would be twice as hot when 20 degrees as it is when only 10 degrees. In such a case the ratio of the numbers do not reflect or are not in direct proportion to the attribute being measured.

Alternatively, in a swimming pool 25m long and one 50m long movement along the scale from 0 to 25m would also be the same as from 25m to 50m. It could also be said that a 50m pool is twice the length of the 25m pool as length has a true zero point and the numbers reflect the ratios of the ascribed measure.

Key point

The difference is fairly subtle and not easy to understand. What is important is to be able to distinguish between what is nominal/ordinal data and what is interval/ratio data.

From a mathematical or statistical point of view most techniques require a minimum level of data to allow the analysis to take place. In the vast majority of instances the dividing line comes at the interval level. The number of methods which require ratio level data are very few (see Table 3.1).

Table 3.1 Categories of data types and characteristics

DATA LEVEL	EXAMPLE	LOCATION	CHARACTERISTICS
NOMINAL	Codes given to gender and other socio-eco groups	User and non-user surveys	Values contain no relative value
ORDINAL	Ranked scales from monitoring sheets, very good, good, bad etc.	Contract monitoring sheets	Can be ranked or put into ascending and descending order
INTERVAL	Water temperature	Contract monitoring sheet	Values are relative
RATIO	Pounds and pence Number of customers	Financial records	Absolute zero point

What average?

As stated earlier managers are often faced with masses of raw data which they need to summarise. One way of making the data more understandable is to reduce it to a single figure which represents all the values distributed within the data set. Such a figure can be found by the use of averages.

The first rule regarding the use of averages is that there is no such thing as *the* average. What there is, is a number of ways in which we can measure the central tendency of a data set, all of which are forms of averaging. None of them is 'the average' and managers should get into the habit of classifying what form of average they are referring to, rather than using the term 'the average'.

Statistically there are several kinds of average of which the most common are:

- the arithmetic mean
- the median
- the mode.

Key point

Reducing any set of data to a single figure is a big step. It is important to be aware of and know when to apply the various forms of averaging.

The data set below represents 50 results from a contract monitoring sheet with scores out of one hundred.

$$
\begin{array}{cccccccccc}
57 & 60 & 61 & 54 & 62 & 24 & 51 & 25 & 72 & 79 \\
80 & 96 & 70 & 64 & 72 & 70 & 72 & 60 & 83 & 80 \\
61 & 67 & 97 & 59 & 60 & 73 & 68 & 66 & 77 & 58 \\
72 & 58 & 72 & 76 & 72 & 47 & 74 & 69 & 89 & 72 \\
49 & 90 & 80 & 81 & 67 & 72 & 62 & 87 & 63 & 61 \\
\end{array}
$$

Such an array of results will form a point of discussion between contractor and client. Let us examine these figures in light of such a discussion using the various forms of averaging.

The arithmetic mean

Definition

The arithmetic mean is more commonly referred to only as the 'mean'. It is calculated by adding all the values in the data set and dividing by the number of items or numbers contained within it.

The calculation may be expressed as:

$$
\text{Mean} = \frac{\text{Sum of all values}}{\text{Number of values}}
$$

For the above data we could produce a mean score by:

$$
\text{Mean monitoring score} = \frac{57 + 60 + 61 + 54 + 62 \ldots \ldots n^{50}}{50}
$$

$$
= \frac{3292}{50}
$$

$$
= 65.84
$$

The mean score from 50 inspections is 65.84.

The median

Definition

The median is the value which lies halfway along the series of values. The value which has 50 per cent of values lying either side of it.

Should the series contain an even number of values (as our example does) the median is found by taking the mean of the middle two values. For example the 25th and 26th values taken from our series when arranged in numerical order i.e. 69 and 70 giving the following median:

$$\text{Median monitoring score} = \frac{69 + 70}{2}$$

$$= \frac{139}{2}$$

$$= 69.5$$

The mode

Definition

The mode of a series is the value which is most common to it, the most frequently occurring.

If we examine our data of monitoring scores again it shows 72 as the most frequently occurring value, appearing eight times.

The modal monitoring score is therefore 72.

Whilst there will always only be one mean or median to a series there is the possibility of having two or more modes. This can occur when different values appear equally as many times as each other. In such cases the data would be said to be either bi-modal or multi-modal.

From this one set of data we have produced three different averages:

The mean	65.84
The median	69.5
The mode	72

The consequences of specifying an 'average' score of 68 as a minimum standard are easy to see. Depending upon the method used a pass or fail outcome could be given.

Averaging has data level constraints which must be observed and are shown in Table 3.2.

Table 3.2 Minimum data levels for averaging

MEASURE OF CENTRAL TENDENCY	MINIMUM DATA LEVEL
MODE	NOMINAL
MEDIAN	ORDINAL
MEAN	INTERVAL

Averages are used extensively in management but be careful of their claims. Reducing data sets in such a dramatic fashion inevitably means losing some detail. Whilst the mode claims to be the most typical score, a quick glance at the original data set highlights just how much detail is lost. The median produces a better summary in saying that at least as many scores were 70 or above as were 69 and below. The mean, often referred to as the centre of gravity of a distribution, gives yet another insight into the data. The total value of items is evenly distributed either side of it, i.e. the total value of our monitoring score data was 3292, the total value either side of the mean would therefore be 1646. In other words the sum of all values less than 65.84 and the sum of values greater than 65.84 would both be equal to 1646.

Key point

Averages can be confusing. Any of the above three averages cannot possibly convey the detail of the individual figures. Use the appropriate average only when you can justify the loss of detail.

Handling percentages

Expressing things as a percentage is often a convenient way of simplifying and clarifying data and is widely used in leisure management. The technique is particularly used for evaluation but if used unthinkingly can be misleading.

Key point

Percentages can be misleading. The wrong interpretation by leisure managers can be costly.

Definition

A percentage expresses something as part of a whole in which the whole is represented by 100. To calculate a percentage divide the part by the whole and multiply by 100, i.e. to express £50 as a percentage of £500 simply share £50 (the part) by £500 (the whole) and multiply by 100:

$$\text{numerator : the part} \quad \frac{£50}{£500} \; = \; 0.1 \; \times \; 100 \; = \; 10\%$$
$$\text{denominator: the whole}$$

The main problem is that managers will react on the basis of an isolated percentage figure. As the manager of a swimming pool you ring the plant supervisor responsible for the quality of the water to ask what percentage of tests have been within the quality limits regarding pH levels. Fifty per cent comes the answer. You react immediately with 'It's not good enough' . What you failed to ask was 50 per cent of what? The truth of the matter was that the supervisor had only taken two measurement that day, one first thing when the levels would be expected to be raised as the pool had been empty all night, he had then taken the appropriate action and on the second test found the levels acceptable.

When used as a management tool the denominator in a percentage calculation is crucial and all parties should be very aware of what the value of the denominator is.

Key point

Understand the denominator. What is its value? And what does it represent?

Often in the management of a leisure enterprise, it will become necessary to compare percentages. It may be the case that this will form part of the evaluation process. Direct comparisons between percentages can be potentially misleading.

One practice to which most leisure mangers are familiar is expressing variances of income and expenditure as a percentage of budget. In such a statement any deviation from a planned budgetary figure is expressed as a percentage of the total budget. For example a £700 over spend on a £14000 budget would give a variance of plus five per cent, i.e.:

$$\frac{£700}{£1400} \ = \ 0.05 \ \times \ 100 \ = \ 5\%$$

Such a practice can become misleading if carried out in isolation. Remember that the purpose of such an analysis is normally to identify to which areas of performance managerial resources should be applied.

Definition

Variance: the difference between a standard or target and the actual level of activity or performance.

Consider the figures below.

ITEM	VARIANCE
Swimming income	−3.5%
Squash income	−16.3%

Based on the above information alone it would appear reasonable to concentrate our efforts into increasing squash usage in an attempt to bring our income figures in line. If we take a look at the whole picture it can be seen that this would have been the wrong decision.

ITEM	BUDGET	ACTUAL	VARIANCE	%VARIANCE
Swimming income	100000	965000	35000	3.5%
Squash income	10000	8370	1630	16.3%

Such a mistake shows lack understanding of the denominator or base figure. The question should be asked: 3.5 per cent and 16.3 per cent of what? The manager should recognise that 3.5 per cent represents £3500 whilst 16.3 per cent accounts to only £1630. The base figure or denominator is the key.

A further trap into which managers can easily fall is the production of spurious figures when computing an average percentage. Consider an example in which it is necessary to examine the percentage of grass in two parks which have not been maintained to the required standard.

East Park has half an acre and South Park half an acre not of the required standard. These represent one per cent and five per cent of the park areas respectively which are not to standard. The contract governing these parks states however that the total area not reaching the specified standard should not exceed two per cent of the total area covered by both parks.

Given the above information it may be tempting to calculate the mean percentage in the following manner:

$$\% \text{ of unkept grass} = \frac{1 \text{ (East Park)} + 5 \text{ (South Park)}}{\text{(Total number of parks) 2}} = 3\%$$

Such a figure is wrong and misleading. The only way the mean amount of sub-quality grass can be meaningfully calculated is as follows:

$$\% \text{ of unkept grass} = \frac{\text{Total acres of sub-standard grass}}{\text{Total acres of all parks}}$$

$$= \frac{0.5 + 0.5}{100 + 10} \qquad = \frac{1}{110} \times 100$$

$$= 0.9\%$$

From this kind of example it becomes easy to see, how the application of percentages can lead to misunderstanding and disagreements between contractors and clients. The first calculation, if used, could well have resulted in a defective work order when it was totally unjustified.

Pareto analysis

Whilst on the subject of percentages it is worth examining a technique called Pareto analysis.

Definition

Pareto analysis is an effective way of examining the relative magnitude of the component elements of an organisation through the use of percentages.

Such a technique is of use to leisure managers in highlighting the importance of various activities within a sports centre to the overall operation of the centre.

47

For example a sports centre offers ten activities which net the incomes shown in Table 3.3.

Table 3.3 Activity and income table

Activity	£ Income
1. Swimming	86,697
2. Sauna	2,015
3. Badminton	4,221
4. Keep fit	10,438
5. Gym	4,079
6. Five-a-side	4,243
7. Squash	8,474
8. Meeting room hire	3,132
9. Creche	516
10. Sunbeds	3,366

In order to carry out pareto analysis the following procedure can be followed:

- First of all rank all of the activities in descending order, according to income and total them (see Columns 1 and 2 in Table 3.4).

- Now calculate the income of each activity as a percentage of the total income. This is easily achieved by the following calculation and recorded in Column 3:

$$\frac{\text{activity income}}{\text{total income}} \times 100 = \%$$

- Having done this calculate each ranked activity as a percentage of the total rank or range of activities. Thus the first item in a rank of 20 represents $1/20 \times 100 = 5$ per cent, the second item represents $2/20 \times 100 = 10$ per cent of the total. This figure will be used as reference or basis of comparison in the final analysis allowing us to make a statement such as 10 per cent of our activities represents x amount of our income. This will become clearer in the next stage shown in Column 4.

- The final column is now calculated to give the cumulative income as a percentage of the total income. This column is achieved by adding the usage as a percentage of total income figures (Column 3) in an accumulative manner, i.e. $68.16 + 8.20 = 76.36$, etc.

The resultant figures are now best represented in the form of a graph as shown in Figure 3.2. By using the vertical or y axis to represent the 'cumula-

Table 3.4 Table for Pareto analysis

1 Activity	2 £ Income	3 Income as % of total	4	5 Cumulative total as %
1. Swimming	86,697	68.16	10	68.16
2. Keep fit	10,438	8.20	20	76.36
3. Squash	8,474	6.66	30	83.02
4. Five-a-side	4,243	3.33	40	86.35
5. Badminton	4,221	3.31	50	89.66
6. Gym	4,079	3.20	60	92.86
7. Sunbeds	3,366	2.64	70	95.50
8. Meeting room hire	3,132	2.46	80	97.96
9. Sauna	2,015	1.58	90	99.54
10. Creche	516	0.40	100	100.00
	127,181			

tive percentage of total income' and the horizontal or x axis to represent the 'cumulative percentage of activities', the results can be seen more clearly.

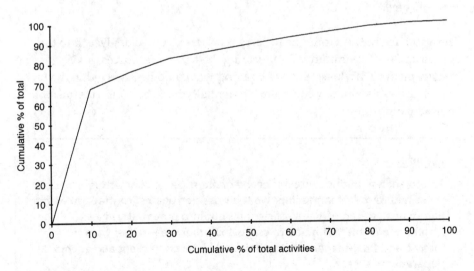

Figure 3.2 Pareto curve of sports centre activities

Key point

The key to examining the results lies in the degree of flexibility in the curve. This indicates the extent to which income and activities are proportioned.

The above curve demonstrates that a high proportion of the income of this particular centre is represented by a small proportion of its activities, i.e. that, 50 per cent of all activities represents nearly 90 per cent of total income or that 10 per cent (one activity) represents 68.16 per cent of all income.

Pareto analysis is best used within a battery of investigative methods. A costing exercise may at the same time show that whilst swimming is the greatest provider of income it also has proportionally high costs requiring a heavy subsidy. Whilst swimming may have to stay as part of the programme of activities for contractual or social policy reasons it makes good financial sense to maintain it as an activity as:

- Firstly, a further investigation of costs is likely to show that an activity with such high activity rates will be making a fairly significant contribution to overheads which the organisation could not afford to lose.

- Secondly, having the information provided by the Pareto analysis suggests that by concentrating management efforts on just 10 per cent of the activities they can potentially affect nearly 70 per cent of total income.

The approach to this would be to carry out more detailed analysis into the cost structure of swimming. By allocating the limited resources of management to this task, any small saving that could be achieved in the unit cost or cost per swimmer could have potentially huge benefits in terms of the contractual position.

Key point

Pareto analysis in this context is of the greatest use to contractors, especially those mid term seeking to improve their position against contract, to whom Pareto analysis can offer an efficient insight into potential savings. Application of the technique to usage and other areas rather than to income and finance make this technique of interest to client and agency departments alike.

Time and trends

In performance review managers are often more interested in trends and patterns than they are in individual figures. Time series offers a useful tool of measurement for this. It can provide a general picture or the underlying trend on some essential performance measures through the passage of time.

Key point

Trends are a main concern in the performance, monitoring and evaluation process.

In plotting a time series it's soon discovered that individual values, be they weekly sales, survey scores or pool temperatures, all have a tendency to move up and down unevenly. There are a number of influences which can be identified as possible contributors to this apparently erratic behaviour. They include:

- seasonal variations

- random variation

- underlying trend.

Definitions

Seasonal variations: a repeating pattern normally on an annual basis which reflects levels of activity. In the leisure industry many operations are heavily influenced by seasonal variations. For example the holiday industry is particularly busy in July and August and not so in the winter, theatres and football are winter activities, etc.

Random variations: movements which follow no pattern are said to be random. Daily income in a swimming pool is unlikely to be exactly predictable. Plotted on a graph the line is likely to rise and fall in a unpredictable manner.

The trend: simply the tendency of a plotted line to behave in a particular way. Often referred to as the underlying trend, it gives insight into the general direction of activity, rising or falling.

It is the trend which is sought foremost. This is described as underlying trend because it is overlaid by random and seasonal variations which must be removed to uncover the trend.

Smoothing

Definition

Smoothing is the process by which we can remove random variations.

Smoothing requires making use of moving averages in the following manner. For example, suppose a cinema owner has the following income for a ten week period (see Column 2 in Table 3.5).

Table 3.5 Moving averages

Week	Income (£.00)	Monthly moving total	Monthly moving average
1	7		
2	3		
		32	8
3	18		
		55	13.75
4	4		
		67	16.75
5	30		
		55	13.75
6	15		
		59	14.75
7	6		
		57	14.25
8	8		
		63	15.75
9	28		
10	21		

There are two stages to carrying out the procedure.

Firstly, calculate the moving total. This is done by adding the income for a four week period. Taking the first four weeks to get the moving total for the first four weeks: 1–4 = 7 + 3 + 18 + 4 = 32 (see Column 3 Table 3.5).

As the series progresses the income for Week 5 is added in and the income for Week 1 subtracted. Doing this maintains a four week period over which calculations are based. Continue to move through the series in the same manner, dropping and adding a figure each time.

This creates a series of over lapping groups of four week periods. As two values from each period will always be carried over into the next, a short cut to calculating the moving totals is as follows:

Moving total for second period = moving total for first period (plus income for Week 5 minus income for Week 1)

Therefore, moving total for second period = 32–7 + 30 = 55

The same procedure can be continued through out the series, next time adding Week 6 and subtracting Week 2 and so forth.

Calculate the moving average. The moving average (mean) is obtained by dividing each moving total by the number of weeks contained within it, in this case 4. The first moving average figure is obtained by:

32 (moving total) divided by 4 (number of weeks) = 8

The same procedure is again carried out on all the moving total figures. The results can be seen in Column 4 of Table 3.5.

The effects of the above calculations are best seen when viewed graphically (see Figure 3.3).

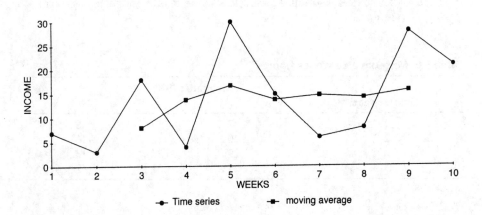

Figure 3.3 Smoothing effect of a moving average

> **Key point**
>
> Graphical presentations are well suited to performance review as they show spatial relationships which are more easily interpreted than numerical ones.

On examination the gradient of the moving average will be seen to be less dramatic than the profile of the time series. The decease in the level of income between weeks 5 and 8 for example are not of such great concern as the original figures may have suggested.

Seasonal variation

The leisure industry is affected by seasonal variations, i.e. repeating patterns in the level of activity the organisation experiences. These variations can often be so severe that they can disguise the real or underlying trend. It is important to de-seasonalise data if the underlying or true trend is to be shown.

> **Key point**
>
> Most sectors of the leisure industry are heavily effected by seasonal variations.

Given the following attendance figures for a museum over a four year period, the figures can be de-seasonalised as follows. The results for each stage are shown in Table 3.8.

Table 3.6 Museum attendance figures

| Quarter year | Attendance (000) | | | |
	1	2	3	4
1	11	17	15	8
2	12	20	16	10
3	15	29	25	14
4	9	29	21	7

1. Calculate the moving totals for the four quarter periods as described earlier (shown in Column 3, Table 3.8)

2. As the year is divided into an even number of sections this results in the moving total being located between quarters as shown below:

```
11
17
-------- 51
15
8
```

It is necessary to locate the moving total figure over a specific quarter so that the relevant adjustments can be made at a later stage. This is achieved by simply using a two step moving total in the following manner (Column 4, Table 3.8).

```
11
17
-------- 51
15 ------------103
-------- 52
8  ------------ 107
-------- 55
12
20    etc.
```

3. Calculate the trend (moving average) by dividing by eight i.e. the number of values contributing to the moving total (Column 5, Table 3.8)

4. Having obtained the trend, subtract this from the actual or series attendance figures (shown in Column 2). The result will equal the seasonal variation plus any residual value. The results of this calculation can be seen in (Column 6, Table 3.8).

5. Now obtain the average variation for each quarter by taking the mean for each period. It is best to display the results of Column 6 on a separate table as below in Table 3.7 to carry out the calculation.

Table 3.7 Calculation for variation

	Year				Total	Mean	Corrected
	1	2	3	4			
Q1	—	−1.8	−3.6	−9.7	−15.1	−5.03	−5.255
Q2	—	5.8	8.8	11.6	26.2	8.73	8.505
Q3	2.2	1.2	5	—	8.4	2.8	2.575
Q4	−5.3	−6.3	−5.2	—	−16.8	−5.6	−5.825
							0.9 (/4) = 0.225

Note, the total of the means should be equal to zero. If not a correction can be made by dividing the sum of the means by n (n = number of cases, in this example 4) and subtracting the result from each mean. This is shown in the corrected column.

6. Finally the seasonal adjusted figure is then found by subtracting the appropriate correction found in Column 5 from the original attendance figures in Column 1. The results can be seen in Column 7, Table 3.8.

The results of the adjustment can be seen graphically in Figure 3.4. It shows how the magnitude of the variations is considerably reduced once the seasonal variations have been removed.

Table 3.8 Seasonal variations table

1 YR.	2 SERIES	3 MOVING TOTAL (4)	4 MOVING TOTAL (8)	5 MOVING AVERAGE	6	7
1.1	11					16.2
1.2	17					8.495
		51				
1.3	15		103	12.8	2.2	12.425
		52				
1.4	8		107	13.3	−5.3	13.825
		55				
2.1	12		111	13.8	−1.8	17.255
		56				
2.2	20		114	14.2	5.8	11.495
		58				
2.3	16		119	14.8	1.2	13.425
		61				
2.4	10		131	16.3	−6.3	15.825
		70				
3.1	15		149	18.6	−3.6	20.225
		79				
3.2	29		162	20.2	8.8	20.495
		83				
3.3	25		160	20	5	22.425
		77				
3.4	14		154	19.2	−5.2	19.825
		77				
4.1	9		150	18.7	−9.7	14.22
		73				
4.2	29		139	17.37	11.6	20.49
		66				
4.3	21					18.425
4.4	7					12.825

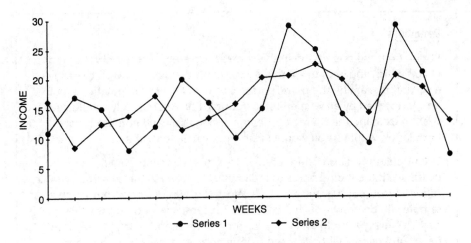

Figure 3.4 De-seasonalised attendance figures

The use of this fairly simple approach to time series analysis allows managers to quickly appreciate the underlying trends of not only income and attendance figures but also to identify an underlying trend.

Obtaining samples

<u>Key point</u>

The point behind taking samples is so that we may make observations from a few which can be generalised to the many.

The use of sampling is widespread in the leisure industry. Unlike the common saying of 'a little knowledge can be dangerous' obtaining samples is an area in which a little knowledge can greatly improve the validity of results. Whether you're taking pool samples, user samples, inspecting the cleanliness of changing facilities or the length of grass, the ability to produce sound samples will be an invaluable skill.

Before examining the different methods of selecting samples it is important to establish the precise meaning of some of the terminology to be encountered.

Definitions

Population: the population in this context represents the members of the group which you wish to examine. For example should you wish to carry out a survey to examine the usage patterns of women, your population would be represented by all women using your facility. Alternatively should you wish to examine the characteristics of women users and non-users, your population would be all women from your catchment area.

The population is also often referred to as the 'sampling frame'. This is possibly a more logical name as it allows us to visualise the concept. What is required is to put a frame around a selected group of items from which a sample will be drawn. Such a frame may encapsulate every person living on earth, or every hour in every day for the last thousand years. Equally it may be around people who wear red swimming trunks, have black hair and swim on a Friday morning at a particular swimming pool. What is important is that a frame is laid down at the outset.

Sampling Unit: the elements from which your population is compiled are known as the 'sampling unit' and it is essential that you identify this early in the process. Depending upon the particular situation the sampling unit will not necessarily be people or categories of people. The sampling unit may in fact be anything, number of open spaces, a set amount of open space, or even a period of time. The sampling units of a particular group, for example hours in the day, users in a year or total acreage of open space, represent the 'population' for the purposes of an investigation.

Representative Sample: as a sample will only gather information from part of a larger population, an attempt to draw a sample which will accurately reflect the characteristics of the population must be made. When this is achieved it is referred to as a representative sample.

The collection of data can be an expensive and difficult exercise for leisure managers. The populations from which they gather data are often very large and intangible making it difficult to collect. It is impossible to gather information from every user or to have someone permanently assigned to checking the cleanliness of the changing rooms. A more efficient approach to the problem is to collect data from only some users and inspect the changing facilities on certain occasions. But to do so in such a manner as to remain confident that the data collected will reflect what would have been found had every instance been monitored. Obeying the rules of sampling theory can ensure this, making considerable savings in time and effort.

> **Key point**
>
> The main aim when obtaining a sample is to ensure that it is representative of the population to which it belongs.

Ground rules for sampling

In sampling inferences are made from the few (the sample) to the many (the population). When sampling is carried out as part of the monitoring process it is essential that ground rules between the contractor and the client are agreed before an investigation is commenced.

Agreed standards for this are difficult to provide as both the level of service and resources to monitor them will be unique to individual situations.

British Standard 6001 provides a sampling procedure which is designed primarily for use in the production industry, but has been successfully adapted for use on grounds maintenance, refuse collection and other local authority services.

> **Key point**
>
> If BS 6001 sampling procedures can be adapted to your particular situation use them.

One of the main reasons for the above key point is that within a contract situation if it does become necessary to provide evidence of defective or sub-standard levels of work, having carried out sampling to a British Standard will provide strong evidence of the reliability of your findings.

Whether using BS 6001 or not, any inspection by sampling requires clients and contractors to agree on, or have specified:

- the unit of analysis
- the acceptable level of the results, to use BS 6001 terminology the acceptance quality level (AQL)
- the level of inspection
- the form of sampling to be employed.

It is of use to expand and explain the above four points in more detail.

Unit of analysis

The unit of analysis for inspection represents what you are going to look at. This may seem obvious but in some situations it does require some classification. In a grounds maintenance contract, for example, it may be necessary to inspect the length of grass to ensure that it is being maintained to specified levels. Blades of grass are obviously an unsuitable unit in this case. What is required is a more practical unit such as a square metre of grass. Similar problems can also arise in the inspection of facilities. What aspects of the facility are being inspected? What are the boundaries of the inspection?

Closely related to the unit of analysis is the sampling frame which has to be agreed, i.e. what is the population of the sampling unit. Identifying a complete sampling frame again requires answering questions as to the boundaries and limits of the investigation. For example agreement upon the extent of a catchment area will be required when surveying non-users. Similarly the time period over which facility inspections are to be based will require agreement. Will the inspection times be selected from a week, month, year or contract duration? The ease with which a complete sampling frame can be obtained is variable, i.e. catchment population can be found relatively easily from the electoral register. User sampling frames are not as tangible.

The acceptable level of results or acceptable quality level (AQL)

In inspection sampling, there should be a target or standard against which the results are compared or evaluated. For example, in the inspection of sports centre's activities it may be agreed that five per cent of inspections would be permitted to fail in a given period. The failure rate to be agreed between the contractor and client will be based on a number of issues:

- the nature of the activity
- recognition that people don't get things right 100 per cent of the time
- recognition of the short falls of sampling
- resources required to respond to individual failures.

A more detailed discussion regarding the basis of pass or failure in inspection can be found in Chapter 6 on Contract monitoring.

The level of inspection

The level of inspection is essentially a trade off between the resources available for inspection purposes and the level of acceptable accuracy of the sample. The result of this relationship determines the sample size, i.e. how many questionnaires to complete or how many inspections to carry out.

One of the main reasons that leisure managers have not become seriously involved in the use of sampling has been fear over the amount of data it is necessary to collect and the sample size required. Such fear is generally unfounded as the size of the population from which the sample is to be drawn has little to do with how accurate the sample is likely to prove.

Without prior knowledge it's possible to imagine that to survey the adult population of a catchment area with 100,000 residents would require at least 10–20 per cent of them to complete a survey if it hoped to maintain any level of representation. A daunting task if this was the case. In fact what is important is the size of the sample not the size of the population or the sample sizes relationship to the population.

The sample size required should be based on:

- the level or degree of accuracy you require
- the extent to which there will be variation in the response to questions
- any requirements of the statistical method to be used in the analysis.

Key point

There will always be limits to the level of error that can be accepted in performance review.

Firstly decide the level of error which is acceptable. As with all survey work it must be pointed out that, there is no definite way of ensuring that the characteristics of a sample will mirror those found in the population. When the level of error is known however statements of the following nature can be made:

'We are ninety five per cent confident that 74 per cent, plus or minus 2 per cent, of our users travel to the centre by car'.

Such a statement shows that whilst it is never possible to be 100 per cent sure (unless a 100 per cent sample is used), it is possible to be 95 per cent sure that between 72 per cent and 76 per cent of users travel by car. Using Table 3.9 it can be seen that the above example was based upon a sample of around 2500 as it cites the sampling error as 2 per cent.

> **Definition**
>
> Sampling error: a predictable amount of error resulting from the sample not being truly representative of its population.

Table 3.9 Sample size and error

Sampling Error %	Sample Size
1.0	10000
1.5	4500
2.0	2500
2.5	1600
3.0	1100
3.5	816
4.0	625
4.5	494
5.0	400
5.5	330
6.0	277
6.5	237
7.0	204
7.5	178
8.0	156
8.5	138
9.0	123
9.5	110
10.0	100

There are several things to be observed from the above table regarding the relationship which exists between the size of a sample and its associated level of error.

From the plot shown in Figure 3.5 it can be seen that the required sample size decreases at a steady rate as the level of error is increased. This essentially means that when using smaller samples a large increase in accuracy can be achieved by a small increase in the sample size. Such a benefit is not gained at the opposite end of the scale. For example by increasing a sample size of 100 to 173 (an increase of 73) the sampling error is reduced from 10 per cent to 7.5 per cent (by 2.5 per cent). Conversely an increase in sample size from 2,500 to 10,000 (an increase of 7,500) only reduced the sampling error from 2 per cent to 1 per cent.

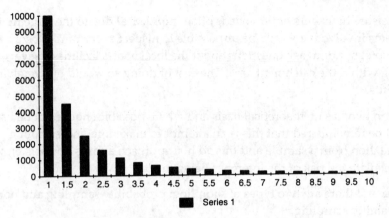

Figure 3.5 Relationship between sampling error and sample size

> **Key point**
>
> The decision regarding the level of error and sample size should be made on a cost/benefit basis.

Sample size is as much to do with resources as it is to do with sound statistical practice but there is a point beyond which the increased costs of extending the sample size will pay poor rewards in terms of accuracy.

> **Key point**
>
> The size of the population from which a sample is taken is not important to the accuracy of a sample survey.

The sampling options

When faced with the prospect of inspecting or surveying the various facets of a leisure organisation, there are three options which may be taken:

- 100 per cent sampling: when every instance or item under investigation is examined
- ad hoc sampling: in which spot checks or a percentage of the population are examined
- probability sampling: which relies on the mathematical theories of probability.

For leisure managers option one is often impractical due to the large number of items involved, it would be impossible to inspect every pint of beer served in a hotel bar or to ask questions about the local sports facilities to everyone living within the catchment area. The cost of doing so would outweigh any benefits.

Option two has no theoretical basis and where possible should not be used. It must be remembered that this is an attempt to make inferences about a population from a sample and this ad hoc approach affords no basis on which to calculate the risk of the inference being made.

In general there are two types of sampling: probability sampling and non-probability sampling.

Definition

Probability : The likelihood of an event occurring relative to the likelihood of it not.

Option 3 probability sampling involves every member of the population having an equal chance of being selected in the sample, whereas in non-probability sampling some have a greater chance than others. Unfortunately, for those who were willing to wrestle with the maths of it, the chance of selection in a non-probability sample is unknown. It is therefore preferable were possible to use a probability sample. They are much more likely to produce a 'representative' sample.

There are a number of methods that can be used to draw a probability sample. The method you use is largely dependent upon:

- whether or not a good sampling frame exists
- the desired level of accuracy
- the resources available to carry out the investigation.

These items together with the topic under investigation will shape your choice of sampling method. What is intended here is to give insights into a number of possible approaches to sampling. Whilst the examples used may never be mirror reflections of your own investigations, they will demonstrate the kind of practical application they are best suited to.

The four main methods of selecting a probability sample are:

- simple random sample
- fractional sampling
- multi-stage sampling
- stratified sampling, which can be applied to all the above.

Simple random sample

A simple random sample is easily obtained, it is the most basic form of probability sampling and offers a simple technique for obtaining samples with a known level of error. To select a simple random sample give every member of the population an equal chance of being included. For example, consider a sports centre which is open seven days a week for ten hours a day. To develop a schedule of random inspection times for a given month, you would need to:

- Assign every opening hour an individual number, the first hour of first day of the month = 1, second working hour = 2, first hour of second day = 11, etc. In a 30-day month this produces a list of 300 hour periods each with an individual number.

- Use a random number generator table to provide a number less than or equal to the total population size, in this case from 001 to 300.

- Identify the time to which the number corresponds, i.e. if the number 050 was generated then the corresponding time would be the first hour of the opening on the fifth day of the month.

- Repeat steps two and three until the desired sample size has been achieved.

Key point

Many computer packages are capable of generating a list of random numbers of a given size between zero and the population size.

Assuming the first of the month to be a Monday and that the centre opens at 9.00 a.m. each day, the following random numbers would give the inspection schedule below for Week 1.

$$110 \quad 121 \quad 008 \quad 017 \quad 281 \quad 187 \quad 073 \quad 081 \quad 039$$
$$073 \quad 269 \quad 247 \quad 372 \quad 174 \quad 096 \quad 175 \quad 261 \quad 195$$
$$170 \quad 002 \quad 177$$

Sports Centre Inspection Schedule Week 1

Monday 1st	10.00 a.m.	(002)
	7.00 p.m.	(008)
Tuesday 2nd	4.00 p.m.	(017)
Thursday 4th	8.00 p.m.	(039)

Multi-stage samples

This method, as its name suggests, requires the collection of a number of samples. In doing so it is hoped that the costs of collecting a widely dispersed sample can be reduced.

Key point

Multi-stage sampling identifies a final sample which is less widely dispersed yet retains its representatives.

For example, in an audience survey to examine customers' response regarding their visit to a theatre, the theatre holds a thousand people and has 50 shows in the forthcoming season.

If a random sampling method was to be employed based on the 50,000 seats available in the season, it may be necessary to have researchers attend every performance even if only to interview one member of the audience. Both practically and economically this would not be a convenient approach.

Key point

In multi-stage sampling as many stages as deemed necessary can be undertaken as long as each unit can be broken down into smaller units of the same thing, i.e. country, county, city, street and household are all large units of people.

This inconvenience can be overcome by firstly selecting randomly a number of shows and then selecting a second random sample of seats which will act as the reference point to the customer. The advantages of this are:

- no isolated respondents
- reduced data collection costs
- representative sample is maintained.

Factorial or systematic samples

An alternative method of selecting a sample is by using the ratio of the total population to the number being sampled. For example in a users survey in a single day a facility expects 5,000 visitors. By calculating the ratio we can stop and interview every *n*th customer, i.e.:

$$n = \frac{\text{Total Population}}{\text{Sample size}}$$

It has been agreed that 100 would be an acceptable sample therefore:

$$n = \frac{5000}{100} = 50$$

In this case we select every 50th customer for our interviews after initially choosing a random number less than 50. For example suppose the initial random number is 26 then the sample would select customer or seat numbers 26, 76, 126, 176, 226, etc.

Key point

Factorial sampling is not recommended when a pattern or trend is likely to exist within the population.

For example in producing an inspection schedule a factorial sample may result in inspecting the same time, on the same day each week.

Stratifing samples

Stratifying samples helps make them more representative by ensuring that sections of the population are relatively represented.

Key point

All forms of sampling can be subject to stratification.

Key point

Stratifying samples is a way of increasing the accuracy of a sample when resources are unavailable to increase the sample size.

For example in examining usage patterns of a facility, a sample was obtained in which people under 21 were under-represented, the results of the survey would be biased towards the behaviour of older people.

The use of a stratified sample can help avoid this problem. For example in taking water samples from a swimming pool, we may find that a simple random sample, especially if the sample size was small, gives a sampling schedule which under represents the peak usage times. As most centres have identified high low and normal usage periods these could be used as the basis of stratification in each period.

Peak	520 hours
Normal	780 hours
Off peak	1300 hours
	2600 hours

To select a stratified sample, a random sample from each stratum needs to be selected, which is proportionate to the size of the stratum in the population.

In the above example there are three strata. If we require a total sample size of 200, by taking the following steps a stratified sample can be obtained:

- calculate the sampling fraction by dividing the sample size by the population size:

$$\frac{\text{Sample Size}}{\text{Population Size}} = \frac{200}{2600} = \frac{1}{13}$$

- once a sampling fraction has been obtained finding the sample size from each stratum is a simple matter of multiplying the sampling fraction by the stratum size. For example the number of samples from peak usage times = 520/13 = 40. Normal and off peak periods can be obtained in the same manner.

Operational Level	Population Size	Sample Size
Peak	520	40
Normal	780	60
Off peak	1300	100

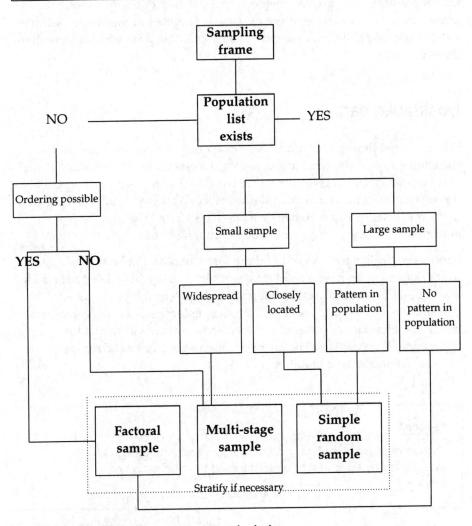

Figure 3.6 Flow chart for selecting sample design

It is possible to draw a representative sample using a number of methods. The flow diagram in Figure 3.6 should help select the most appropriate method for your investigation.

69

The question of sample size within a working environment is as much to do with costs and resources as it is to with sound statistical methods. However, if a job is worth doing it's worth doing right, and if resources do not allow for the use of a simple random sample, then don't use one. Find a method which does not require a probability sample if you cannot supply one. Accept the limitations of non-probability methods rather than produce spurious data; the consequences could be even more expensive. Despite common belief, sample size has nothing to do with the size of the population from which you wish to draw the sample.

Qualitative data

Data collected through the more traditional quantitative techniques is considered to be hard, reliable and precise. Its association with mathematical and statistical analysis gives it a rigour worthy of science status. It is possibly this image which has made quantitative data popular with policy makers in many organisations. Qualitative data is seen as having rich and deep information allowing for a more in-depth investigation.

Leisure enterprises have a need for both forms of data. Public and private sector organisations have a need for quantitative data where direct measures are required in financial monitoring, measuring water temperatures, etc. Yet, the nature of the services provided by leisure enterprises is seen by many as intangible. How do we comprehend if customers are having a quality experience? What makes a theatre performance good or bad? Such questions provide a demand for qualitative data.

Key point

The use of qualitative data, within a performance, monitoring and evaluation process is vital to understanding the true nature of leisure services.

Whilst Table 3.10 shows the differences between qualitative and quantitative data collection, the advantages of qualitative investigations in a leisure enterprise may be seen as:

- qualitative data has more empathy with the phenomenon being investigated, i.e. leisure is a qualitative experience

Table 3.10 Characteristics of qualitative and quantitative data collection

Characteristic	Quantitative	Qualitative
1. Relationship between monitor and subject being investigated.	Distant	Close
2. Monitors stance in relationship to subject	Outsider	Insider
3. Monitoring approach to standards	Confirmation of standards	Emergence of standards
4. Monitoring strategy	Structured	unstructured
5. Scope of evaluation	Confirmation of law-like principles	Accepts unique situation
6. Nature of data	Hard, reliable	Rich, deep

- qualitative methods give more consideration to the people aspect of the service

- the results of qualitative are more easily understood by those without statistical training

- qualitative techniques are better placed to understand people's needs and aspirations — an important element in the provision of leisure services.

Qualitative data collection methods include:

- In-depth interviews — respondents are encouraged to talk at length regarding a subject rather than answer specific questions. Conversations are often transcribed for analysis.

- Focus groups — an in-depth interview involving a number of people.

- Participant observation — collecting information by becoming a participant so as to see things through others' eyes.

- Open ended questioning — free range of response to questions in a self-complete or verbal response format.

- Photography — pictorial data is often more capable of showing levels and standards on issues such as cleanliness and deterioration than indices or discourse.

Analysing qualitative data

The analysis of qualitative data is subjective. Monitoring is required to organise and classify the data collected. This essentially involves examining the data for themes and topics, for example responses to an open ended question regarding visits to a museum may be examined for positive and negative remarks. They may also be divided into comments regarding different aspects of the visit such as exhibits, catering etc. before being cross referenced.

Analysing qualitative data is a long process, which requires the analyst to become extremely familiar with that data. Only by going over and over it can themes be identified.

Qualitative investigations also produce a large amount of data. There are a number of software packages available, such as Ethnograph, which are designed to assist in the process of organising large amounts of material. Alternatively most word processors can at least assist in the process through the use of Cut, Copy and Search facilities.

Qualitative data collection can offer fresh insights into a leisure service even if it is only used as a complementary approach to more formal methods of data collection.

LEARNING POINTS

- Data is the basic commodity of performance, monitoring and evaluation. It is the results of the monitoring process.

- Attention must be given to how data is collected, the type of data and the analysis of data.

- There are four levels of data — nominal, ordinal, interval and ratio.

- There are three types of average — the mean, mode and median.

- Percentages are potentially misleading figures.

- Understanding the denominator is essential to a percentage calculation used in a decision making process.

- Pareto analysis is an effective way of examining the relative magnitude of the component elements of an organisation.

- Trends are a major concern of the performance, monitoring and evaluation process.

- Graphs are well suited for use in performance review as they demonstrate spatial relationships.

- Sampling should allow observations to be made from a few which can be generalised to the many.

- A main aim when obtaining a sample is to ensure it is representative.

- The decision regarding the level of error and sample size should be made on a cost benefit basis.

- There are a number of approaches to selecting a sample.

- The use of qualitative data, within a performance, monitoring and evaluation process is vital to understanding the true nature of leisure services.

REFERENCES AND FURTHER READING

Cuming, M. (1984) *A Manager's Guide to Quantitative Methods*, Elm Publications

Bancroft, G. and O'Sullivan, G. (1981) *Maths and Statistics for Accounting and Business Studies*, McGraw-Hill Books

Edwards, B. (1980) *The Readable Maths and Statistics Book*, George Allen & Unwin

Section 2

The first section of the text has provided the reader with an understanding of what performance, monitoring and evaluation entail. The second section is intended to meet the 'how to' needs of leisure managers and those involved in developing PME systems for leisure related activities.

The importance of the local experience in leisure is well documented and indicates that any PME system will only be relevant to a particular situation. By familiarising themselves with an array of common approaches to PME and the skills to develop their own measures and indicators, readers will be in a position to construct systems appropriate to their specific situation.

The basic skills to undertake PME are now discussed in the next three chapters under the headings of:

- financial monitoring
- contract monitoring
- usage monitoring.

4

Financial monitoring

Introduction

The use of financial information as the basis of assessment is common practice in most organisations. Essentially it represents a measure of efficiency. Leisure organisations of all types will have some interest in their financial performance, and like any other aspect of performance, this will require a system of monitoring and evaluation.

A generally accepted definition of efficiency accepts that both inputs and outputs can be assigned monetary values. In a broad sense it may be seen as the minimising of costs for a given level of output or increasing output for a given level of cost. Financial performance has in the past presented a dilemma to leisure managers as their outputs have not been capable of taking on monetary values for the main part.

The quest for efficiency is the cause of a need for financial monitoring in most organisations. It would be wrong to imagine that such a quest is always in the pursuit of profit. In local government for example the quest for efficiency is often more associated with accountability than profit.

This section is not intended to be a do it yourself guide to accountancy. There are already numerous books which dedicate their whole efforts to this task. What this section will do is introduce the topic of financial interpretation within the framework of performance, monitoring and evaluation.

Income and expenditure

The majority of financial monitoring stems from an interest in either the income or expenditure of an organisation. Whilst we may wish to examine these in relation to a number of other factors, essentially it is the fine balance between what we pay out and what we receive in, that is crucial.

> ### Key point
>
> The basis of all tender bids is made upon the fine balance between income and expenditure. As a result the income and expenditure statement is one of the most commonly used monitoring techniques in contracted leisure organisations.

The exact details of any income and expenditure statement will vary from one organisation to another. There is, however, a general structure which is applicable for most situations. Many managers use this statement on a monthly or weekly basis to monitor their financial performance. Many managers also refer, inaccurately to the income and expenditure statement as the profit and loss account. Whilst the profit and loss account does have some use in the monitoring of performance, managers should not be misled into attempting to construct these accounts in favour of the income and expenditure statement. The profit and loss account is more difficult to construct and of less use in the monitoring of operational performance. There are fundamental differences between a profit and loss account and an income and expenditure statement and they should not be taken to be the same thing.

Profit and loss account

The profit and loss account or the trading profit and loss account, as it is more properly called, is a financial accounting statement. It shows how much profit or loss has been made over a given period of time. Within the statement profit is given on two different levels, gross and net.

> ### Definitions
>
> Gross profit is the difference between what goods are bought at and what they are sold at.
>
> Net profit is any remaining profit after the expenses of running the business have been deducted from the gross profit.

The gross profit is shown in the trading account statement, whilst the net profit is shown in the profit and loss account. Normal practice is to amalgamate these two statements. It is the amalgamated statement which we normally refer to as the profit and loss account.

From the example shown in Figure 4.1 the two statements can be identified. The logical layout is to show the trading account first followed by the profit and loss account. The reason for this is that the result of the trading account is needed (i.e. the gross profit) before the profit and loss account can be calculated.

Trading Profit and Loss Account

	£	£	
Income			
Membership	200,000		
Conference room hire	150,000		
Fees	400,000		Trading
Catering	135,000		Account
		885000	
Direct cost		360000	
Gross profit		525000	
Administration expenses		240000	
Net Profit before interest		285000	
Bank interest payable	5000		
Debenture interest payable	10000		
	270000		Profit and
Corporation Tax	67500		Loss Account
Net profit after Tax	202500		
Less			
Transfer to reserves	60000		
Proposed dividend	60000		
	120000		
Unappropriated Profit	**82500**		

Figure 4.1 Profit and loss account example
Adapted from Whitehouse and Tilley, 1992, Chapter 3

The profit and loss account was developed for a specific purpose and within a specific environment, neither of which makes the trading profit and loss account of great use to the leisure manager in its normal format. Some of the reasons for this include:

- the account is essentially financial, i.e. part of the statutory accounts which satisfy a company's legal obligation and produced fundamentally for external bodies such as the inland revenue

- the development of the account has been for the production rather than service industry.

Whilst there are many branches of the leisure industry that do trade in a manner which is appropriate to the use of the trading profit and loss account there is also a large sector to which the account is unsuitable as a monitoring tool, these include:

- those organisations which produce no tangible outputs, i.e. involved only in the delivery of services

- those organisations operating under contracts

- those organisations which reside within local government.

Many of the organisations operating within the leisure industry would qualify under all three of the above. The reasons for finding the use of the account uncomfortable are for the main part associated with layout. Those organisations delivering only services find it difficult to associate their activities with the trading account. Whilst the sales figure is easily calculated the manager of a leisure centre will not as easily be able to identify the cost of the goods sold. There will certainly be very few stock items and purchases which can be identified as the direct cost of particular activities; shop and catering goods being the main exceptions.

Income and expenditure statement

The income and expenditure statement is more of a management accounting tool than the trading profit and loss account. It provides the type of information which managers can use in operating and controlling their activities.

Its benefits over the profit and loss account include:

- the breakdown of income into appropriate headings

- the breakdown of expenditure into appropriate headings

- the ability to show all headings against a target, tender bid or other basis of comparison

- easy identification of under and over performing areas.

Whilst the individual headings used will vary from facility to facility, the following layout is a standard approach to an income and expenditure statement for a sports facility run under contract. This example typifies the lay out used by many leisure centres and is an approach adaptable to most situations.

	Tender	Present year	Previous year
Income			
Administration	1987	2133	1345
Wet sports	32316	33417	36216
Sauna	7925	7648	8114
Dry sports	34285	32285	34602
Client	42893	42893	42893
Ad hocs	0	240	100
Sponsorship	3000	2500	3200
Total	122406	121116	126470
% of yearly income	10	9.8	10.3
Expenditure			
Staff costs			
Wet sports	20251	19501	21500
Dry sports	17111	17007	17468
Administration	12887	12900	13105
Training	456	550	504
Complex	26895	24741	25222
Total	77600	74699	77799
% of income	63.3	61.67	61.51
New equipment	3102	2113	4237
Cleaning	4250	3728	4237
Refuse	1000	1000	1000
Chemicals	4312	4302	4275
Insurance	564	570	580
Marketing	3521	3600	4200
Telephones	1569	1577	1607
Transport	243	150	300
Central admin	4352	4578	4496
Concessions	18000	18000	18000
Total	40913	36618	43641
% of income	33.4	30.2	34.5
Total expenditure	118513	111317	121440
Total income	122406	121116	126470
Profit/loss	3893	9799	5030
% of monthly income	3.18	8.1	3.97

Figure 4.2 Income and expenditure statement for one month period

The above layout shows clearly the contractor's position against contract for each of the headings. It is also of use to produce additional columns for comparisons with the previous year and possibly the contract's best year to date. Be careful however of cluttering the statement. It should remain as clear and straightforward as possible.

The same applies to the choice of headings to use under income and expenditure. The choice is subjective and influenced by the nature of the facility. You will need to group some items under a collective heading and to break some down into more detailed sub-headings. Again try and maintain clarity and ease of use.

Key point

Working documents of this type should be easy to read and interpret; whilst maintaining a level of detail which can positively inform the decision making process. This is not an easy balance to maintain.

Some items will be of universal interest, such as wages. These should be subdivided into meaningful headings and shown together with a sub total.

Key point

The inclusion of percentage indicators in the income and expenditure statement can assist in clarifying the position, especially when covering short periods of time such as a week or month.

In the above example two types of percentage indicator are given.

- **Percent of total income**—this figure is included under the income for the period. By showing it as a percentage of the yearly or contractual income managers are better placed to assess the magnitude of the income for the period.

- **Percent of income**—by expressing the expenditure as a percentage of income the relationship between the two can be monitored from month to month. The same calculation can also be used on other key figures, such as wages.

Activity

What are the main financial statements used to monitor performance in the organisation you are considering?

Matching income and expenditure

Matching is an important concept in dealing with income and expenditure. Essentially we need a basis on which to match both the income and the expenditure to specific periods of time. The main reasons in doing this are to allow a constant basis of comparison and for the calculation of concession payments.

Matching is important to all organisations for financial accounting purposes, but is particularly important in a client/contractor situation. Very few sport and leisure contracts will operate on a fixed price basis. The majority employing some form of income sharing, deficit guarantee contractual arrangement. The exact details of any such arrangement will of course vary from contract to contract.

The basis upon which this type of contract operates is two fold. Firstly, the contractor having submitted a successful bid, based on the predicted deficit for operating the contract, is awarded the relevant amount of monies on a pre-determined time scale. The amount tendered is the deficit which the client guarantees to pay and is the maximum cost to the client of operating the contract. In addition, any income which exceeds the estimates will be shared. For example, the successful bid for the management contract of a municipal golf course was based on the following estimates:

Expenditure	£500,000
Income	£380,000
Tender bid	£120,000

The authority 'guarantees the deficit' by promising to pay twelve monthly payments of £10,000 on satisfactory operation of the contract. In addition the authority also has an income sharing arrangement in which, income in excess of £380,000 is shared between the client and contractor on a 50/50 basis.

In a good year income may be £450,000. In which case the following concession payment would be made to the client.

Tendered income estimate	£380,000
Actual income	£450,000
Surplus	£70,000

Concession payment to client = £70,000 × 50% = £35,000

Conversely, the income could be below the tendered estimated in which case the contractor would absorb the full amount of any short fall.

The estimates may be broken down to work on a monthly or weekly basis. As such there will be a need for a monitoring process to inform both client and contractor of the level of income being received.

> **Key point**
>
> Where such arrangements exist it is essential that clear guidelines are drawn up to identify the time periods and how income and expenditure is to be allocated.

Prepayments and accruals

One way of matching income and expenditure to a time period it by using a accruals and prepayments procedure.

> **Definitions**
>
> Accruals: an expense incurred within a specific accounting period which remains unpaid until a future accounting period, for example a Christmas buffet which is not paid for until February.
>
> Pre-payments: payments received in one accounting period, which refer to an expense incurred in a subsequent period, for example income received for tickets in July but which refers to shows in August.

The benefits of this are:

- it allows income and expenditure to be apportioned to specific time periods on a consistent basis

- gives clear instructions to the contractor regarding the allocation of income

- allows clients a clear basis on which concession payments can be made.

The purpose of the prepayments and accruals approach is to apportion income and expenditure to the time period to which it refers, to allow for consistency and comparativeness.

Using the earlier example of the golf course, let us now elaborate the picture slightly to show the impact of using an accruals approach. In the first year of the contract income was £360,000 which means the following concession payment would be made to the client:

Tendered income estimate	£380,000
Actual income	£360,000
Surplus	–£20,000

Concession payment to client = *nil*

i.e. there existed a deficit and no payment was made to the client

The second year of the contract proved to be better than the first with income of £420,000, and so the following concession payment would be made to the client.

Tendered income estimate	£380,000
Actual income	£420,000
Surplus	£40,000

Concession payment to client = £40,000 × 50% = £20,000

So over the two year period the client received £20,000 in concession payments. Now consider the same example in which we employ an accruals and prepayments type approach to income.

Further examination reveals that in Year 1 £60,000 of the income was prepayment for next year's memberships and that in Year 2 £40,000 was prepaid membership for the following year.

Year 1

Tendered income estimate	£380,000
Actual income	£360,000
Less prepayment	
membership Year 2	£60,000
Surplus	–£80,000

Concession payment to client = *nil*

Year 2

Tendered income estimate	£380,000
Actual income	£420,000
Less prepayments	
membership Year 3	£40,000
Plus accruals	
membership Year 2	
paid in Year 1	£60,000
Surplus	£60,000

Concession payment to client = £60,000 × 50% = £30,000

> ### Key point
>
> Prepayments are subtracted and accruals added to any actual income received within a period.

In using this method not only does the client receive double the amount in concession payments, but also the income is reflected in the year to which it applies rather than that in which it is received.

The practical arrangements of most sport and leisure contracts will be constructed so that concession payments are done on the basis of income rather than a trading profit. Whilst a trading profit could be used as the basis if so desired, the arguments against it include:

- simplicity, concession payments calculated on the basis of a trading profit are infinitely more complex than those based on income only
- alleviates the problem of agreeing legitimate expenditure
- avoids contractors having to disclose levels of expenditure.

The simplest way of administrating concession payments for income sharing is on an annual basis. For domestic reasons this may not always be possible and can be done on whatever basis the client feels most appropriate, quarterly, monthly or even weekly.

> ### Key point
>
> A main consideration regarding the timing of payment in income sharing will be the contractor's cash flow.

The management of the performance, monitoring and evaluation process is often more concerned with establishing trends and identifying changes. The next two sections on Cusum charts and Ratios help move financial monitoring from a stationary 'snap shot' approach to one encapsulating the dynamics of financial activities within a leisure enterprise.

> ### Activity
>
> The earlier example of matching gives calculations for the first two years. Attempt to calculate the concession payment for Year 3 based on an income of £400,000 of which £42,000 is prepaid membership for Year 4.

Cusum charts

> **Definition**
>
> Cusum charts give a visual display of the accumulated variance from a target or standard.

Cusum charts can provide leisure managers with a powerful aid to highlighting small changes over time. They are particularly useful in controlling and monitoring performance, as the charts indicate the deviation of values from a fixed target.

For example, the manager of a leisure facility employs a number of staff on a casual basis. A budget of £300 per week has been allocated on the basis of the tender bid. Due to the varying and unpredictable levels of activity within the facility it is unlikely that spending will be exactly to budget each week. When expenditure or income is erratic the Cusum chart can assist in monitoring the position.

The following figures demonstrate this:

Week	1	2	3	4	5	6	7	8	9	10	11	12	13	14	15
WAGES	280	310	320	290	310	310	340	320	340	310	290	280	300	280	290
WAGES -TARGET /TENDER	–20	10	20	–10	10	10	40	20	40	10	–10	–20	0	–20	–10
CUSUM VALUE	–20	–10	10	0	10	20	60	80	120	130	120	100	100	80	70

The Cusum value represents the accumulated variance from target and is found by:

- Subtracting the target or tender estimate from the actual spend (wages −target/tender £300).

- Accumulating the variances over the period.

Over this 15 week time scale there are three distinct periods. In the first six weeks the spending on casuals wages, whilst never being exactly £300 deviates just above or below target. Those above, the overspends, being cancelled out by those below, the underspends. This has the effect of maintaining the Cusum figure at close to or actually at zero.

Section 2

During the second period, from weeks 6 to 10 there is a period of constant overspend. Whilst this is often of only small amounts, the cumulative effect can be seen in the increasing Cusum figure. In the third and final period between weeks 10 and 15 spending remains on or under the £300 target, having the opposite effect by decreasing the Cusum value.

These point are best shown when viewed, as they are intended to be, in chart form. The Cusum Chart for the above figures is shown in Figure 4.3 compared with a time series plot using the same figures.

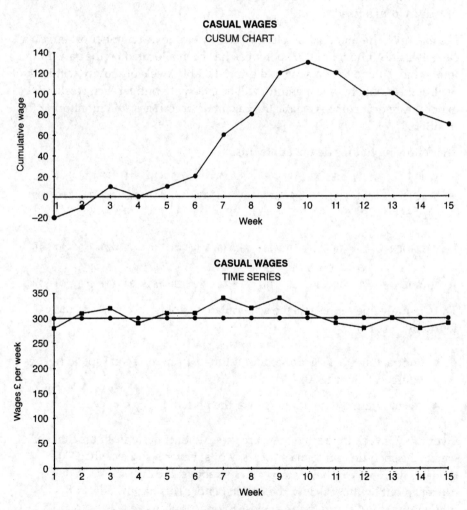

Figure 4.3 Comparison of a cusum curve and time series

The shape of the two graphs is very different as are their interpretation.

> ### Key point
>
> The value given by the Cusum chart is not as crucial, as the shape and direction of the curve, is it rising falling or remaining level.

The plot will demonstrate an upward tendency as long as the present values are on average above the target or tendered figure and conversely a downward tendency if below. The distance of the line above or below the target is essentially a reflection on previous not present levels of expenditure.

Given below are a number of brief interpretations to various shaped Cusum charts. Whilst these charts are easily constructed their interpretation is not as straightforward. The examples below will help the reader to grasp this skill.

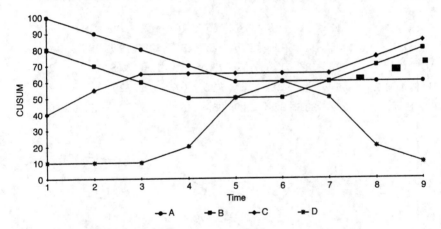

Figure 4.4 Example cusum charts

Brief interpretations:

A. Below target, returning to on target
B. Below target, on target, above target
C. Above target, on target, above target
D. On target, above target, below target

> ### Key point
>
> The interpretation of being above or below target as acceptable or not, will depend upon whether issues of income or expenditure are being examined.

Section 2

In the first example of Cusum charts the target or tender price remained constant at £300. In a working environment it is not always the case that targets would remain stable. Cusum charts can however still be used successfully to monitor position against target or contract when the target is variable. For leisure organisations it is often the case that targets and tender prices will be calculated to reflect the anticipated seasonal variations and will therefore be variable. When this is the case the Cusum value can be calculated using the variation between the tender value or target and the actual value. For example a golf course run under contract has the following estimates of income based on its tender bid.

Week	1	2	3	4	5	6	7	8	9	10
TENDER(£000)	8.2	12.2	12.2	16.2	16.5	9.1	10.2	12	13.1	13.3
ACTUAL(£000)	9.7	14.2	16.1	15	14	16.1	12	7.3	14.3	17.1
VARIANCE	1.5	2	3.9	−1.2	−2.5	7	1.8	5.3	1.2	4.2
CUSUM	1.5	3.5	7.4	6.2	3.7	10.7	12.5	17.8	19	22.8

Week	11	12	13	14	15	16	17	18	19	20
TENDER	14.7	14.2	14.7	12.6	12.2	13.7	12.1	9.9	10.7	10.4
ACTUAL	20.1	18.2	14.9	13.7	13.7	14.3	12.6	7.8	11.4	9.2
VARIANCE	5.4	4	0.2	1.1	1.5	0.6	0.5	−2.1	0.7	−1.2
CUSUM	28.6	32.6	32.8	33.9	35.4	36	36.5	34.4	35.1	33.9

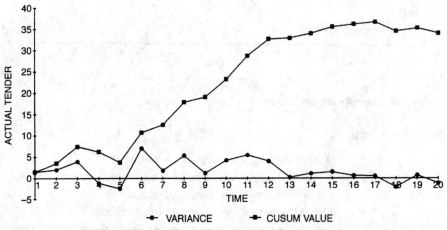

Figure 4.5 Comparison of cusum and variance plots

The plot in Figure 4.5 shows how the Cusum is used to monitor actual income against tendered income and in this case shows a very favourable picture.

90

Cusum charts can assist leisure managers in gaining an overview of financial performance and where possible should be calculated on a weekly basis.

Activity

Using a series of income and target figures from your organisation construct a Cusum chart and attempt an interpretation.

Ratio analysis

Many of the financial statements which are produced including the profit and loss account balance sheets etc. act only as a starting point for further investigation.

Many of which take the form of 'ratio analysis'.

Key point

Ratios indicate the proportional relationship between two factors.

The classes of objects which can be used for ratio analysis in leisure management are infinite and include both financial and non-financial information. It requires intelligent judgement on the behalf of the manager to select the relevant ones from what is an exhaustive list and to be able to produce a battery of measures which reflect the objectives of the organisation.

In designing an array of ratios managers should consider the following points, which apply equally to both the public and private sector, in order to produce a balanced picture of performance:

- are all objectives represented?
- are the different aspects of performance reflected?
- is the information required for the ratios obtainable?
- are the ratios easily understood?
- are they valid — do they measure what you want?
- are they reliable — will they maintain consistency for comparison?

Understanding ratios

Most ratios, financial and non financial, are normally expressed as either:

- a percentage or
- by the number of times one figure can be divided into another.

For example, if the operating expenditure of a sports centre amounted to £70,000 and the income to £35,000. There two options as to how these may be expressed. Firstly, it could be expressed as:

$$\frac{£70,000}{£35,000} = 2:1 \text{ i.e. the relationship between expenditure and income is two to one. For every pound of income two pounds have been spent.}$$

Equally this ratio could be expressed as a percentage which is achieved by multiplying the ratio by 100 i.e..

$$\frac{£70,000}{£35,000} \times 100 = 2 \text{ i.e. expenditure is 200 per cent of income.}$$

Key point

Convention to a large extent guides the format of specific ratios. The uppermost consideration should always be given to the recipient of the calculation.

Categorising ratios

Ratios are often discussed under the headings of the public and private/commercial sector. Such a dissection reflecting the private/commercial sector's primary concern with financial matters, in particular profit, and the public sector's concern with public good and welfare.

Under such headings ratios may possibly be seen as mutually exclusive to either group. Yet most ratios are of interest to both public and private operations. As Taylor and Gratton (1989) point out in discussing the objectives of public and private sector leisure organisations:

> It is apparent that there is no simple split in such objectives according to ownership. For example, a public sector supplier is likely to be interested in financial objectives, even if profit is unlikely; and a private sector supplier will be interested in serving the community's needs, not least because this is seen as consumer demand and is a source of revenue and growth for the supplier.

> **Key point**
>
> The objective in terms of ratios is to establish an array of relationships by which operational performance can be judged relative to organisational objectives.

Ratios should be seen as appropriate for all sectors of the industry. Whilst ratios can obviously be constructed which reflect different facets of the organisation, it is the mix between these which will reflect the overall priority of the organisation.

In searching for alternative headings from public and private sectors, under which to list ratios a solution is not easily found. One alternative is to use:

- financial ratios

- non financial ratios.

Such a spilt is again not ideal, as it suggests that ratios are developed using either financial or non financial data. Such a suggestion, of either or, is not strictly true because as will be shown later many ratios combine financial data with non financial data.

For example the ratio cost per visit involves using financial information regarding the operating cost of a facility and non financial information regarding the number of visitors (throughput) of the facility. When information is combined in this manner managers need to be able to assess whether the ratio reflects a measure of financial performance or usage.

For example: if a facility has an operating cost of £200,000 and attracts 100,000 people visitors per year, the ratio of cost per visit could be calculated as follows:

$$\frac{\text{Operating cost}}{\text{Number of visitors (throughput)}} = \frac{£200,000}{100,000} = £2.00 \text{ per visit}$$

Is this essentially a measure of financial performance or is it a measure of usage, i.e. capacity utilisation?

When doubt exists as to what the ratio is actually measuring, the validity can normally be established by examining how the ratio responds to change. For example, consider what would happen should a price cut be implemented. The normal response to a reduction in price is an increase in demand. As the majority of costs associated with leisure provision are fixed, the effect on the ratio will be to reduce it, i.e. if demand rises to 150,000 visits per year there is unlikely to be a proportional increase in operating cost as a result, giving:

$$\frac{\text{Operating cost}}{\text{Number of visitors (throughput)}} = \frac{£200,000}{150,000} = £1.33 \text{ per visit}$$

Such a calculation shows that this ratio is primarily concerned with capacity utilisation or usage rather than finance as it is the variations in the number of visitors which will be more significant and therefore hold more influence over the outcome of the ratio.

Given the changes that have taken place within the leisure industry within the last decade the most dramatic of which can be attributed to CCT, it no longer seems appropriate to categorise ratios as being of either public or private sector. For the large part there has been a merging of the sectors, due predominantly to the imposed free market environment in which public leisure organisations now operate, but in part also to the private sector being drawn into the public environment as contractors.

As such, the notion of public and private sector ratios no longer seems appropriate. The headings of financial and non financial ratios also have some obvious failings. The ratios discussed here are essentially those which can make a contribution to financial monitoring. The majority are applicable to both the public and private enterprises. When adjustments for individual sectors are necessary these are given.

Ratios for leisure enterprises

As stated earlier there is an infinite number of ratios which can be demonstrated by most organisations. A leisure enterprise is no different and it is often difficult to select relevant ratios. In the use of ratios this task is made somewhat easier by the fact that some can be arranged in a hierarchical order, in which the relationship between them can be demonstrated. This 'ratio map' allows for a systematic approach to identifying problems within an organisation. Such a map, shown in Figure 4.6 shows ratios on three levels:

- primary
- secondary
- tertiary.

Whilst this ratio map represents a convenient approach to ratio analysis, local government enterprises may have difficulty in identifying some of the values, for example the capital employed. Alternative calculations are given later where this problem is anticipated.

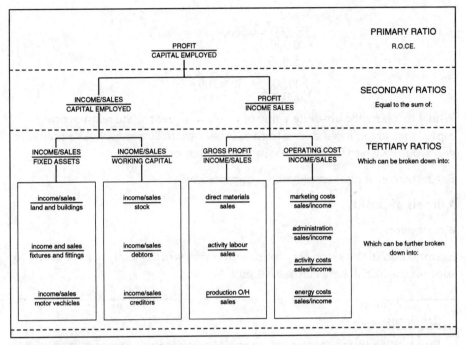

Figure 4.6 Ratio hierarchy map

By starting with the primary ratio of profit to capital employed, and moving through the secondary and tertiary levels it is possible to plot a route to areas of under and over performance. To demonstrate the point at a basic level consider the following example.

A Theme Park has the following levels of activity for two separate years.

	Year 1	Year 2
Income	1,500,000	1,500,000
Net Profit	350,000	500,000
Capital Employed	600,000	1,000,000

Using the above information we can calculate the primary ratio of profit to capital employed often referred to as the Return on Capital Employed (ROCE).

Key point

The ROCE ratio indicates to what extent resources have been employed to generate a profit.

Year 1

$$\frac{350,000}{600,000} = 0.583 \times 100 = 58.3\%$$

Year 2

$$\frac{500,000}{1,000,000} = .50 \times 100 = 50.0\%$$

Whilst in Year 2 the absolute value of profit was greater, the relative profit to capital employed has reduced from 58.3 per cent to 50 per cent. As a manager you would wish to investigate why this has happened.

The return on capital employed is supported by:

- levels of profit

- turnover.

Examination of the secondary ratios will reveal which elements have failed to support the ROCE between Years 1 and 2.

Definitions

Profitability: the ability to produce revenues in excess of expenses for a given period.

Turnover: the absolute volume of sales within a given accounting period in relation to the volume of investment.

Secondary ratios

Profitability ratio

	Year 1	Year 2
$\dfrac{\text{Profit}}{\text{Income}}$	$\dfrac{350,000}{1,500,000} = 23.3\%$	$\dfrac{500,000}{1,500,000} = 33.3\%$

Turnover ratio

$\dfrac{\text{Income}}{\text{Capital employed}}$	$\dfrac{1,500,000}{6,000,000} = 2.5$	$\dfrac{1,500,000}{1,000,000} = 1.5$

In this example the profitability ratio has increased and the turnover fallen. This has resulted, as the fall is proportionally larger than the increase, in a downward trend for the rate on capital employed.

As a manager you would more than likely be pleased to see the increase in profitability but have some concern over the decline in the turnover ratio.

Further investigation, using the 'ratio map' should be undertaken to investigate income to fixed assets and income to working capital in an attempt to locate a possible cause of the decline.

The relationship which exists between the secondary and primary ratios can also be demonstrated as follows:

$$\frac{\text{Profit}}{\text{Income}} \times \frac{\text{Income}}{\text{Capital employed}} = \frac{\text{Profit}}{\text{Capital employed}}$$

Therefore:

$$\frac{350,000}{1,500,000} \times \frac{1,500,000}{600,000} = 0.58 \times 100 = 58\%$$

Further explanation of the workings of a financial ratio hierarchy as described can be found in any good accountancy text (see further reading).

Whilst local government leisure services are now adopting many of the techniques of financial control previously associated with the commercial sector, there are limitation to this, due mainly to the financial structure and organisation of local government finances. For example it is difficult to define capital employed in the local government environment.

These together with a number of nuances of leisure operation necessitate the calculation of some additional ratios in the examination of financial issues in local government leisure enterprises. The ratios outlined below have been adapted from *Managing Sport and Leisure Facilities* (Sayers, 1992).

Recovery rate

Some leisure enterprises are not profitable e.g. local government. In such instances the additional calculation of a recovery rate ratio can be used to demonstrate the extent to which entry fees, or tariffs charged to use the facility cover the operating costs. The ratio is calculated as follows:

$$\frac{\text{Income}}{\text{Operating expenditure}} \times 100$$

The ratio expressed in this manner represents the operational recovery rate as opposed to the gross recovery rate (sometimes referred to as the service recovery rate) which is expressed by:

$$\frac{\text{Income}}{\text{All expenditure}} \times 100$$

The essential difference being the exclusion of debt charges together with profit centres such as bars and catering from the operating ratio.

Subsidy rates

The converse of the recovery rate is the subsidy rate. Again this can be examined on both a gross and operating basis in a similar way to the recovery rate.

The subsidy rate is conventionally expressed in terms of 'per user' meaning every person using the facility required a subsidy of a given number of pounds.

Gross subsidy (service subsidy):

$$\frac{\text{Gross expenditure} - \text{income}}{\text{Number of attendances or throughput}}$$

Operating subsidy:

$$\frac{\text{Operating expenditure} - \text{income}}{\text{Number of attendances or throughput}}$$

(See Chapter 6 on usage for calculation of throughput figure.)

Measuring income

It is useful to be aware of how different activities contribute to the total income of a facility. In Chapter 3 on data it was seen how this could be achieved for individual activities using 'Pareto analysis'.

Pareto analysis essentially produces ratios. Other additional areas of income may also be identified by ratio analysis including:

$$\frac{\text{Income from activities}}{\text{Total income}} \times 100$$

$$\frac{\text{Income from catering}}{\text{Total income}} \times 100$$

$$\frac{\text{Income from special events}}{\text{Total income}} \times 100$$

$$\frac{\text{Income from special events}}{\text{Total income}}$$

Additional elaboration can be given by comparing income to the number of square metres within the facility or income per hour of opening. It is common practice to calculate income as an average spend per head as:

$$\frac{\text{Income (excluding bar/catering)}}{\text{Number of admissions or throughput}}$$

All major sources of income should be identified and measured separately.

Measuring expenditure

The breakdown of expenditure can be examined by ratio analysis and is useful in examining the cost structure of an organisation. Measures of expenditure could logically be achieved by further developing the probability side of the ratio hierarchy. The more relevant measures of expenditure for use in leisure organisations are:

$$\frac{\text{Energy costs}}{\text{Operating expenditure}} \times 100$$

This ratio can also be broken down into its component parts of gas, electric, etc:

$$\frac{\text{Repairs and maintenance}}{\text{Operating expenditure}} \times 100$$

A further facet of expenditure which warrants special attention is that of employees' costs. Salaries and wages often represent the greatest single element of expenditure and as such should be monitored closely.

The simplest measure is:

$$\frac{\text{Energy costs}}{\text{Operating expenditure}} \times 100$$

Again where possible the elements of this cost should be sub-divided into relevant sections, for example in an arts centre all wages, i.e. the variable element of employees costs could be examined under the following headings:

- front of house stewards
- reception cover
- event stewards
- technicians
- duty manager cover.

All the above being expressed with operating expenditure of total employee costs.

Turnover

Whilst the ratio hierarchy deals extensively with the issue of turnover, there is one nuance of the leisure sector associated with local government which is worthy of explanation.

Section 2

The Secretary of State, under the rules governing Compulsory Competitive Tendering sets 'target levels' regarding profit expressed in terms of turnover. The following example shows how turnover is handled in this situation:

Facility income:

Income from users	250,000
Income from local government revenue budget (i.e. net deficit)	250,000
Total income (i.e. turnover)	500,000

Should the target for net profit on turnover be set at five per cent the tender price would be calculated as follows:

$$Turnover + profit - income\ from\ users$$

Categories or ratios

It helps when using ratios if they can be grouped into categories. The following eight categories highlight the key areas of performance which leisure organisations may wish to examine:

Profitability — ratios which demonstrate how successful the organisation has been at generating income either as a profit or recovery measure.

Asset utilisation (turnover) — ratios which examine the operating efficiency of the organisation. Such ratios look at how well the organisation has used the resources at its disposal.

Liquidity — ratios regarding liquidity examine the immediate availability of cash and attempts to assess the organisation's ability to meet its present financial arrangement.

Capital structure — ratios examining capital structure attempt to assess the risk of financial implication of the structuring.

Investment — investment ratios examine the return on investment for those organisations in which stages can be purchased.

Effectiveness — ratios dealing with effectiveness examine the attainment of output targets, but the cost of achieving these targets is given little consideration.

Efficiency — ratios considering the relationship between inputs and outputs and concern themselves with achieving objectives at a minimum cost.

Economy — the concern here is with achieving inputs at a minimum cost, and so considered in isolation there exists the possibility of false 'economy'.

As stated earlier the number of ratios that can be calculated is infinite. Figure 4.7 contains a summary of a number of ratios in each of the above categories.

It is not exhaustive and is meant as a indication of the possible combinations which managers may develop. All are shown with a comment regarding their use.

Profitability

$$\frac{\text{Gross or net profit}}{\text{Income}}$$ Variable, no standard

$$\frac{\text{Gross or net profit}}{\text{Income}}$$ Definitions regarding measure of profit and assets vary and therefore are unreliable in comparison.

Asset Utilisation

$$\frac{\text{Income}}{\text{Fixed assets}}$$ Also effectiveness measure.

$$\frac{\text{Gross or net profit}}{\text{Income}}$$ Indicates the revenue productivity of employees.

Liquidity

$$\frac{\text{Current assets}}{\text{Current liabilites}}$$ Often called the current ratio. Rule of thumb 2:1

$$\frac{\text{Current assets} - \text{inventories}}{\text{Current liabilities}}$$ The acid test, a more austere test of ability to meet debts. Rule of thumb 1:1.

$$\frac{\text{Balance sheet trade debtors}}{\text{Total credit sales} \times 365}$$ Shows average number of days for accounts payment.

Capital structure

$$\frac{\text{Borrowing (fixed interest capital)}}{\text{Net worth (ordinary share capital)}}$$ 'Gearing an indication' of risks of the capital structure.

Investment

$$\frac{\text{Dividend per share}}{\text{Market price per share}}$$ 'Dividend yield' rate of return on investment in shares.

$$\frac{\text{Net profit preference shares dividend}}{\text{Number of ordinary shares}}$$ Earning per ordinary share

Effectiveness

$$\frac{\text{Dividend per share}}{\text{Market price per share}}$$ Used on target groups indicates this effectiveness of catering and can be used as a survey of the wider population.

contd . . .

Effectiveness (contd)

$\dfrac{\text{Throughput}}{\text{Catchment population}}$	Participation rate (See usage section).
$\dfrac{\text{Bookings}}{\text{Total booking available}}$	Capacity utilisation (See usage section).
$\dfrac{\text{Marketing expenditure}}{\text{Throughput}}$	Use on any major area of expenditure which assumes relationships.

(Please see section on usage for more information including calculations on usage, utilisation and occupancy.)

Efficiency

$\dfrac{\text{Net operating expenditure}}{\text{Catchment population}}$	Per capita subsidy, this is often used but is an imperfect indicator. High subsidy does not necessarily mean an inefficient service.
$\dfrac{\text{Net operating expenditure}}{\text{Total throughput}}$	'Subsidy per visit' is best applied if desegregated into different types of users/activities.
$\dfrac{\text{Direct income (fees/charges)}}{\text{Gross operating expenditure}}$	'Cost recovery' not perfect as an indicator of efficiency. It may be the authority's intention to have a highly subsidised service.

Economy

$\dfrac{\text{Staff costs}}{\text{Gross operating expenditure}}$	Use on any cost items within the organisation, e.g. energy administration.
$\dfrac{\text{Cleaning expenditure}}{\text{Floor space}}$	Only assesses input, no indication of quality.

Figure 4.7 Ratios for key areas of performance
Adapted from: Economics of Leisure Organisation, Taylor and Gratin.

There exists a number of problems which may be encountered in establishing and operating a set of ratios including:

- The ability to state organisational standards. Variations in the level and type of use between facilities, will result in resources of all types, being distributed in a different way in the various facets of the organisation. Direct comparisons of ratios therefore are misleading as to relative performance.
- Ratios can over simplify the situation. When inadequate sources of data are resources feeding into ratios the result can be an over simplified and misleading measure or indicator. Ideally any information to be used should be available directly from a facility's records.

- The information used in ratios can often be calculated in a number of ways. For example profit and capital employed figures can be constructed quite legitimately in a number of ways, with various outcomes. Consistency of calculation should be checked when comparisons are being made.
- Getting people to use ratios appropriately.

Activity

- Take an overview of the financial stewardship in your organisation and consider how the information in this chapter can help to improve it.

- Obtain a copy of a leisure enterprise's aims and objectives, consider what ratios could be used to best reflect how the organisation is performing against them.

LEARNING POINTS

- Tender bids for sport and leisure contracts should reflect the balance between estimated income and expenditure.
- The income and expenditure statement has a number of advantages over the profit and loss account for leisure managers monitoring at an operational level.
- Financial stewardship is an essential element of the monitoring process.
- The inclusion of percentage indicators in the income and expenditure statement can help clarify performance.
- Matching allocates income and expenditure to specific time periods.
- Income sharing is best calculated on a revenue basis rather than a profit basis as it is easier to monitor in this form.
- Ratios are an expression of how one item exists proportionally to another i.e. profit to expenditure, etc.
- Ratios should be developed as a battery of measures which reflect the organisation's aims.
- Ratios are conventionally expressed as either a percentage or by the number of times one figure can be divided into another.
- The ratio hierarchy allows a systematic approach to identifying areas of under and over performance.
- Cusum values show the accumulated effect of variances from target.
- The value given by a Cusum chart is not as crucial as the shape and direction of the curve; is it rising, falling or remaining level.
- Many financial statements act only as the starting point for further investigation.

Section 2

REFERENCES AND FURTHER READING

Audit Commission (1988) *Performance Review in Local Government*, HMSO

Fox, R., Kennedy, A., and Sugden, K., (1990) *Decision Making: a management accounting perspective*, CIMA Butterworth Heinemann

Sayers, P. (1992) *Managing Sport and Leisure Facilities*, E. & F. N. Spon

Taylor, P., and Gratton, C. (1989) *Economics of Leisure Organisations*, Longman

Weswick, C. A. (1987) *How to Use Management Ratios*, Gower

Whitehouse, J. and Tiley, C. (1992) *Finance and Leisure*, Longmans

5

Contract monitoring

Introduction

A large segment of today's local government leisure facilities are run under contract, as a result of the compulsory competitive tendering imposed by Government. To ensure that contractors are maintaining the standards laid down in the specifications of a contract, it is essential that a contract is monitored (see Figure 5.1).

Contract monitoring particularly attends to:

- contractual compliance
- validation of payments between contractor and client
- indicates how well the enterprise is doing
- general quality of service
- quality of equipment and materials used
- response to complaints.

Key point

The contract monitoring role is the responsibility of the client.

An integrated system for the monitoring of sport and leisure contracts will form the bedrock of good contract management. As a process of performance, monitoring and evaluation contract monitoring is made easier by a detailed specification. The specification represents a very precise description of the tasks required of the contractor, for example one aspect of performance for a swimming pool contract may be associated with maintaining given levels of water temperature. This may appear in the specification as follows.

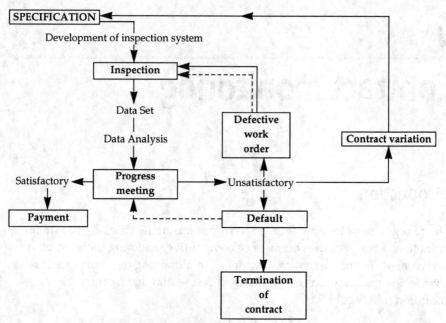

Figure 5.1 The contract monitoring process

The contractor shall ensure that the pools within the centre are maintained in accordance with these standards to ensure safe and hygienic water conditions at all times.

	Water temperature °C	
Swimming pools	28	30
Swimming pools (galas)	26	26

Such a specification spells out exactly what is expected of the contractor in terms of water temperature. For this type of specification it is relatively easy to find an appropriate tool for measurement purposes. Not all specifications are as straight forward as this. The problems of measuring contract specifications are essentially:

■ the number of individual specifications is often large

■ some specifications would require continuous monitoring, i.e. levels of cleanliness, staff behaviour

■ the measurement tool is not always obvious, i.e. on what basis do we measure concepts such as equity, comfort or quality?

Whilst these problems are real they are not insurmountable.

Key point

The starting point for all contract monitoring should always be the specification.

The specification document will not only give the aspect of performance which is to be measured, but will often give a basis of comparison by stating an acceptable or expected standard. For example the above specification referring to the temperature of swimming water, firstly indicates the basis of performance, i.e. swimming pool water temperature and gives the basis of evaluation by stating minimum and maximum temperatures for different forms of usage. All that is required is the measurement tool to allow completion of the PME process. In this instance this can be achieved relatively easily through the use of a thermometer. The problem of sampling, how many times and when do we measure the temperature, can be solved by the use of maximum–minimum thermometers which constantly measure the temperature. Not all specifications are as easy to monitor.

The importance and use of contract monitoring

Whilst normally carried out by the client or agency department contract monitoring produces information which is of use to both the client and the contractor.

Use of monitoring to the client:

- to ensure that the conditions of the contract, for which payments will be made, are completed

- to safeguard the use of public money

- to provide evidence that the authority or client has established that the obligations of the contractor have been completed under the conditions of the contract.

Use to the contractor:

- to draw contractor attention to areas of high, poor and improving performance, including areas of potentially greater income and growth

- to allow negotiation and flexibility of the contract

- acts as a free research service as to levels and standards of service.

The monitoring process is the client's responsibility and is fundamentally for the benefit of the client.

Key point

When there is under performance it is the client's responsibility to identify the reasons and take the necessary action.

The inspector

The inspector or monitor of contracted leisure services is faced with a difficult task. Leisure services have in the past been measured on the basis of inputs (money), as the outputs (people's experiences) of leisure services are often intangible. In terms of measurement the task is considerably easier in the production industry. Inspecting cars as they roll off the production line is relatively easy compared to inspecting the quality of a person's leisure experience. All too often in leisure the product is instantly consumed and intangible thereafter. Inspection can only identify the tangible items which surround and hopefully contribute towards ensuring a quality leisure experience, pool water, cleanliness of the building, etc.

Key point

The monitoring process should as far as possible never interfere with the contractor's ability to perform the conditions of the contract.

The above key point puts monitors in a difficult position, they are often restricted in access to the most fruitful source of information, the customer — yet need to monitor the position in a fair manner. The methods which can be used are numerous including photographic evidence, visual inspection together with techniques designed to get the monitor close to the service without interfering, so that a general picture of the service can be developed.

> **Key point**
>
> All monitors should have access to examine or inspect any facet of the service performed under contract at any time without prior notice.

Many specifications require constant, around the clock, monitoring. This is obviously impractical in many instances. As a result a common practice in monitoring activities is sampling (see Chapter 3 on the use of samples).

> **Key point**
>
> Sampling allows us to accurately measure many aspects of an organisation with the least possible disruption to activities.

Whilst the monitoring process endeavours to produce measures in as precise and exact a manner as possible, such a stringent approach should not be adopted to the client/contractor relationship. The need for precise, reliable and valid measurement is required so that both sides of the contract are able to agree on the position. A flexible approach is the best route to an effective partnership.

Developing an observational inspection system

In contract monitoring 'observation' or going and looking is an important method of data collection. Unlike areas such as finance, in which data is compiled essentially from documentation and on which decisions can be made without stepping in the facility to which they refer. There are however many aspects of contract monitoring which do not generate data in such a readily usable form and so require observation.

Veal (1991, page 85) gives us an eight point plan which he suggests constitute the main tasks in devising an observational project. Its worth re-iterating these points but, with a more specific application to contract monitoring. The tasks Veal suggests are:

- choice of site
- choice of observation points, within or outside the site
- choice of time period

- decision on whether to observe continually or undertake spot counts/observations
- if sampling, decisions on the number and length of sample
- decisions on what to observe numbers or behaviour, etc.
- where spatial behaviour is involved decisions on the areas into which the site is to be divided and the preparation of site maps
- design of a recording sheet.

Some of these points will have more relevance to contract monitoring than others, but the general scheme remains good in the observational situation. We will now examine each aspect in a little more detail, keeping in mind the purpose to which they are to be applied.

Choice of site

The choice of site may be fixed in that there may only be one swimming pool or facility which has to be observed. It may also be fixed by the specification of the contract. The choice of site may also need to be decided upon via a system of sampling. For example when inspecting play areas or bowling greens of which an authority may have many, it would be necessary to make choices about which ones could be practically observed. Similarly a national cinema chain may have to select which to inspect should it not be feasible to travel to all sites.

Choice of observation point

The monitoring process should as far as possible never interfere with the contractor's ability to perform the conditions of the contract. All inspecting should attempt to give the least possible interruption to the activities being observed and any other activities taking place nearby. Inspectors should therefore give apt consideration to the activity and position themselves accordingly. It may also be the case that covert or undercover observations may be necessary when observing staff behaviour or simply wishing to experience the facility through the eyes of the user.

For example hotel and tourist operators have for many years used 'mystery visitors' to sample the level and quality of service offered by the hotels they use.

> **Activity**
>
> Consider how any part of the monitoring process could be inhibiting to a contractor.

Choice of time period

Serious consideration needs to be given to the choice of time period in which the observations will take place. Depending on what is being observed, it will be necessary to vary the amount of attention given to this. For example in making observations regarding the efficiency of the reception area it may be desirable to observe how long people had to queue before being served. There would be little point in observing this activity every Saturday evening, which happens to be the quietest time of the week. Such problems may be solved by the application of sampling techniques (see Chapter 3). Be careful, however of the consequences of using fractional sampling on such problems and to take account of the seasonality of the leisure sector's activities.

Continuous observation or spot counts

Whether to undertake continuous observation or spot counts will depend on:

- the resources available
- the level of accuracy required
- the subject and intended outcomes of the observations.

All observation uses the valuable resource of manpower which will affect the nature of observation. Using the reception example the commitment in terms of resources would be greater if we observed how long it took customers to be served than it would be if we took a spot count on the length of the queue. It may be argued that the two methods measure different aspects of that service. Whilst you may feel that the length of time each customer has to wait is a better indicator of service, if you have limited resources the spot count may have to be used.

If a high level of accuracy is required then continuous observation will be necessary. When less accuracy is sought a number of spot checks may suffice. The nature of the observation will affect the decision. For example; If observing pool staff behaviour, a momentary spot check is unlikely to give any real insight. Continuous observation, however, over a longer period of time is more likely to allow a true insight into behaviour.

Length and number of observations

The number of observations we make of a particular subject is again dependent upon the resources available and the level of accuracy required. It may be useful to calculate the necessary number of observations (i.e. sample size) by the method described in Chapter 3, in the first instance based upon the ideal level of accuracy. If resources will not allow for this number of observations reduce the target level of accuracy until they do. By using this method it will be possible to assess the results in terms of their accuracy. Always keep in mind the level of accuracy that has been accepted when acting upon the results.

Sampling

Due to volume of events, activities and facilities, sampling methods may need to be employed. In contract monitoring it is particularly important that representative samples are obtained. The reason for this is that through the process of monitoring, in the case of defective work, it will be the client's responsibility to prove non-compliance. The use of statistical evidence in such matters would without doubt come under scrutiny as to its reliability and validity. The employment of sound sampling techniques is therefore necessary. Sampling methods are used in a number of areas covered in this text and Chapter 3 gives a detailed description of sampling.

British Standard 6001 gives sampling procedures and tables for inspection by attributes. The use of a British Standard when sampling has obvious benefits if and when the contract needs to be enforced. Unfortunately BS 6001 was developed with industrial production in mind. Whilst this makes BS 6001 unsuitable in many leisure situations, this is not to say that the spirit of the standard can not be maintained and followed where possible.

BS 6001 has been adopted in spirit by local authorities in the monitoring of other contracted out areas including refuse collection and grounds maintenance.

Key point

It is important that the boundaries of sampling are agreed between the client and contractor before sampling commences.

What to inspect

Due to the wide range of work being carried out in any sport and leisure management contract, it is not possible to monitor every item of work every time it's performed. It remains the client's responsibility as to what to inspect.

Key point

Clients need to be aware of the pitfalls of only monitoring highly visible activities.

Contractors, both in-house and private sector operators, operate on a financial bottom line. As a result both, given the opportunity, can be prone to the furtive operation of contract specifications. It is only human nature to concentrate on the high profile areas often at the expense of other areas. It is the client's responsibility to put into place a system of monitoring which ensures attention to the whole range of activities.

The problems in achieving this are:

- the selection of a cross section of activities/facilities to be inspected.
- the frequency of inspection
- establishing a coding or rating procedure for the measurement of different activities.

Key point

In the initial setting up of a monitoring system the contract documents should be examined for all specifications which may warrant inspection. These should then be listed as brief short statements.

The specifications for each sport and leisure contract will vary, therefore the list of items to be monitored will also vary from contract to contract. Many will however have a common core of activities. It is this list which will form the basis for the development of an inspection sheet. Below are a number of examples of the kind of statements which can arise from the more formal language of the specification.

- are opening hours displayed?
- are forthcoming closures displayed?

- is the price tariff displayed?

- are the floor markings in good order?

- are the showers working?

- are all the staff wearing uniform?

- is all equipment in good order?

- are staff monitoring pool behaviour?

Activity

Consider how you would approach any aspect of a monitoring process under the following headings:

- choice of site
- choice of observation point
- time period
- how you sample
- what you observe.

Can you improve the way you do any of these?

From the monitor's point of view the easiest type of inspection is that which produces a dichotomous response range — yes or no, is it or is it not. Where possible the monitoring process should be brought down to this basic level. It is however the client's responsibility again to decide upon the level of response required.

To inspect by attribute or by variables

Due to the vast array of items which may come up for inspection as part of a sport and leisure contract it is feasible that inspection may take place using both an attribute and variable approach.

For any item under inspection there should be pre-determined standards or benchmarks for evaluation purposes. Such a benchmark or standard can be set on one of two bases, by attribute or by variables.

Definitions

Inspection by attribute — this means that the item under inspection is classified on a dichotomous basis of either pass or fail, acceptable or defective. When inspecting by attribute no indication of the degree of

---

acceptability or defectiveness is given, i.e. a lifeguard either has a whistle or not; no degree of measurement is possible.

Inspection by variables — Conversely inspection by variables takes into account the degree of acceptability or defectiveness and relies on being able to take measurements of the items under inspection, i.e. pool water temperatures and grass length both have degrees of measurement. When an item can be measured, it is still possible to classify each item under inspection as having the attribute of either acceptability or defectiveness by placing a demarcation point on the measurement scale.

Designing the recording sheet

The monitoring list obtained above is the starting point in the design of the recording sheet. In reality the list would contain many more headings than the example. What is required is to organise all these headings. There are several ways of doing this. The chosen method will be up to the individual depending upon how they prefer to work. It is practical to categorise the headings by either:

- activities
- facilities.

For example a swimming pool may be inspected as a facility, in which case the sheet would contain any headings associated with the pool, including anything to do with cleaning, staffing, notices, equipment, etc. Conversely, a sheet could be created on which all observations regarding a specific activity would be made, i.e. the notice boards in reception, poolside, sports halls and corridors would appear on the same sheet. Example headings for each approach are given below.

Activity monitoring sheets:

- staff behaviour
- notices
- cleanliness
- equipment
- safety
- building.

Facility monitoring sheets:

- pool complex
- driving range
- sports hall
- reception area
- changing areas
- sauna suite.

The manner in which these are organised is not as important as recording the data correctly. Cross references can always be made at a later date. There is no reason why you cannot have a combination of both. What is important is that all areas are included.

Activity

Examine an existing monitoring sheet for its validity, e.g. do the questions asked measure what they are intended to? How could you improve its validity?

Using scales

Some specifications may be abstract in that they can not be monitored by the use of only one factor. For example a specification may require that changing areas must be kept clean, tidy and comfortable for users.

With specifications of a more intangible nature a picture of the general condition is built up. When monitoring this is done in much the same manner as by a customer. By observing different aspects of the facility, do the showers work?, are the lockers working?, is the area clean?, is there adequate lighting? All of these factors make up an overall impression of the facility.

The monitoring process works in exactly the same manner only it requires a more systematic method of recording this information.

Scales are useful for the following reasons:

- they help to simplify complex situations and concepts
- the validity of the measure is increased by numerous observations

- the reliability of the measure is increased

- they enhance the precision of the measure

- they help to simplify information for reporting purposes.

For example in monitoring a gymnasium the following aspects are identified as contributing to the general service on offer and used to develop a scaled score:

Gymnasium Inspection Sheet

Cleanliness	1	2	3	4
Maintenance of equipment	1	2	3	4
Supervision	1	2	3	4
Lighting	1	2	3	4
Room temperature	1	2	3	4

Where
1 = Work carried out above specification standard
2 = Work carried out to specification standard
3 = Work below specification standard
4 = Unsatisfactory work

The scale score will vary depending on how well the monitor considers each aspect of the work has or is being carried out. To obtain the scaled score simply add the score for each aspect (see Table 5.1). Each time the gym is inspected the results can be added to develop a data base of information. When a volume of information has been accumulated then trends and patterns can be identified.

Table 5.1 Example of scaled scores for inspections of gymnasium

Inspection	Cleanliness	Maintenance	Supervision	Lighting	Temperature	Score	interpretation
1	4	4	1	2	2	13	unsatisfactory
2	1	3	1	3	2	10	satisfactory
3	1	2	2	3	2	10	satisfactory
4	2	1	1	2	2	8	very satisfactory
5	4	3	2	2	3	14	unsatisfactory

Key point

The data obtained when using this type of scale building is often only of an ordinal nature and consideration must be given to any further analysis.

Accepting and rejecting

The basis by which you either accept or reject an inspection also requires consideration.

Following the spirit of BS 6001 this decision can be made on the basis of defectives or defects.

Definition

Defect: a deviation from requirement, an item or score which is below the required standard.
Defective: a unit or object of analysis that contains one or more defects.

In monitoring a decision is required as to whether the agreed level of outcomes is to be made on the basis of defects or defectives. This is something that needs to be agreed between the contractor and client before monitoring begins.

The distinction is of little or no importance if the item under investigation is not capable of having more than one defect. A light bulb works or it does not!

It has been shown that many aspects of a leisure contract require the building up of a picture through the examination of a number of characteristics. Such as in the gymnasium example in which cleanliness, maintenance, supervision, lighting and room temperature were all considered. In such a situation as in Table 5.1 it may be said that there are two defects (cleanliness and maintenance) but only one defective. When a number of possible defects are possible in this manner the distinction becomes essential.

The out come of a series of inspections can be expressed as either:

■ Percentage defective or

■ Number of defects per 100 inspections.

For example, consider a series of inspections of a swimming pool, in which, a number of aspects of the service are under examination including, pool temperature, air temperature, lifeguards, etc. From 25 inspections only 20 were found to be totally acceptable, two have three defects (i.e. water, light etc. not to required level) one has two defects and one has one defect. The two expressions can be given as follows for the same data.

Percentage defective:

$$100 \times \frac{\text{Number of defectives}}{\text{Number of inspection}}$$

$$= 100 \times 5/25 = 20\%$$

i.e. 20% of inspections would be failed.

Number of defects per 100 is given by:

$$100 \times \frac{\text{Number of defects}}{\text{Number of inspections}}$$

$$= 100 \times 9/25 = 36$$

i.e. for every 100 inspections we would expect to find 36 defectives.

Which method is employed is for consideration by individual monitoring systems. BS 6001 gives a number of factors which may be taken into account in making that decision:

- Percentage defective analysis assumes no distinction between an article under investigation having only one or having more than one defect. An inspection will be classified as either acceptable/ not acceptable with no other distinction.

- Inspection for defects per 100 units makes the assumption that an inspection with three defects is as significant as three inspections with one defect in each.

- It is desirable to maintain a constant approach throughout the monitoring process so that comparisons can be made.

- The percentage defective approach can have economic benefits. Inspection could cease when one defect is identified and only resume after confirmation from the contractor of amendment. Whilst the saving in both manpower and financial terms may be appealing, this is not recommended especially when scores/results databases are being developed.

In a text such as this it is impossible to recommend which approach to adopt. Individual monitors will need to assess their own needs and circumstances. The outcome being as much to do with the nature of the activity being monitored as with the assent under which the contract is being managed as all contracts have a unique set of circumstances.

Key point

When the basis of inspection has been decided, acceptable outcomes need to be defined.

Activity

Take any aspect of the service you are familiar with and explore how a system based on defects and defectives could be developed.

Appendix 1 gives a number of example monitoring sheets. The sheets cover monitoring of the areas below. Due to the varying needs of different authorities the sheets shown are unlikely to be readily transferable. They will however serve as a basis from which sheets can be developed for individual situations.

- **General observation sheet** — all monitors should be equipped with a general sheet of this nature to record any observation which are not part of a routine inspection. Observations not part of a specific are often forgotten.

- **Activity monitoring sheet** — the example shown is for the inspection of outdoor pitches.

- **Marketing monitoring sheet** — monitoring sheets can be developed for any facet of the service which management or the client deem necessary. Monitoring marketing activities is one such activity.

Whilst all these sheets have been designed to address different needs of the monitoring process where possible all should contain a number of common features which include:

- **A space for comments** — no matter how well thought out the monitoring sheet is, there is still likely to be occasions when the monitor feels that further comment is necessary. By providing a space on each sheet to facilitate this, inspectors will have total freedom of response outside those elicited by the forced response questions. For interpreting such responses read the section on open ended questions in chapter 6.

- **Date and weather recording** — such information is vital to the valid monitoring of services. It is important that monitoring is undertaken with due respect to the prevailing conditions and environment. For example, it is unreasonable to expect the reception area to remain as clean and tidy during wet, slushy weather as it does on hot, dry days. Similarly, the level of queuing, or average waiting time will be understandably increased, compared to other Mondays, on bank holidays. The same principle applies to special events which affect the usage directly or indirectly such as galas, road runs, local carnivals, festivals etc. All such information should appear on the monitoring sheet so as it may be taken into account in the evaluation.

The monitoring of secondary services, such as catering, can be very productive. Not only does this allow insights into other monitored areas but is important to the overall assessment of the facility, contributing to the general impression gained from an inspection, i.e. in monitoring outdoor areas it is necessary to give consideration to the state of rivers and streams, footpaths and buildings which may form part of the experience but are not within the responsibility of the contract being monitored. This practice is particularly important when separate leisure DLOs are in operation and the monitoring of secondary services is normally carried out in isolation.

Activity

Do you think that monitoring by facility or monitoring by activity is best for the facility you are considering? What are your reasons for this?

Supplementary monitoring methods

Photography

The use of photography in the monitoring process is widespread. As the song says 'a picture paints a thousand words' and is certainly better at conveying certain aspects of a service than not only words but indices also.

Photographs are particularly useful for illustrating:

- levels of cleanliness
- levels of tidiness
- extent of damage

- levels of deterioration

- congestion

- aesthetic values.

Used together with text and indices, photographic evidence can provide convincing support to other forms of data.

Key point

Warning: Whilst it is done, use of photography in the observation of staff is possibly unethical and certainly demoralising for employees and can be embarrassing for some members of the public.

Participant observation

When an inspector appears in a facility armed with a clipboard and pen, it is only natural that staff and management will ensure, if only temporarily, that things appear as they should be. It is for this reason that it may be useful for monitors to see the facility through the eyes of the customer. By becoming a user a real picture of the facility may be observed. In social science this technique of observation is often used and is termed 'participant observation'.

The technique of participant observation is very useful in providing initial insights into the workings of an organisation. Use of the technique in monitoring a leisure organisation is compromised by:

- Social interaction with other users being difficult, although it is not impossible, for example, the inspector could join the squash league or keep fit class.

- The ability to remain anonymous. Staff and management of a facility are quite likely to know who you are. Even if you just happen to play at the golf club any way, you will certainly create the state visit effect when seen.

The above difficulties should not deter observation . Even if you are known by staff and if the people you participate with are aware of your position, by being a participant you will still see things from a different angle; through the eyes of the customer.

Recording information from participant observation can be difficult. Essentially there is no alternative than to make notes immediately after participation. The longer the recording process is left the less accurate and less detailed it will be. If taking part in an activity during an evening, don't wait until you get to the office the next day before making notes.

Advantages of participant observation:

■ the activity is 'experienced' rather than observed

■ the experience is complete, i.e. the whole visit is seen from start to finish, from booking office to showering

■ any immediate response from other users is seen. Mutterings in changing rooms and entrance ways can reveal many things about the quality of service on offer.

Customer complaints

Despite the monitor's efforts there will inevitably be times when the facility will not be monitored. It is therefore essential to the overall monitoring process to employ a degree of self-monitoring.

Key point

The process of self-monitoring relies on customers speaking out when they are not happy with the level or standard of service.

To allow for self-monitoring to be facilitated, a system for customer comments needs implementing which is both:

■ accessible — who do you complain to? How do you complain?

■ effective — the complaint results in something being done.

All complaints should be recorded and copies sent to the client or agency department responsible for monitoring. Records should contain the following information:

■ contract to which the complaint is associated

■ location and to whom the complaint was initially addressed, whether personally by post, telephone, etc.

■ nature of the complaint

■ location of complaint

- name and address of complainant

- date of complaint

- time of complaint

- any circumstances surrounding the complaint.

Additional space should also be allowed to:

- record client and contractors comment

- record the action taken as a result of the complaint, e.g. reply to customer, defective work order issued, variation order issued.

Such records should ideally form part of a quality management system which would ensure a prompt response to all complaints.

Defective work and variations

Should the standard or level of work be found to be of an unsatisfactory nature it is important that this be conveyed to the contractor.

> **Key point**
>
> Defective work orders should only be issued on the basis of a continual trend rather than a single instance: except under extreme circumstances.

One-off items of a less serious nature are better resolved in a less formal manner through a progress meeting. It is also best to discuss the issue of defective work notices prior to the issue being raised at a progress meeting.

The monitoring process will no doubt from time to time produce results of an unsatisfactory nature which can not be attributed to the contractor's efforts. For example, if the level of cleanliness being observed in the changing rooms of a swimming pool prove to be unsatisfactory, but the contractor is found to be fulfilling his obligations to the contract regarding the number and intensity of cleans. Clearly in such cases the contract specifications are at fault. Extra cleaning is required if the level of cleanliness the client desires is to be achieved. Any additional work to the contractor will have a cost implication. A variation order acts as an official notice to carry out this work at an agreed price.

The dynamic nature of leisure in which the service is constantly changing and developing to accommodate new needs and markets, requires that amendments to the contract will need to be initiated in the same manner. Contracts written for the management of sport and leisure facilities are relatively new and in the early years will require constant amendment and change as they develop.

Data analysis

The monitoring process should produce through the inspection sheets, information which can be collated for purposes of analysis. Ideally information should be capable of being entered directly into a computer.

Earlier we saw that not all data could be treated equally and that there are restrictions on the analysis depending upon the level of data possessed. Trends are particularly useful in contract monitoring and where possible time series and other trend identifying techniques such as Cusum charts could be used. Chapter 3 gives a full explanation on handling data.

LEARNING POINTS

- Contract monitoring is the formal process of stewarding sport and leisure contracts with benefits for both contractor and client.

- The setting up of a monitoring process similar to that shown in Figure 5.1 ensures effective communication between contractor and client.

- The contract specification is the basis of developing a monitoring system.

- Monitoring is the responsibility of the client.

- Monitoring indices should endeavour to be as precise and reliable as possible, however the management of the monitoring process should adopt a flexible give and take approach.

- The extent, level and boundaries of sampling need to be agreed between all involved in the process before monitoring begins.

- The majority of inspections require generalising from the few to the many in the evaluation stage.

- The monitoring process can be divided into manageable sections on the basis of either facilities or activities.

- The use of scales helps to simplify complex situations whilst increasing validity.

- Beware of the level of data generated in the monitoring process.

- Participant observation gives a customer's eye view of the service.

- Variations to the contract are inevitable as it is a dynamic working document.

- A main concern of the monitoring process is with trends rather than isolated instances.

- Regular progress meetings are the key to an effective partnership between contractor and client.

REFERENCES AND FURTHER READING

Veal (1991) *Research Methods for Leisure and Tourism*, a practical guide, Longman

6

Usage monitoring

Introduction

Usage monitoring can be seen as a similar activity to market research. It is the process by which a leisure enterprise gathers information regarding its customers. Who they are? How they are consuming the service, etc. In leisure organisations use of market intelligence has management implications for both public and private enterprises.

Usage has for a long time been considered a variable worth examining in the assessment of a leisure facility. How well used is this leisure facility? A question that managers have long been required to find the answer to. For all leisure managers the need to collect information regarding usage of the facilities still exists and in many areas of the industry has increased.

Key point

The advent of CCT has evoked a more 'mandatory' approach to examining usage.

Key point

The more we understand about the customer the more likely we are to make the correct decisions concerning them.

Usage monitoring is not simply a matter of counting the number of people using a facility. Although that is often used especially when dramatic effect is required. Half a million users a year sounds fairly impressive, especially when the catchment area only has around 100,000 people. The obvious assumptions to which many people would jump given this information is 'what a great community building' most people in the area must be making use of it!. In reality probably less than 10% of the catchment population actual use the facility; 10% just happen to go once a week all year. The management implications of this are great for both the public and private sector, for both social policy and market development reasons.

For such reason, usage monitoring needs to be explicit in what it reveals:-

- who used the facility?
- what activities are they doing?
- how often do they visit us?
- what SOC/ECO background do they come from?
- are we attracting special needs groups?
- what use do they make of the centre?

As with many other areas of monitoring, usage has been lacking in any pre-determined targets or standards. For those running facilities within a CCT environment, this problem has to some extent been overcome, local government officers now have to commit at least some level of usage to paper as part of their contract specifications which make the job of monitoring somewhat easier.

Key point

The most important elements in any leisure service are users. Leisure managers make many decisions, all of which directly or indirectly affect them.

In 'Managing a leisure management contract', Rogers and Chaytor examined the topic of managing the social conscience. They looked at how the 'public good' could co-exist within an economically viable business, pointing out the often unseen benefits to the client. Within the same section they also identified some of the key responsibilities of managing this potentially conflict ridden area in which commercially minded contractors are put in the position of pursuing customers with less ability to pay or who require a special effort, normally at a cost, to accommodate them. In such situations the client obviously holds the trump card in terms of being able to specify the contract. But as Rogers and Chaytor rightly point out there are benefits for both sides in pursuing such groups. One of the key responsibilities in managing this situation is that of monitoring the effectiveness of such schemes. This section will pick up where they left off and begin to examine how we may monitor this and other issues to do with usage.

Usage is controlled or specified in contract documents with three purposes in mind:

- to protect access for deprived groups
- to maintain levels of public access
- to restrict commercial and non-sporting use of the facilities.

Public facility provision and catering for special needs are both worthy social policies, either one taken to the extreme however, can become a threat to the other. Too much public access can deprive disadvantaged groups in the same way that too many special needs sessions can restrict general use. In addition to the threat that these groups pose to each other both could have their access to facilities restricted if contractors were allowed to pursue commercial and/or other sporting activities freely.

The only way of controlling the levels of activity for these different interests is to include them within the contract specification and implement a system to monitor this particular aspect of performance.

Key point

Usage monitoring provides both commercial and social intelligence.

The next section of this chapter is divided into two areas, secondary and primary analysis, which represent the two broad areas which act as sources of information in usage monitoring.

Definitions

Primary analysis: uses the market to answer specific questions regarding the service and relies on field research i.e. asking users and non users direct questions regarding their behaviour, beliefs, attributes and attitudes. Surveys are the main source of data collection.

Secondary analysis: uses data and information which is generated internally. Leisure enterprises, in the course of business, generate vast amounts of information which when analysed can give insights into usage. Sources of such information include:

- booking sheets
- booking forms
- till transaction records
- computerised booking systems.

Whilst it may appear more logical to discuss primary analysis first, the more pragmatic approach is to undertake the secondary analysis first as it often gives insights into the more direct areas of primary investigation.

Secondary analysis

The basis of usage

It has already been seen how the total number of users is not always an appropriate statistic for examining usage. This is not, however to say that it is of no use at all. There are basically three areas upon which the level of usage can be based. All of which have a contribution to make to the overall examination of usage. These three areas are:

- occupancy
- utilisation
- throughput.

Definitions

Occupancy: examines whether, or to what extent a particular facility is being used. For example a sports hall will be in use for a given percentage of its available time.

Utilisation: looks at how well any occupied space is being used. A badminton court may have two people playing singles or four playing doubles, the same space may also be used for a small aerobics class of a dozen people.

Throughput: total number of people passing through the facility . Whilst use of the throughput figure is often abused it is still a worthwhile statistic for inclusion in a number of operational ratios as we shall see later.

Key point

Don't rely on throughput to tell you the full story regarding usage.

Historically, the majority of leisure managers have collected usage figures. For many this has developed into an integrated part of the daily routine. Yet until the advent of CCT very few managers developed them beyond the throughput level. For those managers who did begin to explore usage in more detail they found they had a practical application in a number of areas including:

- programming issues
- the effect of marketing efforts
- the effect of cost control exercises
- the ability to give goals and targets for levels of usage.

The three basic of usage forms discussed, utilisation, occupation and throughput are not mutually exclusive in a monitoring system. A balanced system will find occasion to use all three measures.

Forms of analysis

In addition to the above three principles upon which measures of usage can be based, different aspects of the operation also need to be considered. The most common approaches are:

- analysis by facility
- analysis by user groups.

In practice there will probably exist a need to undertake both. Analysis by facility explores usage of a particular area or space and is more likely to be of interest to operational managers for example in the identification of cost or profit centres. Analysis by user group however is more likely to be undertaken as part of the contract monitoring process and explores usage by specific groups.

Analysis by facility

The units of analysis

Having explained the basis of usage, the process is further complicated by having to now give attention to the unit of analysis. That is what it is intended to represent usage in terms of. In doing so consideration needs to be given to two aspects of usage:

- the facility in which the activity takes place — is it single use or multipurpose?

- the type or form of usage — is an activity bookable?, is it all casual use? and does it have a set time period?

Both the above factors can greatly affect our ability to calculate occupation and utilisation measures.

When an activity has a predetermined length and takes place at a facility in which only that activity occurs, the calculation for occupation and utilisation is relatively straightforward, e.g. tennis courts and squash courts. However when no set time period exists and/or when the same area is used for a number of different activities monitoring usage becomes much more complex.

The complexity of the situation is a trade off between the activity range and activity duration as demonstrated by Figures 6.1 and 6.2.

Let's now begin the task of determining usage figures. To begin with the process of producing occupation and utilisation figures for simple single activities with set time periods will be examined and then how to deal with the problems of indeterminate time periods and multi-purpose facilities will be considered.

Activity duration

		fixed	*casual*
	single	Tennis Squash Bowls	Swimming Golf Gymnasium
Activity range	*multi-purpose*	Sports hall activities	Parks

Figure 6.1 Matrix showing forms of usage for sample of leisure activities

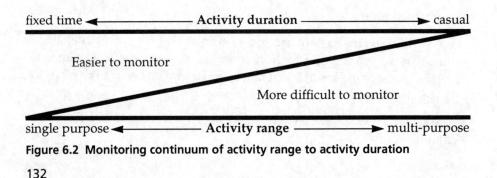

Figure 6.2 Monitoring continuum of activity range to activity duration

132

Activities

Where on the usage monitoring continuum shown in Figure 6.2 would you place the following activities:

- squash usage
- parks usage
- golf usage?

What are the sources of secondary data in the leisure enterprise you're considering? Who has this information?

Single activities within set times

When undertaking usage analysis by facility the task is at its easiest when the facility in question houses only one activity and that activity also has a set time period. For example let us consider the occupancy of four tennis courts. The courts are only used for tennis and may be hired for 40 minute sessions. To establish the occupancy we need to take the following steps.

Step one, select the unit of analysis: this should be given careful consideration. What needs to be determined is, what do we wish to express usage in terms of, and what is the base unit of examination? In this instance it would be logical to use 'tennis courts' as we are essentially asking what percentage of tennis courts are being used?

$$\text{Base unit} = \text{tennis courts}$$

Step two, establish the maximum value of the base unit. What is the maximum number of tennis courts that could be used in the period under investigation?

In cases where the activity has a pre-determined duration, i.e. where the facility is hired or admittance to it charged for a set time period, as in such activities as five-a-side or squash and as opposed to activities such as the use of parks or golf courses, it is a simple matter of dividing the activity duration into the total opening or available time.

$$\text{Maximum value} = \frac{\text{Total available time}}{\text{Activity duration}} \times 100$$

To continue with the tennis courts example, given the following open times and an activity duration of 40 minutes a maximum value could be established as follows for a one week period.

$$\text{Tennis court opening hours}$$

Mon–Sat	10.00a.m.–6.00p.m.
Sun	10.00a.m.–4.00p.m.

$$\text{Maximum Value} = \frac{\text{Total available time}}{\text{Activity duration}}$$

$$= \frac{54 \text{ Hours} \times (\text{No. Courts})}{40 \text{ mins}}$$

$$= \frac{3240 \text{ minutes} \times 4}{40 \text{ mins}}$$

$$= \frac{3240 \text{ minutes} \times 4}{40 \text{ mins}}$$

$$= \frac{12960 \text{ minutes}}{40 \text{ mins}}$$

$$= 324 \text{ sessions}$$

Step three, collect the actual level of the base unit — how many tennis sessions were booked or used. This information should be available from booking sheets or computerised records. Simply count the number of allocated sessions including club use, school hire, etc. Let's say in this instance it came to 261 sessions.

Step four, carry out the following calculation to convert to a percentage occupancy statistic:

$$\% \text{ occupancy} = \frac{\text{Actual usage within period}}{\text{Maximum value for period}} \times 100$$

$$= \frac{261}{324} \times 100$$

$$= 80\%$$

Key point

It may be the case that it is not advisable to have club, school and other block bookings included in the calculations. In which case it must be remembered to extract such usage time not only from the actual figure, but also from the maximum value figure before calculating the percentage.

Utilisation

To elaborate the information obtained in the occupancy figure, utilisation of the facility can be examined. Using the tennis court example again, if all four courts were in use, 100% occupancy for that session could be claimed. However, to obtain 100% utilisation this would require all four courts to have doubles games in progress. Allowing the maximum number of people to use the facility. If all courts were to only have singles games in progress, utilisation would fall to 50% . Utilisation can be calculated in the following manner:

$$\text{Utilisation} = \frac{\text{Actual number of participants}}{\text{Maximum participants per session} \times \text{total number of sessions}} \times 100$$

Assuming the actual number of participants as 444:

$$\text{Utilisation} = \frac{44}{4 \text{ (doubles games)} \times 324} \times 100$$

$$= \frac{444}{1296} \times 100$$

$$= 34.25 \%$$

A variation on this figure, which is often more meaningful, is to examine the utilisation of occupied space, rather than total available space. Using our example the adjustments would be as follows:

$$\text{Utilisation} = \frac{\text{Actual number of participants}}{\text{Maximum participants per session} \times \text{Number of occupied sessions}} \times 100$$

$$= \frac{444}{4 \text{ (Doubles games)} \times 261} \times 100$$

$$= \frac{444}{1044} \times 100$$

$$= 42.5 \%$$

Replacing the total number of sessions with the total number of occupied sessions has a fairly dramatic effect upon the utilisation statistics.

Key point

Utilisation often requires physical counts of participants which can be difficult to administer.

Key point

Which calculation is used is a domestic decision. Be careful to ensure however, that consistency is maintained in its production especially when used for comparative purposes.

Activities of an indeterminate length

In many cases the activities offered do not have a pre-determined duration and may have no real restrictions surrounding the length of participation, such as golf. When dealing with activities with such characteristics it is necessary to find an alternative to the activity duration, so as to establish a maximum usage figure.

If it exists, the minimum duration offered by a centre for an activity may be used. For example if a centre offered at least 40 minute sessions for swimming and the capacity of the pool is known, it's possible to work out the utilisation/occupancy (note that in individual activities such as swimming, saunas, use of parks etc. utilisation and occupancy are essentially the same thing) as follows:

$$\% \text{ usage} = \frac{\text{Actual number of swimmers in period}}{\text{Maximum number of swimmers in period} \times \text{Number of sessions in period.}}$$

For example, in a pool offering 40 minute sessions over an eight hour day with a capacity of 125 swimmers it is possible to establish the maximum number of swimmers in a day by:

$$\frac{480 \text{ minutes}}{40} = 12 \times 125 = 1500 = 100\%$$

This calculation assumes that all swimmers stay at least 40 minutes and does not consider that anyone leaving the pool before their 40 minute period is up may allow another swimmer to be admitted. The result is that whilst 1500 swimmers would represent 100% usage it is quite feasible to have usage in excess of 100%. This is not necessarily a problem if the figure is viewed as an index of comparison.

Consider another example. Golf is an activity which has a variable duration. How can measures of occupancy and utilisation be devised in such a case? Firstly the problem of what can be used as a base unit needs to be considered. Can usage can be expressed as rounds of golf? Unfortunately golf has an undetermined duration which makes it difficult to calculate the maximum number of rounds.

The only insight into this, is by using the tee times. This tells us how many games may start in a period, whilst there may be an imposed maximum, like a five ball game, from which a maximum value of rounds could be established. However, it is the game that occupies the tee booking regardless of whether it is a two or five ball game. Therefore, 'games' rather than 'rounds' needs to adopted as a base unit in the measurement of occupancy.

To find the maximum value of 'games' one must first calculate:

$$\text{Maximum value (possible games)} = \frac{\text{Duration of period being investigated}}{\text{Tee interval}}$$

and then:

$$\text{Percentage occupancy} = \frac{\text{Number of booked tee times}}{\text{Maximum value (possible games)}} \times 100$$

If given information regarding the total number of rounds played and the maximum ball game, we could calculate the utility usage by:

$$\text{Percentage utility} = \frac{\text{Actual number of rounds}}{\text{Maximum ball games} \times \text{Maximum value (possible games)}} \times 100$$

Multi-purpose facilities

The Audit Commission (1983) recognised the problems in addressing usage for multi-use areas such as sports halls, which normally have the ability to accommodate a number of activities. There are varying units of analysis on which to base our usage figures. For example consider a single court sports hall which has the capacity to accommodate various activities.

The possible use of the hall at any one time would be as follows together with the maximum number of people.

	Equivalent badminton courts
Badminton × 4 courts	4
Tennis × 1 court	4
Gymnastics sessions × 1 area	4
Five-a-side × 1 court	4
Aerobic sessions × 2 areas	2

	People
1 tennis court	4
1 gym session	25
4 badminton courts	16
1 five-a-side	10
2 aerobic sessions	50
1 aerobic and 2 badminton	33

The Audit Commission recommend that in such circumstances the smallest unit possible should be used. For sports halls the smallest unit is the badminton court and should be adopted as the base unit. In such a case the hall would be said to be 100% occupied when all four badminton courts are in use, a gymnastics session is in progress or a five-a-side game; 75% if an aerobics session and one badminton court; 50% with only an aerobics session and only 25% when only one badminton court is in use etc.

So for a sports hall with bookings for the equivalent of 93 badminton courts in a day, percentage occupancy can be calculated as follows:

$$\% \text{ occupancy} = \frac{\text{Actual used badminton courts (units)}}{\text{Number of courts in facility} \times \left(\dfrac{\text{opening hours}}{\text{session duration}}\right)}$$

$$= \frac{93}{8 \times \left(\dfrac{13.5}{45 \text{ mins}}\right)} \times 100$$

$$= \frac{93}{144} \times 100$$

$$= 0.646 \times 100$$

$$= 64.6 \%$$

In calculating the utilisation of a multi-purpose area one should adopt the approach of using 'occupied' space rather than available space as the denominator of the calculation. The main reason for this is as usage will vary between activities and as the space is available for a number of activities, the use of utilisation figures based only upon the activity giving the greatest possible usage could encourage managers to seek bookings primarily in that activity.

To calculate the utilisation figure the following procedure may be adopted.

Create a table as per Table 6.1 showing maximum numbers of participants based upon an activity.

Table 6.1 Maximum value of participants based upon activity

Activity	Max values (people)	Number of sessions in period	Total
A	10	5	50
B	16	20	320
C	40	15	600
		Maximum value based on activities	970

Then assume 506 actual participants.

$$\text{Utilisation percentage} = \frac{\text{Total number of participants}}{\text{Possible number of participants based upon activity}} \times 100$$

$$\frac{506}{970} = 52\%$$

Varying activity lengths

Activities vary in the amount of time they occupy. This may be due to a number of things including:

1. The nature of the activity — whilst 40 minute sessions may be acceptable for badminton, 1 hour sessions are required for five-a-side football.
2. The programming arrangements — a facility may decide to offer different session lengths, even for the same activity, at different times of the day. For example a common practice is to compress activity duration at midday. This is convenient to the participant as shorter sessions fit more comfortably into lunch breaks. The same principle could apply to any peak period. Table 6.2 shows a typical sports hall's sessions throughout a day.

Table 6.2 Session variations in multi-use sports hall

Time	Duration	No. of Sessions	Courts (Units)	Max. available	Actual courts
9–12 a.m.	1 hour	3	4	12	8
12–1.40 p.m.	40 mins	2	4	8	8
1.40 p.m.–6.40 p.m.	1 hour	5	4	20	14
6.40 p.m.–10.25 p.m.	45 mins	4	4	16	12
				56	42

Maximum time (mins)	Actual time
720	480
320	320
1200	840
720	540
2960	2180

There are essentially two calculations required to produce an occupancy figure for this situation.

1. Using courts as the base unit:

$$\text{Occupancy} = \frac{\text{Total courts used}}{\text{Total available courts}} \times 100$$

$$= \frac{42}{56} \times 100$$

$$= 75\%$$

2. Using time as the base unit:

$$\text{Occupancy} = \frac{\text{Actual time in use}}{\text{Total available time}} \times 100$$

$$= \frac{2180}{2960}$$

$$= 73.6\%$$

Both are legitimate approaches but give different answers. For this reason care should be taken to ensure consistency of use and comparison. Both measures have arguments in favour of their validity. When varying session lengths are introduced as a programming concern, the issue is mainly one of utilisation rather than occupation; it is known that peak period sessions will sell but how can we make best use of that demand.

Possibly the best approach is to use both figures. Where session duration has been compressed for programming reasons this is normally to cope with high demand. In such cases the 'court' figure will logically be higher than the 'time' figure.

Using both figures it's possible to make statements of the nature:

Occupancy = 75% of available courts representing 73.6% of available time.

By doing so, progress over time can be monitored (see section on Time Series in Chapter 3) in which managers would hope to see the 'time' figure approach the 'court' figure. Should the time figure exceed the court figure this is a direct indication that peak period programming is not effective. This is due to the fact that peak periods would be shorter representing less of total time. A time figure which is greater than the courts figure therefore suggests that occupancy is greater in the longer off peak periods.

Activity

■ What measures of usage are collated for the facility you are considering—occupation, utilisation or throughput?

Analysis by user groups

Analysis by user groups can be carried out at two levels:

- those classifications or groups which may be considered overt and would appear within contract documents, etc. i.e. schools, clubs and societies' events and other highly visible groups.

- those groups which are essentially covert or hidden groups, i.e. groups classified on a social and economic basis such as sex, age, where people live, how they travelled to the facility, etc.

For example within a sports and leisure contract specification the difference between these two groups is highlighted by the manner in which they are covered. Overt groups such as schools, clubs etc. are likely to have detailed quantifiable specifications such as those shown in Table 6.3 for a swimming pool complex. Overt groups' specifications are probably to be found having a more qualitative nature. Specific levels of usage for men and women or differing areas of the catchment areas are unlikely to be specified. What may be specified however is something more general regarding some form of action, often between the contractor and client, to carry out research as the basis of discussion on how to promote capacity equity in participation.

First we will consider overt user groups as they can be observed and monitored in much the same way as 'by facility usage' and offer the opportunity to give a more comprehensive example of how this type of monitoring may be achieved in the working environment. Information regarding covert user groups requires field research which will be addressed in the section on primary analysis.

Monitoring recommended levels of usage

In order to maintain the correct balance of usage, as seen fit by the client, certain restrictions can be included within the contract specification. Table 6.3 shows how this can be achieved for a pools complex by firstly identifying the types of activities that we wish to control:

- courses and activities
- events
- school usage
- clubs and society use
- casual use.

141

> ### Key point
>
> The basis upon which usage is controlled will of course vary from facility to facility depending upon the local situation.

One then needs to decide on the restriction levels, i.e. how much time are we willing to give to each of these interested parties? This can be done by either stipulating a minimum or maximum level of usage. This again is subjective and needs careful consideration before being entered into the specification.

Table 6.3 Recommended percentage usage for swimming pool

Activity Areas	Monday to Friday						Saturday and Sunday				
	Courses	Events	Schools	Clubs	Casual use	Total	Courses	Events	Clubs	Casual use	Total
Main pool	0%	2%	0%	17%	81%	100%	0%	5%	0%	95%	100%
Diving pool	1%	2%	0%	0%	97%	100%	0%	5%	18%	77%	100%
Training pool	38%	0%	50%	4%	8%	100%	40%	5%	0%	55%	100%

As is the case in Table 6.3, this will include developing a pattern of usage throughout the facilities when more than one facility is concerned. For example it's recommended that 50 per cent of time in the training pool can be used for school use Monday to Friday which would not be the case if there were not three other pools in operation at the same time.

Additionally the table shows how levels of usage for the different groups is changed during weekend periods. This elaboration could be taken even further by further breaking the time periods down into peak and off peak periods.

Overt user groups

If a contracting situation exists the starting point is the contract specification which would reveal a programming policy regarding use by specified groups. In non-contractual situations it is still possible that a programming policy will exist and when possible this should be consulted first.

An elaboration on the simple calculations in the previous sections on 'by facility analysis', and one recommended by the Audit Commission is to do separate calculations for peak and off peak times normally reflected in the programming policy. For example consider the following programming policy of a sports facility:

Table 6.4 Recommended percentage occupancy for various user groups

Activity Area	Monday to Friday							
	Off Peak				Peak			
	Courses	Schools	Casual use	Total	Courses	Casual use	Leagues	Total
Sports Hall	45%	10%	45%	100%	0%	85%	15%	100%

Saturday and Sunday					
Competitions	Organised sessions	Clubs	Leagues	Casual	Total
10%	0%	0%	20%	70%	100%

Notes: 1. Non sporting or social events to be limited to 5% of the hall's availability.
   2. Organised sporting events and competitions are restricted to weekends.
   3. Peak sessions are 5 p.m.–8 p.m. Mon–Fri and all sessions Saturday and Sunday

The nuances of the programming policy will be decided on a local level and no two facilities are likely to be identical. The method of investigation should always be the same. As previously shown when calculating occupancy it's necessary to:

- Establish the unit of analysis — as this is a multi-purpose hall we will use a badminton court as the base unit, for the reasons described earlier.

- Calculate the maximum values of the base unit—What are the maximum number of badminton courts that could be used in the period.

  For simplicity purposes let us also assume that opening hours are 13 hours per day, seven days per week and that all sessions are one hour in duration. Our maximum values would then be as follows:

Maximum courts bookable per session	8
Maximum courts bookable per day	107
Maximum courts bookable per week	728
Maximum peak courts	328
Maximum off peak courts	400
Maximum weekend courts	208

- Establish the actual level of usage from the booking sheets. This essentially means counting the number of courts used by each of the groups. Even if computerised booking systems are used some of this information may still have to be collected manually and is possibly best done on a daily basis by reception or other customer service staff.

It is from the recommended usage or programming policy that groups of interest are identified, in this case:

- Course and activities
- Schools
- Casual use
- Leagues
- Competitions
- Organised sessions
- Non-sporting social events.

Data is best recorded in a matrix against the various constraints in peak/off peak, weekend sessions etc. Remember to record in base units.

It is possible to collect this information in more detail, i.e., by session throughout the day. Whilst this does have a number of advantages identifying patterns of usage and determining peak and off peak periods, it is also extremely time consuming. It is recommended to collect data in as much detail as is practically possible; as it is much easier to simplify data in the analysis stage rather than it is to elaborate it.

On such recording sheets it is always advisable to have a space for notes. Usage always needs to be considered within as wide a context as possible. It is therefore useful to know about anything that may have affected usage in that period — was there six foot of snow that day? is it the schools' half term?, etc. Record such notes at the time as such things are often forgotten six months later when usage is being reviewed.

The period of time over which an analysis is to be taken is again a domestic issue. It is important however to have clear cut guidelines regarding the period of investigation. Are the recommended levels of usage per week, per month, year or contract duration. It's particularly important when dealing with activities which may be seasonal. For example galas in swimming pools. Occupancy in the 'gala season' may be as high as 20% but over the year only be three. For this reason its often useful to monitor the underlying trends of such usage (see section on trends in Chapter 3). The information collected on a daily basis needs to be transferred to summary sheets until the maximum period of analysis is reached.

The necessary calculations to obtain the actual occupancy figures by user groups are then as follows:

$$\frac{\text{Monday–Friday}}{\text{Off peak}}$$

$$\frac{\text{Actual courts booked for course activities}}{\text{Maximum off peak courts}} \times 100$$

$$\frac{\text{Actual courts booked for schools}}{\text{Maximum off peak courts}} \times 100$$

$$\frac{\text{Actual courts booked for leagues (Mon–Fri)}}{\text{Maximum week day peak courts}} \times 100$$

$$\frac{\text{Actual courts booked for competitions}}{\text{Maximum weekend courts}} \times 100$$

$$\frac{\text{Actual courts booked for leagues}}{\text{Maximum weekend courts}} \times 100$$

$$\frac{\text{Number of courts booked for non-sporting events}}{\text{Maximum total courts for period}} \times 100$$

When occupancy is being examined in this manner and calculations are being made under a number of constraints, total usage, peak/off peak usage, weekends usage, etc. careful consideration must be given to the denominator or maximum value used in the calculations. Only by studying the brief, specification programming policy or what ever document has initiated the calculations can you be sure of using the right one.

Once the calculations have been carried out the results can be laid out in a similar manner to the recommended usage showing recommended, actual and variance as in Table 6.5.

Table 6.5 Comparison of recommended and actual levels of occupancy for various user groups

Activity Areas	Monday to Friday							
	Off Peak				Peak			
	Courses	Schools	Casual use	Total	Courses	Casual use	Leagues	Total
Recommended	45%	10%	45%	100%	0%	85%	15%	100%
Actual	40%	11%	47%	98%	0%	89%	11%	100%
Variance	–5%	+1%	+2%	–2%*	0%	+4%	–4%	0%

* 2% Social and non sporting events

Most of the hard work involved in producing these figures can be avoided by use of a computer. Widely available spreadsheet packages can quite easily be set up to deal with such calculations. An added advantage of using the computer is that graphical presentations are easily obtained.

The production of a utilisation figure in 'by user group analysis' is as important as 'by facility analysis'. The obvious difficulty in providing such an analysis is the requirement of head counts. Whilst use of an area by a particular club or group will provide 100% occupancy, utilisation is not guaranteed. Client officers in particular may wish to monitor the utilisation of clubs and groups who have been included in contract specifications. Whilst the encouragement of minority activities may well be a general policy of a centre, officers and members need information on which to base decisions because these will be limits under which some activities can no longer be supported on the grounds of poor utilisation. Such a process should form part of a flexible approach to contract management and where necessary result in amendments to the contract.

Activity

Calculate an occupancy figure for a facility you are familiar with. Make any relevant adjustments for activity and time alterations.

Covert user groups

Covert user groups are those which we need to collect information directly from the customer or potential customer. Information referring predominantly to personal characteristics, attitudes, beliefs and behaviour. To obtain this information requires the transition from secondary sources of information to primary sources. Collecting information directly from users and non-users is examined in detail in the following section.

Primary analysis

Definition

Primary research uses the market to answer specific questions regarding the service being offered by a leisure enterprise. Its concern is with information which is generally covert in nature; things that are not obvious or directly observable such as attributes, beliefs, attitudes and behaviour.

Information of this nature is of use to management for a number of reasons including:

■ identifying catchment areas

- profiling of users/non-users

- attaining user opinions.

The type of questions to which primary analysis can assist leisure enterprises include:

- where do our customers live?

- are there particular social and economic groups who use our facilities?

- are there any patterns of behaviour regarding usage?

There are a number of methods by which data can be collected directly. The more popular of these include:

- face to face interviews

- telephone interviews

- postal surveys.

Which method to use will depend upon a number of things including:

- the resources available both financial and human

- how precise or accurate the findings need to be

- the location of the people to be surveyed

- the expected response rate.

Possible methods

The face to face interview

The face to face interview is a common method of collecting information from users. It is often the only way of obtaining information in the absence of membership or mailing lists. The use of postal and telephone surveys on users is problematic as information, even when mailing and membership lists exist, is unlikely to encompass all users and will therefore be unrepresentative. Face to face interviews are therefore used more or less exclusively for surveys undertaken at the site of participation.

Telephone survey

The use of telephone surveys in leisure enterprises is limited. Whilst having advantages over the face to face interview, mainly on the grounds of cost especially when the sample is widely dispersed, it has little if any advantages over the postal survey.

Postal survey

The postal survey is best suited to larger studies. Postal questionnaires can reach widely dispersed individuals at a relatively low cost. They are particularly useful in surveys attempting to analyse levels of participation throughout a community or catchment area, but they also produce a poor response rate.

Constructing questionnaires

Questionnaire surveys are a popular method of collecting data on both users and non-users. Whilst not the only means, they do offer a highly organised approach.

Key point

Surveys can only inform the decision making process not replace it.

Before embarking on a questionnaire survey the following questions should be asked:

- what is the purpose of the survey?
- are other key people in the organisation in agreement that such a survey is required?
- what will the results achieve?
- do the necessary technical skills to carry out the survey exist in-house?

This section of the text is intended to give managers the tools to construct valid and reliable questionnaires which should only be undertaken once the purpose of the survey is known.

Framing the question

What do you want to know? Unless there is a clear idea about this, it becomes a very difficult task to design and develop a questionnaire. The type of question to which surveys can be applied include:

- what are the personal characteristics of our users?
- what do users think of the quality of service offered at a facility and how do they think it could be improved?

- what are the characteristics of non-users?

- longitudinal or repeat surveys on any of the above points can also help answer questions regarding changes in participation levels, attitudes to facilities and services etc.

The questions that will be asked to answer the problem will be influenced by:

- what indicators are available to measure the concepts involved?

- what hunches do we have regarding possible links?

- what level of data can be produced?

- how is it intended to carry out the questionnaire — postal, interview or telephone, etc?

Key point

Identify the question you wish to answer at the outset of the investigation.

Aspects of a questionnaire

Questionnaires are essentially made up of two distinct areas:

- questions relating to the dependent variable, the measure of the topic that is to be explained, such as participation

- questions relating to the independent variables, those items which will explain levels in the dependent variable, by attempting to explain participation (the dependent variable) as a consequence of sex, age and geographical location (independent variables).

The level of participation is in some way dependent upon age, sex, age and geographical location. A survey should suggest to what extent levels of the dependant variables are affected by changes in the independent variables. It is essential that questionnaires contain questions designed to measure both.

Example questions:

1. Why do people use sports centre A rather than sports centre B?
(dependent variable = sports centre usage)

2. Does income and/or car ownership affect membership of the country club?
(Dependent variable = membership)
(Independent variable = income and car ownership).

Content of questions

How a question is asked can affect the kind of response achieved. It is important that in developing questions consideration is given to what is being sought. The question content should aim to achieve information regarding either:

- Behaviour
  - why do people go to the theatre?
  - do people use the bar after swimming?
  - do people play golf more at the weekends rather than week days?
  - why do the majority of people choose hot destinations for their holidays?

- Beliefs
  - do you believe we offer a high quality service?
  - do you think the pool temperature is adequate?

- Attitudes
  - should more women's activities be on offer?
  - should under three's go free on most summer activities?

- Attributes
  - what ethnic background are you?
  - are you male or female
  - what is your occupation?

In the use of surveys for examining usage the foremost focus of questionnaires tends to be around behaviour and attributes. Behaviour here refers to and acts as a dependent variable. Social and economic attributes act as the independent variables.

Having decided upon the focus of the questions and identified the dependent and independent variables, the time comes when it is necessary to write the individual questions.

Writing questions requires careful consideration to the following points:

- Simple language — the use of elaborate language will have the effect of either making the question difficult to understand or act as a turnoff to respond, e.g.
  - are you fiscally challenged by the tariffs levied by this facility?
  - do you find money a barrier to using the local sports centre?
  - do you think our prices are high?

- Question length — the attention span of respondents is often very short. Most people have better things to do. Lengthy and difficult to understand questions will lose the respondents interest very quickly, e.g.

— have you ever, whilst holding a concessionary card, visited more than one of the authority's existing facilities, in a given week for the purpose of recreation?

Short, straight to the point questions are best.

- Only ask one question — all too often questions ask more than one question, e.g.
  — Would raising the water temperature and bigger lockers improve your visit to the centre?

  Such a question should in fact be two separate questions, one asking about water temperature and one about locker size. Someone who found the water temperature more than adequate but that locker space would benefit from improvement would find this question difficult to answer.

- Does the question introduce bias — does the question force or persuade the respondent to answer in a particular manner, e.g.
  — would you agree, that with the finest greens in the country, the 'Hole in One Golf Club' is a first rate course?

  Such a question leads the respondent into agreeing by providing evidence as to why they should agree.

- Ability to answer — it is important to remember that respondents are not likely to have a deep understanding of the leisure enterprise you are asking them to consider. For example the ability of respondents to answer the following question would be somewhat limited, e.g.

  How do you think the introduction of CCT has affected the service of the centre?

  The majority of people would not know what CCT is, and therefore be unable to comment.

- Ambiguous wording — it is best to avoid any words which may have different meaning to different people.

- Respondent kudos — it must be remembered that respondents are people not information/data generating machines. Avoid wording questions in a way which may embarrass the respondent. Direct questions on potentially embarrassing subjects should be avoided and a more subtle approach adapted, e.g.

151

Direct: Are you unemployed?

More subtle: Many people in this area are unemployed, often through no fault of their own. Do you happen to be one of them?

■ Context — in all questions it is important to make clear to the respondent the frame of reference. If you ask:

How often do you visit this facility?

It is important that you clarify the time period, per week, month, year etc.

Question types

Essentially there are two types of questions:

■ closed or forced choice questions

■ open questions.

Closed questions

Closed choice questions force the respondent into selecting from a list of alternative answers. The most simple form of closed question is one which produced a dichotomous response by giving only two possible answers, for example:

Is this your first visit to the theatre?
Yes [ ]   No [ ]

When the response range is only yes or no this presents little problem. However when the range of possible responses is larger or not a simple yes/no response, it becomes essential that considerable thought is put into ensuring that the list of possible responses is exhaustive. For example there would be little point to the following question:

What is your favourite leisure pursuit?
(Please tick one box)

1. Swimming   [ ]
2. Reading   [ ]
3. Walking   [ ]
4. Football   [ ]

The list is far from exhaustive and therefore inappropriate to a large number of people. To overcome this problem it is useful to include a 'do not know' or 'other' category at the end of the question.

There are three basic forms of closed choice questions:

■ Likert scales

■ semantic differential scales

■ ranking formats

Likert scales: this commonly used technique get respondents to indicate the extent to which they agree or disagree with a statement, for example:

> Theatre tickets are good value for money?
>
> | | |
> |---|---|
> | Strongly agree | [   ] |
> | Agree | [   ] |
> | Not sure | [   ] |
> | Tend to disagree | [   ] |
> | Strongly disagree | [   ] |

Activity

■ Is it possible to develop a Likert scale to examine how often someone uses a facility?

Semantic differential scales: this approach uses a continuum with two extreme responses at either end and asks the respondent to mark the continuum at the appropriate point to indicate their response:

> Friendly   1 2 3 4 5 6 7 8   Unfriendly

or

> How do you rate these aspects of your visit to the cinema?
>
> | | | |
> |---|---|---|
> | Good sound quality | 1 2 3 4 5 6 7 8 | Poor sound quality |
> | Auditorium too hot | 1 2 3 4 5 6 7 8 | Auditorium too cold |
> | Good quality picture | 1 2 3 4 5 6 7 8 | Poor quality picture |

Ranking format: using a rank format asks respondents to show preference for a number of items in a list. It is often unnecessary and off putting to ask a respondent to rank all items. The following type of format may be used to shorten completion time.

> Which of the following are the first and second most important to you in deciding to visit this theatre (circle only one first reason and one second reason)?

	First	Second
Good parking	1	2
Credit card booking	1	2
Auditorium comfort	1	2
Bar and catering facilities	1	2

Open-ended questions

In many instances the information to be collected from respondents is so subjective that prompting answers does not feel totally appropriate.

In such cases use 'open-ended' questions to assist responses. Open ended questions allow respondents total freedom of response. Questions contained on questionnaires would normally be followed by a number of lines in which the respondent is totally at liberty to record their response, for example:

What was your overall impression of your visit to Funland?

....

....

....

The advantages of open end questions include:

- interviewer's influence is kept to a minimum
- information of a richer and deeper nature may be obtained.

There are also disadvantages:

- response rate is usually lower than that of closed questions
- analysis is more difficult, time consuming and subjective than coded questions.

Questionnaire layout

Once an array of questions has been selected they will need to be arranged into a questionnaire. Consideration will need to be given to a number of areas when so doing including:

- method of answering
- instructions to respondent
- how the questionnaire will look
- maintaining a logical sequence.

Method of answering

With closed or forced questions ticking boxes, brackets or parentheses are the most common methods. Ticks tend to be preferable to circling answers as this method can be less accurate and lead to doubt as to which answer had been selected.

With open-ended questions the concern is mainly with judging the amount of space to leave for the response. Too much space promotes non-response and too little crammed or incomplete answers.

Instructions to respondents

Whatever method of answering is chosen it is important that clear instructions on how to complete the questionnaire are conveyed to the respondent. Instructions to respondents can be given in four areas:

1. Introducing instruction — the purpose of these instructions is to introduce the respondent to:

   - details of any enticements to complete
   - purpose of the questionnaire
   - why they have been selected
   - confidentiality if necessary
   - response procedure: Please tick one box only [   ] unless otherwise asked

2. Area or topic instructions — questionnaires are often compiled with the intention of answering more than one question. For this and other reasons it is sometimes necessary, and desirable to have a number of sections within the questionnaire. It is important for reasons of clarity that respondents are instructed and informed that the topic is changing. They can then be ready to adjust to a different style of questioning. Such information keeps the respondent informed and hopefully interested.

3. Instructions for individual questions — there will be occasions when the respondent may need to be instructed to deviate from general instructions, for example:

   (tick as many boxes as you like)
   (please write in)
   (tick as many activities which apply)
   (tick more than one box if appropriate)

4. Completion instruction — depending how the questionnaire has been

155

administered it will be necessary to give instructions regarding what to do with the questionnaire once completed:

- Return to given address

- Hand to reception

- Place in boxes at exits

- Give to tutor/instructor.

Activities

- Establish a research question regarding a leisure enterprise and design a questionnaire to answer it.

- Compare throughput figures obtained from secondary analysis with any levels of usage obtained from primary sources. What are the strengths and weaknesses of each?

Analysing the data

Once we have collected data using an appropriate questionnaire we will wish to analyse it. The main influences on how the analysis is carried out include:

- The number of variables on which we have information

- The level of data

Chapter 3 gives a detailed account of how to handle data. Sampling, surveys of this nature inevitably require the use of sampling techniques. Once again consult Chapter 3 for a detailed account on how to select a representative sample for use with surveys.

LEARNING POINTS

- The demands on management to produce detailed accounts of usage are increasing.

- Usage monitoring provides both commercial and social market intelligence.

- Secondary analysis examines data generated internally by the leisure enterprise.

- Primary analysis asks questions to users and non-users by carrying out surveys.

- Occupancy examines to what extent a facility is being used.

- Utilisation looks at how well an occupied space is being used.

- Usage can be measured by throughput, occupancy and utilisation.

- It is important to establish the base unit of analysis first.

- A conscious decision as to whether block bookings should be included in a percentage occupancy figure needs to be made by management.

- Try to ensure consistency when comparing statistics on usage.

- Occupancy and utilisation figures need adjustments in their calculation when facilities deal with more than one activity or the duration of activities is variable.

- Questionnaires should be designed to answer specific questions regarding usage.

- Frame the research question before you do the survey.

- There are a number of ways to collect information when carrying out a survey including face to face interviews, postal surveys and telephone surveys.

- Questions can give insights into respondents attitudes, beliefs, attributes and behaviour.

- Questions can be either closed/forced choice or open ended.

- Open-ended questions are much more difficult to evaluate.

REFERENCES AND FURTHER READING

Audit Inspectorate (1993) *Development and Operation of Leisure Centres*, Department of the Environment, HMSO

National Endowment of the Arts (1985) *Research Division Manual*, National Endowment of the Arts, Washington DC

Section 3

So far the reader has been provided with a thorough understanding of what PME is and how the mechanics and techniques can be applied. PME however does not function in isolation. Organisations involve people and no aspect will work without the people dimension. This section therefore takes a rather different viewpoint to the technical perspective of the first two sections. Section 3 is concerned with implementing the new or changed PME system; the interface between what makes an organisation work (the people) and the system (PME) which determines how the organisation is working.

Implementing a PME system is very much like implementing any other project so the reader has the added value of being able to apply many of the principles outlined in this section to any change that might be brought about in an organisation.

This section is primarily divided into two. The first part, Chapter 7, sets the scene for implementation. It briefly looks at the ethic and cultural aspects of an organisation before examining a number of techniques that can be used to persuade and encourage employees to change. Chapter 8 explains within the context of the people dimension how a PME project can be implemented as an operational facet. The approaches and stages are described as are the potential pitfalls.

7

Preparing for implementing performance, monitoring and evaluation

Introduction

This chapter will emphasise the importance of understanding people and their working environment in the leisure industry and will look at some of the techniques that are used to reward, motivate and control employees in the work place.

The leisure industry is fortunate in that many of its employee posts are interesting, non-repetitive and dealing with people. This is rather different from the manufacturing sector where repetitive, often boring tasks are undertaken on a production line or the white collar sector which is required to shift mountains of paper. This is not to say that the leisure industry is devoid of repetitive tasks e.g., selling tickets, pool attending, silver service — but even here the item of production/service is different. The leisure industry therefore has a head start on many other sectors of business. Another asset that the industry has is that many employees entering the leisure business are well qualified and interested in the employment they are about to take up.

Performance, monitoring and evaluation is not new to the Leisure Industry or other sectors of economic activity. The term representing PME might be slightly different, e.g. management information system (MIS). The commercial sector has used such systems to determine the success of their businesses for generations and local authority leisure departments have calculated budgets and subsidy ratios for almost as long. What has happened is that major external economic and legislative changes have shuddered through the Western World. Massive external influences have come about like the cheap production methods of the Far East and the changing demographics of the older more economically advanced nations of the UK, USA and Western Europe. The reality is that if economies do not become competitive national income generation will fall and there will be insufficient funds to support the current standards of living or make provision for the ageing population.

The resultant emphasis in the UK during the last 15 years has been to make 'UK Ltd' more competitively productive in both manufacturing output and services provided and to reduce costs in all sectors. The comfortable post war years between 1945 and 1980 have gone and are unlikely ever to return. The leisure industry has been part of this massive cultural and directional change.

Some of the symptoms in the Leisure Industry are:

1. Within the commercial sector:

   - increasing size of aircraft to enable economies of scale

   - increased mechanisation in hotels e.g., self-service breakfasts, self tea making facilities, shoe cleaning machines etc.

   - multi-functional aspects of hotel use e.g., tourist market, events, conferences and seminars

   - merging and takeover of groups on a national and multi-national basis

   - the emergence of the economy hotel.

2. Within the public sector:

   - clearer policies required to clarify 'public good' and support for the disadvantaged

   - greater emphasis on income and realistic pricing policies

   - closure of swimming pools

   - the introduction of Compulsory Competitive Tendering (CCT)

   - subsidy reductions in real terms.

There are a number of more mechanistic changes that have taken place which more directly affect both managers and employees. With the growth of leisure centres in the mid 1970s and early 1980s demarcation between tasks was considerable. For example a wet and dry leisure centre would have two sets of staff — one to look after the pool and associated facilities and another set of staff to operate the dry facilities. Only management was multi-functional. Those days have gone with multi-tasking across the whole enterprise.

Diminishing income and subsidies have brought about massive pressure to reduce costs. This happened through 'downsizing and delayering'.

Downsizing and delayering are particularly important in the leisure industry because it is a people intensive business and salaries and wages form a high proportion of revenue costs. Actions like CCT legislation or mergers and takeovers provide management with the opportunity to restructure and develop new cultures within organisations. This is exactly what has happened with CCT and it is quite clear superficially that costs have been driven down and usually at the expense of the human resource asset.

The employee is an integral part of the leisure industry process. Because the industry is client experience based rather than product purchased based, the role of the employee plays a particularly important part. Clients/customers make judgements about the activity/visit/holiday experience they have just completed. That experience will be considerably flavoured by the quality and performance of employees with whom they have come into contact. Local government leisure departments (both client and contractor) have been forced to recognise this quality of service issue through CCT which in turn is reflected by the further attentions of the Audit Commission and by the Citizen's Charter. In practical terms performance, monitoring and evaluation have been kick started into the management of modern organisations, particularly the public sector, through the massive pressures to reduce costs.

Local government therefore finds itself in a dilemma. It requires better and more skilled employees who can raise standards of service whilst clamping down on costs. The commercial sector faces similar problems although it has historically functioned on a much more cost conscious regime and so the impact on personnel is probably not so great as for local authorities. Certainly, employees have taken the brunt of the cost cutting exercise in order that new PME targets can be met. Employees have been affected in the following manner:

- redundancy
- short-term contracts
- split shifts
- reduction in income
- multi-skilling
- increased range and types of responsibility
- reduction of perks

- checklist driven rather than self-organised
- tension between task and quality of performance
- pressure to hit and surpass targets
- stress because of matters being externally driven rather than internally driven
- lack of ownership
- a job rather than a career — reduction of job enrichment
- lack of security
- increase in numbers of part-time employees.

It is not difficult to come to the conclusion that the employee people dimension of local authority leisure particularly has taken a hard knock. On the positive side it can probably be argued that the leisure manager's job has become more focused, those still in jobs are likely to receive more direct payment and the client officer still has a function with an attached career pattern.

The discussion above suggests that in the leisure industry today the emphasis on reactive change leads to its greatest asset, 'people' not receiving the attention they might deserve. This is not such a dissimilar position to the nursing or teaching professions.

The reader surely has by now noted that changes have come about as a reaction to particular pressures rather than as a proactive approach. It is inevitable that when a crisis arises which brings about massive change the human resource element can be lost. It happens with bankruptcies, mergers, takeovers and cutbacks in government and local government funding. There is a distinct need to put human resource management more fully into the picture as part of the process of change rather than just a reactive element. It is also apparent that there is a need to redress the balance between employer and employee if improved quality of performance by employees is to be achieved. External pressures appear to be encouraging more stringent targets to be set within a PME system whilst management reduces the quality of the working environment and conditions. Management, particularly in the leisure industry needs to carry employees with them if the evaluation part of a PME system is going to show progress.

There are two distinct aspects that need addressing. The first is the ethic and culture of the business and the second is what tools and mechanisms can be used to motivate employees to participate wholeheartedly in the running of the business — including performance, monitoring and evaluation.

Organisational culture and ethic

This is an area of human resource management (HRM) which is largely misunderstood, not given enough emphasis and needs serious attention by managers. It is only possible in this text to give the briefest outline to the issues concerned and if readers are not conversant with some of the background theory of HRM, they should highlight it on their next appraisal form and include such study in their action plan. The ethic and culture of a business is essential to its operation especially in a people driven business.

There will be a number of names that are familiar to some readers, like Fredrick Taylor, Elton Mayo, Chris Argyris, Abraham Maslow, Douglas McGregor, Fredrick Hertzberg and Rensis Likert. All, with others, have made their contribution to HRM thinking. This text briefly mentions three, not because their theories are any more important than anybody else's, but because they best illustrate the span and dimension of thinking.

Early in the 1900s, F. W. Taylor put forward what was to become known as the Scientific Management approach. The concept was that management should be divorced from human affairs and emotions within the organisation and should reorganise operations and tasks for efficiency. The design of the system was technological by nature and rationally planned and executed with the purpose of efficient administration and production processes. The techniques and methods used by workers were improved and it heralded the first efforts at time and motion studies. On the establishment of the production line, workers were offered incentives to increase units of production above a set target rate — piece rates! The manager's task was to set the scheme up and enforce the performance criteria in order to meet organisational goals. The stress was always on meeting organisational goals and targets rather than on individual ones.

It might be asked what has this to do with the leisure industry? The late 1970s saw the introduction of time and motion study into the parks department of local authorities e.g., 25 minutes to mow a cricket square. Bonuses were provided for work above target. In the hotel sector, daily income figures at all Holiday Inns are communicated to HQ in America. Managers are answerable for deviations over and above certain target limits and managerial salaries are linked to performance.

The pressure is again on the work place, especially for local government direct service organisations to rationalise and reach targets set by or through 'specifications'. Nearly a century to turn full circle. Taylor's Scientific Management System, although showing concern for the employee, has been regarded as the most severe interpretation of hard line management.

Rensis Likert is an organisational theorist who represents the opposite end of the spectrum to Taylor. He strongly belongs to the Human Relations Movement whose watchword is a statement made by J. D. Rockefeller, 'I will pay more for the ability to deal with people than any other ability under the sun' (Berg and Manley, 1966, page 3). After previous work such as the Hawthorne experiments and McGregor's X and Y theories, Likert examined the managerial approaches to running organisations. From his studies he came up with the following four methods/systems of management.

SYSTEM 1

- management has no confidence or trust in subordinates
- subordinates not involved in decision making
- decisions made at the top and issued down the chain of command
- subordinates forced to work through fear, threats and punishment
- reward only given at the physiological and safety level
- any interaction is made with fear and mistrust
- the control mechanism is highly concentrated at the top
- there generally develops a subversive informal organisation which opposes the organisation's goals.

SYSTEM 2

- management has a condescending confidence and trust in subordinates
- bulk of decisions are made at the top
- some decisions are made at lower levels but in a prescribed framework
- rewards are used to motivate workers
- some actual or potential punishments are used
- superior–subordinate interaction takes place with condescension by superiors and fear by juniors
- main control process is at the top
- some control mechanisms delegated to middle and lower levels
- informal organisations develop but not in direct opposition to the formal organisational goals.

SYSTEM 3

- management has substantial trust and confidence in subordinates
- broad policy and general decisions kept at the top
- subordinates delegated more specific decisions
- communications flow up and down the heirarchy
- rewards and some involvement used to motivate workers
- infrequent use of punishment
- moderate amount of interaction between levels with trust and confidence
- significant aspects of control delegated downwards
- informal organisation develops which may support or partially resist the goals of the organisation.

SYSTEM 4

- management has complete confidence and trust in subordinates
- decision making throughout the organisation is integrated
- communications flow upwards, downwards and laterally
- workers are motivated through participation, developing economic rewards, setting goals, improving methods and appraising progress
- extensive, friendly, trustful superior subordinate interaction
- widespread responsibility of control
- the formal and informal organisation are often one and the same and social forces are in support of organisational goals.

From the work of Likert and McGregor it is clear that there is a continuum of approaches to managing organisations from authoratitive, highly prescribed and structured through to participative. This continuum is very much buried in the social behaviour of man. Another dimension is given by Abraham Maslow. He concluded that human behaviour was goal orientated e.g. the obvious one — people worked for money or the less obvious — high quality performance for self pride. These goals might be conscious or subconscious and are sometimes described as needs, wants, drives or impulses. If goals were blocked, people became frustrated, e.g. an over qualified pool attendant developing 'coping behaviour' or technically 'cognitive dissonance.' Maslow concluded that there were five basic levels of human need or goal orientated behaviour operating at different levels viz:

- physiological need — to sustain life
- safety — security of existence, safe from physical dangers and deprivation, self preservation
- social affiliation — the need to belong, the establishment of meaningful relationships, being a member of a group
- esteem — respect from others, recognition of self-worth
- self-actualisation — maximising one's potential, 'what a person can be, he/she must be'; this could change over time, e.g. an athlete at a young or old age.

These five needs are referred to as 'Maslow's Heirarchy of Needs'. The skill of the manager is to keep the level of needs satisfied which would be different for every individual and prevent the onset of 'cognitive dissonance'.

The ethic and culture of an organisation is very much reflected by the position that management takes in the triangle of authoritarianism, participation and psychological needs. If a PME system is to be introduced or changed within an organisation, it is essential that the operating nature of the organisation is calculated. It forms a backdrop to all managerial change.

Illustrative example of hygiene factors and motivators at work

A supervisor was appointed to a new urban park where all the park labourers reported directly to the supervisor. There was no intermediary foreman. On settling down it came to the notice of the supervisor that there was a history of complaints about the condition and tidiness of the park. On investigation this was confirmed to be true. The labourers seemed to be lazy, unreliable and generally de-motivated. They were walking examples of the Theory X assumption of human nature (authoritarian).

The supervisor called a meeting and stated that he noted that there were a number of problems and that he confessed he did not know how to deal with them and did the employees have any solutions — long pause — one made a tentative suggestion which was followed by many more from an increasingly participative labour force. The supervisor jotted down the ideas and suggestions. At the conclusion of the meeting, the suggestions were summarised with tacit acceptance by all including the superintendent.

After the meeting, the superintendent passed any problems in the labourers' remit over to them. For example, when a material salesman came to the park, the labourers decided on the best materials and equipment within the budget they were given. In fact they were given a room to use as their office. All this had a tremendous influence on the behaviour of the people. They formed a cohesive production team, took pride in the park's appearance and work and the sources of complaint became silent. In fact, the supervisor was asked frequently what he had done to those 'lazy, good for nothing labourers'.

The exercise had taken time but it had not detracted from their work. The labourers worked harder and more effectively than previously and to such an extent that the change was noticed by external sources.

Activity

Consider your organisation or one with which you are familiar. Decide where on a continuum of System 1 to System 4 the organisation might lie. Consider the following elements before making a decision — confidence and trust superiors have in subordinates, how the workforce is motivated (fear, threats, rewards, involvement, progress towards goals and participation), interaction and communication between personnel (upward, downward and laterally) and what nature is the informal organisation within the enterprise.

The illustrative example is a simple one which demonstrates how a change in attitude towards employees can have a dramatic effect on the way people behave and perform their tasks. Too often, organisations evolve into what they are on an incremental basis with little thought or planning. Because heirarchical authoritative structures are perceived as easier, the movement of organisational culture and ethics tends to be in that direction. The activity is designed to make the reader stop and think about his/her own organisation. Managers wishing to introduce or change a PME scheme, must fully understand the ethic and culture within their own working environment. Failure to do so can spell disaster for the project before it even begins.

The employees are an integral part of the performance, monitoring and evaluation process and often, the process is perceived to have brought about discomfort. Therefore there is often a distrust between employees and the PME. So how do employees become committed to such processes? Part of it is understanding, part is involvement and training and part is the reward system. The intention of this chapter is to uncover some of the techniques and mechanisms that can, not will, motivate employees to be productive in the full sense of the word i.e., to participate willingly in all aspects of the business, including the performance, monitoring and evaluation process. A blend of the techniques can be used within an HRM strategy/policy to keep employees committed to a changed 'Management Information System' or new measurements or standards. Below a series of techniques are briefly explained.

Recruitment and selection

Recruitment and selection has the underlying purpose of 'ensuring that the qualities of the individual to be appointed, or promoted are well matched to the human resource requirements of the organisation' (Goss, 1994). Promotion is very much linked to succession planning, appraisal and development which will be discussed in the next chapter. Recruitment and selection are fundamental to having an appropriate manpower resource. For example, in the vast majority of appointments in the leisure business, it would be most unwise to select a member of staff who did not like people. Similarly if they are to be involved in a measurement system they would need empathy and skills in that direction. Too little effort is spent by organisations in selecting the right staff. In times of high unemployment the task is easier but at any time it may be worth spending that little bit more in order to appoint the right person. It is not the intention in this text to explain the whole of the recruitment and selection process. Enough to say, it is fundamental to the whole of the welfare of an organisation and should be thoroughly operated, involving:

- job analysis
- drawing up a job description
- devising a person specification
- promoting the post appropriately
- selection through testing, interviews etc
- induction and support on appointment.

Key point

Appoint the right people to match the human resource needs of the organisation.

Performance related pay

Initially it might be considered that performance related pay is inappropriate for a non production line enterprise. It is easy to count the number of girders or cars that come off a production line. In the leisure industry there are a number of tasks that can be directly related to finite measurement e.g., making up beds in a hotel, cleaning particular areas, mowing areas of grass or taking a number of people in a coaching class. But 'ah!' says the purist, 'that's all well and good — what about the quality issue?'. The leisure industry has been concerned with the issue of quality as is reflected in centres establishing BS 5750/ISO 9000 and discussion concerning Total Quality Management (TQM). (See Badmin, 1993, Operational Management, Vol. 2 for details of BS 5750/ISO 9000 and TQM). Quality is just as important in the steel industry. Sample girders are selected and tested for accuracy of measurement, strength and faults with expensive machinery and skilled staff. There seems to be little difference in sampling rooms for tidiness and cleanliness or the recording of cutting grass to the right standard. Client (user) satisfaction is a little more difficult but by using sampling techniques, questionnaires and attitude surveys as described earlier, it is possible to obtain valid and reliable results.

The reader will note here how intertwined PME has become with the issues of reward/performance. It is possible to see how sensitive employees can be when measurement and performance directly relate to pay. Firstly what factors should be listed when considering a performance related pay system? Why might it be introduced?

- solve skill shortages
- satisfy disgruntled workers
- buy in new methods of working
- moving from single skills to multi-skills
- buy in flexibility.

Straightforward financial reward can have distinctive benefits as a ploy and has been used for example in encouraging wet and dry staff in leisure centres to effectively become multi-skilled. Financial increases are not always the panacea for acceptable change. The right reasons might be:

- increase in productivity
- more effective use of labour
- flexibility and mobility of labour

171

- less overtime
- reduce waste and costs.

Situations where matters might go wrong when paying reward systems for performance could be:

- lack of interest in machinery, e.g. people to control queues rather than have a sensible reception area or ticket issuing units
- poor maintenance leading to non productive time, e.g. leaking roof or poor maintenance of trampoline puts services out of action and the supporting staff could be on overtime
- failure to improve working methods, i.e., ineffective use of assets
- restrictive practices with industrial relations difficulties
- shortage of suitable employees
- high labour turnover
- interruption of supply of materials
- fluctuations in demand
- absenteeism
- poor co-ordination between different parts of the organisation.

Activity

The first two negative reasons given are examples of why the best answer to the problem would not be linking performance to pay. Provide examples of either invented situations or ones that you are aware of in your organisation that might illustrate the other negative reasons.

There are different types of incentive payment schemes that might be constructed for a particular organisation. Some of these might be as follows.

Piecework

Characteristics: paid according to units of output; simple to operate and understand; oldest type of wage incentive.

Advantages Employer: system runs itself; easy and quick to introduce; supervisors can concentrate on bottlenecks; can make a substantial positive difference to productivity.

Advantages Employee: can control the pace of output; little supervision; scheme easy to understand and can predict earnings.

Disadvantages Employer: little control over output and hence the wage bill; quality may suffer; the need to renegotiate rates each time there is a change in procedure; small units of work have a high cost; shop stewards can have a strong influence on the shop floor.

Disadvantages Employee: earnings can fluctuate; social and work contact reduced; fragmentation of tasks.

Work measured payment by results (PBR) schemes

Characteristics: this system is based on the standard time to produce or service units. An average unit day forms the basis for calculating the bonus which might approximate to a third of the payment rate for units of service where 75% of the unit day output is agreed as average. It requires more sophisticated techniques to set up but can be used where more complicated tasks are involved. It can be applied to contractual cleaning and might save considerable downtime.

Advantages: increased output; lower output costs; higher earnings for employees; incentive to reduce inefficiency and waste; allows employees to control effort; easy to understand; less direct supervision and labour and total costs per unit of service/production can be estimated accurately in advance.

Disadvantages: fluctuation of earnings and the associated feeling of insecurity; difficult to calculate and predict earnings and the cost of collecting the data; quality diminishes unless there is stringent checking and inspection; safety rules can be disregarded by employees; difficulties of introducing new procedures or capital equipment; inter-employee group jealousies re differing earnings on similar but differing skill type tasks.

The scheme of measured day work (MDW)

Characteristics: the system of measured day work is a 'system of payment under which a fixed sum is paid for achieving any work performance at or above a pre-determined level'. Stability of output and earnings is the hall mark. This is a more sophisticated scheme which produces a high fixed wage and can be applied to bonus and stepped schemes.

Advantages: High guaranteed earnings; improved flexibility in deploying labour giving a better average output per employee; removes sources of discontent such as different payment systems and hence inequalities of earnings and reduces the haggling over task prices, timings and allowances.

Disadvantages: incentive element taken too much for granted; more difficult to understand for employees; pressures on supervisors to ensure that the process of service/production is maintained because interruption to flow (e.g. an unrepaired lawn mower or dishwasher) are blamed on management and the downtime has a cost; supervisors must support the scheme and accept the responsibility and it restricts the role of shop stewards who tend to be distanced from the day to day bargaining.

Bonus schemes

There are a whole variety of bonus schemes which vary according to the purpose of the organisation. It might be to maximise output which would give a scheme of increasing bonuses. On the other hand the organisation's purpose might be to stabilise output — in which case increased output would be penalised by a decrease in bonus payments. Because of the variety of schemes they are presented in Table 7.1.

Multi-factor schemes

Characteristics: these are complicated systems involving different facets of the above schemes which are scaled and then related to performance and pay. They are used to improve output, quality, reduce waste and inefficiency and increase service/product cleanliness.

Advantages: it is useful for solving specific problems and it acts as incentive to employees.

Disadvantages: it is complicated and difficult to understand; difficult to operate, implement and administer.

Group profit and share schemes

Characteristics: this system directly reflects the organisation's profitability or agreed budget target. Rewards are on the basis of share awards to an Approved Deferred Share Trust (ADST). The Trust holds the shares on behalf of the employees and there are tax benefits. The scheme is designed to avoid divisiveness.

Advantages: it develops a closer link between the employee and the organisation; there is a greater realisation of the individual's effect on profitability through their effort; reduction in the 'them' (managers) and 'us' (employers) syndrome; flexible and tax efficient way of rewarding loyalty and effort and the possibility of softening the impact of economic downturns.

Table 7.1 Types of incentive bonus schemes

Scheme	Characteristic	Advantages		Disadvantages	
		Employers	Employees	Employers	Employees
Proportional schemes	■ Bonus goes up in direct proportion to effort — e.g. 6 standard hours of work completed in 5 hrs equals 6 hrs of pay	■ Simple to explain and easy to to understand ■ Supervision and administration kept to a minimum ■ If incentive right, then productivity up ■ Raising standard rate takes care of annual increases rather than negotiating piece rate	■ Similar to piecework ■ Easy to understand ■ Control earnings	■ Little control over production ■ Little control over level of wages ■ Wage drift — if shop steward a strong bargainer ■ Disputes over fixing job times ■ Dispute over changing materials, machinery etc. ■ Quality suffers	■ Unstable earnings ■ The problems of waiting time
Progressive schemes	■ Bonus increase proportionately more than output	■ Increases productivity ■ Overheads as a proportion of costs goes down and employees get a large share of savings	■ Popular with employees ■ Good control over earnings	■ Direct labour costs high ■ Range of wages may vary widely because of workers' ability — hence ■ Potential for friction ■ Loss of quality	■ Good control over earnings ■ Fluctuating range of wages ■ Reluctant to switch jobs ■ May encourage unsafe working practices
Regressive schemes	■ Lower bonuses for output above standard performance ■ To encourage worker to keep to target either to stabilise production or improve quality	■ Mistakes in rate fixing are less costly ■ Higher production levels give lower wage costs ■ Stabilise production ■ Better quality	■ Don't like sharing benefits with employer ■ Earnings spread narrower	■ Workers build up pools of finished items to use at the most advantageous times	■ Poor incentive to increase production

contd . . .

Table 7.1 Types of incentive bonus schemes — contd

Scheme	Characteristic	Advantages		Disadvantages	
		Employers	*Employees*	*Employers*	*Employees*
Variable schemes	■ Payments alter proportionately differing production levels ■ Perhaps a bar on maximum ■ Encourages an employee to reach a specific level	■ Encourages employees to reach specific targets ■ Better way of relating incentive to productivity ■ Tailored to company needs ■ Greater control over the workforce	■ At times get a relatively large jump in earnings for little effort e.g., going through the bar	■ Complicated scheme to plan, install and administer	■ Can require a great deal of effort to get to next standard for pay increase
Banded bonus scheme	■ Bonus based on a work measured performance scale ■ Groups scale points into bands ■ Worker receives payment for band reached over a period of time ■ Designed to reduce fluctuations in earnings	■ Wage bill more predictable ■ Output more predictable ■ Bonus calculation relatively simple	■ Steadier earning levels ■ Can predict earnings ■ Easy to understand	■ With constant higher performance (bonus) pressure to consolidate bonus into pay scale ■ If bands wide then little incentive ■ Narrow bands defeat objective ■ Can generate more wage drift especially if such precise measurement is not required	■ Difficult to cross band if not properly balanced ■ Not a real incentive

contd . . .

Table 7.1 Types of incentive bonus schemes — *contd*

Scheme	Characteristic	Advantages		Disadvantages	
		Employers	*Employees*	*Employers*	*Employees*
Measured day work with bonus	■ Similar to MDW but a fixed bonus paid in addition ■ Payable for all hours when standard performance is achieved ■ Usually does not apply to overtime or shift working	■ If standard not achieved — bonus not paid therefore prevent employer taking disciplinary procedure ■ Discourages overtime working and reduce employees' temptation to manoeuvre overtime	■ Some incentive	■ In practical circumstance very little evidence to show that financial penalties were used	
Stepped measured day work schemes	■ Attach different levels of pay to different performance standards ■ Payment only changes after a sustained increase in the level of performance ■ MDW usually has fewer steps than banded bonus schemes	■ More scope to bring in changes	■ Provides an incentive ■ More flexibility	■ Need accurate measurement to set the performance standard ■ Accurate monitoring ■ Detailed records need keeping to record changing payment levels	

Disadvantages: there may be only small motivational gains; it is not a good scheme in times of recession; the benefits can be outweighed by the costs of administration and management.

Can the reader imagine running any of the above schemes without a PME process? Such incentive payment systems clearly demonstrate that it would be impossible to operate without a sophisticated measuring scheme. It will also be noticed how a relationship is being established with 'Taylorism' and 'Scientific Management'. As incentive systems become more complicated, so the detail of tasks are broken down and the costs/time of performance measured more accurately in order to form the basis of reward. However this does not necessarily mean that the operating ethic of the enterprise has to be authoritarian. Issues concerning the conditions for bringing about incentive payment schemes will be outlined in the next chapter. Here we are looking only at what the techniques are.

Activity

Refer to the organisation within which you work or to one with which you are familiar and consider:

(a) if you have a payment incentive scheme how would you classify it and how could the scheme be improved or
(b) how to devise a payment incentive scheme for your organisation. (*Note*: this theme will be developed in the next chapter.)

Appraisal

Appraisal is a term that is more frequently used in the management and operation of facilities. It can be used just in the context of incentive related pay, for example, the reappraisal of targets either because the workforce has become more skilful or because new processes or machinery has been introduced. The problem is that the term appraisal have been given a threatening tone and is associated with knocking the employee back by not giving them a pay rise or promotion. It is however difficult to argue that there should not be appraisal. Business, especially the leisure business is repeatedly told that its human resource is its greatest asset. Does that mean this asset should not be serviced? Of course not. It is logical that all employees should have regular appraisals probably once a year. There is a degree of coercion in the process. If you consider your workplace it is probable that you can identify one or more employees that do not pull their weight. Should they be given the same reward as everyone else? There is also the situation where dedicated employees do over and above their job profile at a very high quality. Should they not be rewarded? There are two broad approaches to appraisal — judgemental and developmental.

The judgemental approach

Such an approach tends to assess both social behaviour and performance in the workplace. The types of topics that might form the appraisal agenda are: job knowledge and ability, adaptability and willingness to be flexible, output, quality of performance, attitude towards work and the customers, interaction with other employees, initiative, creativity, use of resources, attendance, timekeeping, safety awareness, need for supervision, supervisory ability and ability to meet objectives.

It is likely that subjective and objective (qualitative and quantitative measurements might be used to measure performance (e.g. number of late arrivals — quantitative; opinion of your supervisor — qualitative). The reliability and validity of such measurements are often controversial and rely very much on the culture of the organisation, the nature of the job and the thoroughness of the appraisal system. This is another key area where techniques discussed in earlier chapters might be used. There is much opportunity for managerial manipulation and control which is distrusted by employees. This is even more the case when appraisal is linked to pay. The arguments for and against appraisal systems being linked to pay involve the following.

Arguments for:

- all personnel take appraisal performance more seriously

- it enables fairness to be applied to personnel so that the better staff can receive just rewards

- it is more likely to encourage a performance related culture.

Arguments against:

- the pay aspect dominates the whole of the appraisal system

- it does not encourage employees to introduce negative information to the appraisal system

- employees attempt to reduce goals

- good performers may be encouraged to underperform by not exploiting their own potential

- appraisal may overrate employees if they think the financial consequences might be adverse.

Activity

Consider how you might measure the factors that may form the agenda for a judgemental appraisal scheme.

The developmental approach

This approach to appraisal is less confrontational and is usually carried out through the vehicle of an interview which is qualitative in tone.

The emphasis of the content is away from the mechanistic perspectives of pay and measured performance and towards competence and individual development. The interview is about identifying weaknesses and how such problems can be solved and how the individual can improve performance through a development programme. The authoritarian view of appraisal is that it should be a personnel function with closed records. The developmental approach shifts the focus to a more open relationship between appraisee and the appraiser with the employee having access to most of the documentation. The appraiser is likely to be the line manager which follows the concept of devolving responsibilities nearer to the workforce. This approach makes the assumption that the line manager is adequately skilled and receives appropriate task training to fulfil his or her role as appraiser.

It is probable that the appraisee might be asked to consider a number of aspects prior to the interview. These aspects might be:

- what the individual has done well
- what performance has been weaker
- what difficulties have been met
- what qualities has the individual which are not being used
- what aspects of the person's job might be improved by further training or experience
- what could help the individual's personal development by the person's manager, the company and the individual
- where may future developments lie.

It is clear how very different these aspects of appraisal are from the judgemental approach. An agenda for the appraisal interview might be:

- positive comment made about achievements
- appraisee's own performance assessment
- appraisee's response to self-appraisal
- action to improve subordinate's performance
- appraisee's assessment of the appraiser's assessment
- appraisee's ambitions
- agreeing development targets
- developing an action plan to match targets
- agreed written summary of interview.

Activity

- Consider your own organisation in the light of appraisals.
- As an appraisee examine your own performance in the light of the agenda above.
- If you are really forward looking, decide on an action plan that would further develop your potential.

It is interesting to note that appraisal systems span the authoritarian and participative philosophies. The judgemental approach is a very much a top-down system and like incentive payments is looking for hard quantitative evidence. The developmental approach reflects the human relations ethic. The focus is on improving and developing performance with the emphasis on soft and qualitative information. The reader should also note that appraisal is another PME process. Both the judgemental and developmental appraisal approaches use PME. Quantitative and qualitative data is used to indicate performance and the interview provides the focus for the evaluation which is recorded with an action plan of developmental targets noted to use in the next appraisal interview.

Commitment

Managers frequently wish their workforce to be committed to the employing organisation be it of a local authority nature or one in the commercial sector.

Section 3

What is commitment? Definitions include:

> *Commitment is typically conceived as an individual's psychological bond to the organisation, including service, job involvement, loyalty and a belief in the value of the organisation* (Reilly, 1991).

or

> *the bedrock upon which flexible and quality-conscious attitudes and behaviours can be built* (Goss, 1994).

These are pretty strong statements and one might be wonder how a business enterprise could function at all without recognising that the symptoms of low commitment might be:

- high labour turnover
- high absenteeism
- poor performance
- sabotage of output
- irregular promotions
- little in the way of development
- strong punishment regimes.

Personnel, however, can be overcommitted to a position within an organisation and this can be equally damaging, for example:

- personnel can take illegal actions to sustain or prevent damage to the organisation (safety)
- it can stifle creativity and innovation
- it can be resistant to change
- it can bring about stress
- it can dominate life giving role overload.

Individuals should have a range of balanced commitments both within and outside the organisation. Family, friends and the community should play an important part in an individual's life. There are also a whole range of people and organisations to whom the employee should have commitment within the work environment — management, workers, professional associates, the union, customers and clients. These need to be in balance.

Activity

What type of Likert System (1-4) would you expect an organisation to adopt if it were to encourage the commitment of its workforce.

A commitment model might be as shown in Figure 7.1

**Structures/systems/cultures
of the organisation**
- Symbolic action from the top
- Employee involvement
- Flat organisation and structure
- Shared goals and values
- Horizontal communication flow

**Commitment and
optimised output**

**Employee — organisation
relationships**
- emphasis on mutual benefits
- comprehensive reward system intrinsic and extrinsic
- individual pay linked to skills/performance
- emphasis on mutual benefits
- high level of trust
- strong social emphasis

Job design
- multi-tasking and skilling
- flexible job definition
- work in teams which are the accountable unit
- emphasis on completing the task

Figure 7.1 A Diagram to illustrate the components of an employee commitment to organisation model

From the diagram it is not difficult to see that the answer to the activity is System 4. The question still arises how commitment is brought about. Does it just happen or does management give up its right to direct? Management needs to be proactive and fully supportive of any human relations approach adopted by an organisation. There are a number of techniques that can be applied in order to develop workforce commitment. We will now outline three applications — others will be examined later.

Attitude survey

This is a technique developed during the 1980s to evaluate the opinions of the workforce. Such an approach is more about gauging the current commitment of employees rather than encouraging involvement. It is a snapshot of opinion at the time of taking. What happens as a result of the survey is more appropriate to the encouragement of participation and involvement. Even so, employees do like to feel that their opinion is sought and generally value the process of the seeking their views and opinions.

Attitude surveys can check on how the organisation's policies are being applied, e.g., how do recreation attendants/officers feel about wearing a standardised form of dress. Morale is often raised by such exercises but there is a need for feedback and management should be prepared to act on the findings or at least be able to present convincing arguments as to why action might not be taken. Attitude surveys are best applied to policy or less clear issues than technical matters. They are better for softer, more qualitative findings, for example the quality of senior management, the system of communications within the enterprise or how efficiency might be improved. One aspect concerning attitude surveys is certain and that is if senior management are not committed to the process and it is 'only a sop to keep the workforce happy' then surveys probably do more harm than good.

The reader will no doubt have noted that the technique of applying attitude surveys to the workforce is the same as seeking the opinions of the customer. The results of a workforce survey equally become part of the performance, monitoring, evaluation system. Over time, a sequence of surveys will develop patterns which will be evaluated, and the results will act as a focus upon which management will make decisions. The performance in this case will be the degree of commitment indicated by the survey not performance in the usual sense of output like number of persons attending a theatre performance.

Team briefings

Team briefings are a downward communication designed to bring about some employee involvement.

Definition

Team briefings are a system of communications operated by line managers to enable employees to know what and why they are undertaking

---

Each morning, when the Tall Ships Race commenced from Newcastle, the operating team were gathered together by the co-ordinator for a team briefing with the purpose of:

- rectifying any mistakes from the previous day

- outlining the schedule of deliveries for each ship — food, fuel, support materials, special orders, etc.

- arranging visits to and from each ship

- collecting the requirements for the following day

- checking schedules for the day

- arranging the detail of special events — protocol, etc.

- fending off any potential future errors.

Team briefings therefore have the purpose of:

- reinforcing management (downward communication)

- increasing commitment

- preventing misunderstandings

- enabling and helping change — by making time for the 'why' of things happening

- improving upward communication to some degree.

Team briefings are mainly downward communication and if applied in large organisation need consistent application across all the teams to prevent lack of misunderstanding and duplication. For example when events are being organised it is very important that each of the groups is absolutely sure where their boundaries of responsibility lies — the responsibilities for competitors for Group A hosts ceases at the stadium where Group B hosts take over. Such clarity of detail and information should be consistent across all briefing teams, if not, chaos will ensue. Finally, team briefings do not really encourage upward communication. The individual within a team is required to have the necessary confidence to speak up. Even if he/she does there is no guarantee that the briefing supervisor will pass the message upwards.

Suggestion schemes

Definition

Suggestion schemes are dependent on the morale and ambience of the organisation to encourage employee suggestions to improve the running, organisation and output of the enterprise. Such suggestion schemes usually operate in the technical sphere.

Suggestion scheme have a number of advantages which might be:

- they encourage upward communication
- rewarding employees
- encouraging a climate of change
- they enable the identity of skilled thinking employees
- immediate line managers can be circumvented legitimately
- to assist management development
- that the types and natures of responses reflect employee morale
- providing significant financial savings.

The success of such a scheme very often lies in the ethic of the enterprise. If it is a token attempt by management at participation and ideas are not rewarded, employees will soon become disenchanted. There needs to be a good relationship between management and employees and real commitment by senior management. The individual leisure facility lends itself well to such an approach where positive and proactive relationships can be established within a relatively small workforce (up to 100 or thereabouts). Where chains of enterprises are established such as within the hotel system or a series of leisure centres within the remit of CCT, it is more difficult. Central headquarters or/and experts can become too detached from the operating situation and figures and profiles become more important than people. Management must take a much more proactive role in such chain circumstances.

In order to operate a suggestion scheme successfully, there are a number of aspects over and above the commitment of senior management and the enterprise's ethic that need attention. These might be:

- Avoiding lengthy delays in evaluating and rewarding suggestions. Complicated suggestions might need some serious investigation. Try to involve the employee who made the suggestion. Delays lead to frustration, suspicion and disenchantment

- The eligibility of the scheme, for example is it all staff, both full and part-time? The scheme is usually applied to the workforce rather than the managers

- The suggestion scheme can be counterproductive if for example group problem solving techniques are already being operated

- it might be necessary to exclude certain areas of the workforce or sites from such schemes because of collective bargaining arrangements with the unions

- Reward needs to be given for effort rather than the implementation of the suggestion. Stepped rewards can be established but it can be difficult to calculate the savings and hence quantify a reward.

Very often suggestion schemes are driven through technical elements rather than through systems, organisation and structure. This particularly applies if management is excluded from the scheme because they have a broader holistic and conceptual view of the enterprise. In a leisure centre one would expect suggestions to be put forward in such areas as reorganising storage areas, changes to schedules to minimise down time or the design of a certain piece of equipment to undertake a particular function such as clean windows that are difficult to reach. As part of the direct monitoring system it is not an infrequent occurrence for customers to be asked for suggestions in conjunction with a complaints scheme.

Quality

Quality is a term that has had a major impact on the public leisure services recently. The commercial sector has always been aware of quality issues and has come to the conclusion that they strongly relate to price, for example, a night at the Ritz will cost a great deal more than a stay in a suburban hotel. The difference in the experience for the customer will be quality i.e., service will be better, a wider range of food selection, ambience, quality of furniture and bedding, etc. However, high price does not always mean high quality and a third aspect enters the equation, that of 'value for money'. This element is particularly relevant to public sector thinking where accountability to the taxpayer at both local and national level replaces the idea of profit and rate of return for commercial enterprises.

This book is not primarily concerned with quality. Readers should refer to Chapter 5 of Badmin's *Leisure Operational Management* vol 2, 2nd Edition for such an account. We will concentrate on some of the techniques that can be applied to a leisure business to encourage full participation in change, for example, the introduction or change of a PME system. Such a system might be to measure quality under the auspices of BS 5750/ISO 9000. The start should be, what is quality?

Definition

Quality is 'the totality of features and characteristics of a product or service that bear on its ability to satisfy a given need i.e., fitness for purpose' (CIRIA 1989) The concept might be applied to a product, a trampoline or a service such as a customer visiting a restaurant for a meal.

The introduction of a quality ethic in local authority leisure departments has had a number of driving forces viz:

- the political emphasis being put on the idea of value for money
- introduction of the Citizen's Charter
- political defence of direct labour organisations for the next round of CCT specifications and tender
- the real quest for quality
- competing with the commercial sector.

In reality, quality is a marketing weapon which provides added value to a service or product that a competitor might be delivering. The old adage that one should open a fish and chip shop in a road full of fish and chip shops still applies, but only if the quality is above that of your competitiors.

There are a number of techniques that can be used to bring about quality which are explained below. However an underlying principle that applies to them all is that if the workforce is not committed to the process or top management is not fully behind such a scheme then all the techniques in the world are likely to be unsuccessful.

BS 5750/ISO 9000 British Standard Quality Assurance

The BS system can be viewed as being highly mechanistic with standards set by the hosting organisation. As such, low standards can be set. It can however be argued that this approach to standard setting is a stepping stone towards higher ideals such as the total quality management (TQM). Because BS 5750/ISO 9000 is so mechanistic it is a PME system within the enterprise itself. It should be a system within a total integrated PME system that would have marketing, financial and operational subsystems running parallel.

Total quality management (TQM)

Total quality management relates much more to the quality ethic of an organisation, and improving the quality of all aspects of the organisation in a continual process. Often problem solving groups are formed which are the agents of change or for improving quality. Such groups are very similar to quality circles, the mechanics of which will be explained later.

TQM is management driven but may effectively involve the employee and commit them to the goals of the organisation. A TQM process is likely to present fewer political and organisational barriers to implementation than say BS 5750/ISO 9000 or suggestion schemes because it involves the whole ethic of the entire organisation. The whole workforce, senior and middle management plus the hourly paid employees are working towards improved quality performance.

There are employees that view TQM with suspicion because it is considered a way management can be empowered through the quality surveillance process, much of which is peer group led. The question is therefore, is there real employee empowerment? The answer to this question can only be answered within the actual context of the situation. A Likert System 4 approach might be fine but one in the range of System 2 to System 3 could be very suspicious.

Quality circles

Definition

Quality circles are voluntary groups usually numbering between 6 and 12 members who meet to solve work related problems and implement the solutions. They are led by a supervisor or team leader and management attends by invitation.

Quality circles have developed in Western industrial society as a result of the Japanese success at using the technique. The Japanese were always accused of copying Western products badly. Post-Second World War, the Japanese have changed their philosophy to a high productivity, high standard, low cost nation. The strong competition of the Japanese has severely threatened Western industrial production and the quality circle is one of the techniques used to combat the developing Pacific countries. Quality circles developed particularly in the 1980s and if applied successfully are believed to:

- improve the quality and reliability of the service or product

- make suggestions that may lead to cost savings

- increase employee interest and commitments to the job

- encourage awareness of, and response to problems

- enhance supervisory and leadership skills

- increase trust between management and workforce

- improve communications, involvement and job satisfaction

- stimulate personal growth and breed new, better attitudes.

Needless to say there are difficulties in implementing quality circles which might be reviewed as follows:

- TQM is an alternative means of addressing the problems of quality

- the difficulty of sustaining enthusiasm on a voluntary basis — many employees displayed indifference and participation was disappointing

- the honeymoon effect — the most obvious or difficult problems might be solved early followed by a vacuum where little in the way of problems could be identified or results achieved and groups tend to wither away

- middle management could see quality circles as a threat because they were transgressing on their operational territory

- related to the above — the difficulty of integrating quality circles into the existing structure.

It should be remembered that it can be very difficult to transpose a system from one culture (Japanese) to another (Western industrial). The Japanese took an holistic approach to developing quality circles which was founded on a different work culture. In the UK for example, there were already established strong management/workforce relationships. Rightly or wrongly these were primarily based on an adversarial approach fed by liberal helpings of mistrust. At best, quality circles in the UK have been seen as fragile successes and research has been inconclusive.

Each technique that is applied has advantages and disadvantages. The next devised approach eliminates some of the problems but creates new ones. For example, the quality circle is voluntary and therefore by its very nature bottom up. TQM work groups are activated by management and hence top down. In TQM employees feel that management and peers are spying through quality surveillance. With quality circles, the reverse happens with junior and middle management being threatened. On careful examination it is not the technique that is at fault but the people participating. If there was mutual trust and common goals supported by a fair reward system, most techniques would work — back to Likert System 4. The problem is that few organisations have a work ethic above System 2.

As stated earlier, which technique might be applied in your organisation or what you might try to apply as a manager, will depend upon the actual circumstances of the moment. Even with relatively favourable 'causal factors' it may be that external factors provide dramatically opposing tensions.

Example

The control managers of a local authority leisure centre wish to develop an ethic of involvement by staff in operations. It is recognised that because of the tight specifications being applied by the client's department a more severe and accurate management information system will need to be constructed (PME). At the same time, subsidies are being reduced under Government and local government financial cuts and the recession is reducing the user demand and hence income. Because a high percentage of leisure centre operations are staffing costs and most other revenue expenditure is essential, the manager sees no other alternative but to split shifts, reduce staff, employ more part time staff and drive wages down. How in this climate can staff be encouraged to trust management and become involved in constructing a tighter performance, monitoring and evaluation process?

Unfortunately it is not recognised that PME goes hand in hand with quality. As stated before PME is an integral part of any business. The question is not should there be such a system because all businesses have them, but how effective the PME system is and how it can be made more effective. PME is very often pushed to the forefront of management thinking when an external factor forces change, e.g. bankruptcy threatens or CCT is imposed. Both situations produce cost cutting exercises which create an operating environment which is the least suitable for the introduction of a PME system. PME systems need to be established when business is buoyant and the system can become part of the accepted ethic of the enterprise. If the reader remembers in the Introduction it was suggested that economic indicators were called for in the late 1970s so that local authority leisure departments could measure the 'public good' of policies for disadvantaged groups. If that advice had been accepted by the leisure sector CTT may never have been introduced some ten years later. Much of the justification for CCT was based on the lack of defence that a PME system could have provided for local authority leisure departments if it had been in place.

Activity

Refer either to your own workplace or a facility with which you are familiar. Consider the issues that might have to be resolved if as manager you were required to upgrade the quality of operations (e.g. from BS 5750/ISO 9000 to TQM). What techniques would you introduce and apply? How would you counteract the disadvantages? How would you relate it to PME and how would you get employees to commit themselves to such changes?

Welfare, health and efficiency

Hygiene factors reflect such matters as working conditions, social relationships, money and status (see Hartzberg, 1966 for more information). Part of the hygiene equation is the welfare and health of the employee. There is a direct link between the well-being and especially the health of employees and output in the workplace. A 'well' workforce will be far more likely to have sympathy and commitment to organisational goals if the organisation subscribes to an ethic of care for the employee. There are valuable tools in the welfare and health package which can enable employees to support the rigours of a PME scheme. The text will briefly examine well-being, health promotion, substance abuse, drugs, stress and counselling.

Well-being

Well-being is part of the reward and development package that can be used to support employees. These might involve:

- holiday entitlements
- sick pay arrangements
- health schemes

- access to education and training

- job satisfaction.

Welfare

Welfare usually refers to the 'physical and emotional health' of the employees. The old style personnel rationale to welfare had three strands:

- the legalistic and reactive approach, for example, responding to Health and Safety at Work legislation and directives

- corporate conscious — this concept has its roots in the 19th Century Social Reform movement and the 'need for social cohesion in a potentially alienating work environment' (Goss, 1994)

- Paternalism — the concept developed from the large Quaker manufacturers such as Cadburys.

The above assumes a static urban population, but this no longer applies. Work security and continuity has changed and new methods of supplying welfare are necessary by human resource managers. Welfare support needs to be individually directed, flexible and adaptable. Schemes reflect the philosophical approaches to servicing human resources which are broadly defensive or humanitarian. The defensive approach assumes a threatening stance which is applied mechanistically and often as a result of surveillance (measurement). The humanitarian scheme would be typified by an open door policy, education of employees, direct access to assistance and agencies, confidentiality, counselling and sustained support. It must be remembered that welfare schemes are ultimately for the benefit of the business organisation and as such should have the following characteristics:

- the needs of the leisure business must come first

- employees need to be developed

- a 'tough love' approach rather than a 'soft love' support. The scheme must be realistic and practical

- respect for the individual does not mean pandering to the employee

- a 'care' driven by organisational needs.

The whole concept of a welfare scheme is that an employee with a healthy body and mind is more likely to work towards organisational objectives than an unhealthy employee. This is particularly important where employees are directly related to a service provided, as is very often the case in the leisure industry. There is little joy for the customer who is greeted by a coughing, diffident front of house employee.

Health promotion

Health promotion is self-explanatory in that it is about promoting good health and preventative medicine. It sets out to educate employees and is aimed at staff morale and fears to prevent a reduction in performance rather than an improvement.

A new development within the context of health promotion is Acquired Immune Deficiency Syndrome (AIDS). This has had an important impact on the workplace. In the 1980s there was prejudice against sufferers in the form of recruitment, non-promotion and dismissal, anxiety and fear amongst the workforce; and the need to confront issues and attitudes in the difficult areas of sexuality. There are now corporate AIDS policies which are mainly in the public sector. They should cover the following:

- a general statement of the businesses commitment to non-discrimination
- commitment to employee education policy
- confirmation of normal hiring procedures
- assurance of continued employment
- equity benefits
- confidentiality of medical records
- access to employee assistance plan.

These are important implications to the running of leisure organisations, particularly with regard to swimming pools, saunas and spa baths, etc. Organisations have a responsibility to:

- prevent new infection
- alert and train new managers and supervisors regarding discrimination and violations
- raise morale and prevent fear and anxiety.

The issue of health promotion might not seem to have a connection with PME but it does. Firstly it is a subsystem in its own right which requires performance records and their evaluation. Much of this monitoring would need to be confidential. Secondly a good support system for employees will give them confidence in the organisation; and thirdly a person seeking employment could partially evaluate an organisation through its caring services and as a result join the enterprise.

Substance abuse

Substance abuse is another modern phenomenon which infiltrates the workplace. Where large numbers of people are entertained and the sale of liquor is encouraged because it directly relates to profits, it is pertinent that substance abuse can be recognised. Substance abuse might be through alcohol or drugs. Both will impair employee performance. Symptoms are likely to be accidents, time off, poor relationships with peers and line management and poor co-operation decisions and judgements. There are two approaches to tackling substance abuse:

- the disease model which emphasises prevention and treatment

- legal and social responsibility model — this relates back to Health and Safety at Work legislation.

Each leisure business should have a policy and it should reflect the 'soft' and 'tough' love ethic mentioned earlier. The policy should outline in writing specific procedures detailing the handling and referral of employee, line management and supervisor responsibilities; qualified referral personnel or access to diagnostic facilities and rehabilitation agencies; and clear confidential recordings so that programme effectiveness can be evaluated.

Stress

Stress is not a new ailment but new working conditions and the shake up of the employment market during and from the late 1980s to the mid 1990s has brought about insecurity, job overload, changes of task, de-skilling and multi-skilling, etc. Stress related symptoms within the business could be any combination of the following:

- Absenteeism — emotional and physical strain

- High staff turnover — leaving as a means of escape. Often many employees in stressful posts are poorly trained

- Health — stress related disorders like heart or mental illness. In 1985, 111 million work days were lost through stress

- Litigation — this is a growing symptom in the USA where work induced stress is compensatable in law. Litigation has already taken place in the UK and will no doubt increase.

- Productivity/output falls — a difficult relationship to establish because some stress indicates an increase in performance. Excessive stress will bring about poor performance.

There is an implied need for a performance, monitoring and evaluation system, otherwise the leisure business concerned would not know it had a stress problem. Once detected, there is a need to monitor the situation so that patterns and evaluations can be established. Having detected a stress problem, what can an organisation do to solve it? Briefly develop a stress management programme which would entail:

- raising awareness of stress related symptoms

- individual training to cope with stress

- provision of special skills, e.g. a dedicated stress counselling service

- Stress audit — identify organisational stress sources for example extended lengths of poolside watching. Stress flashpoints should be defused to acceptable levels.

Counselling

An effective and confidential counselling service is a valuable asset to any business. Such a service can relate to all the subheadings above and can be extended to such matters as financial worries, bereavement, legal problems or redundancy. There are two basic forms of counselling:

- support or welfare type — this approach talks through the client's feelings and experiences relative to the problem. The role is that of a sounding board rather than making up the client's mind. The provision of benefit schemes and information has a high profile.

- outplacement counselling — particularly concerned with giving redundant employees the resources and skills to get themselves back to work.

The preceding text has provided a number of services and issues that are associated with the welfare and health of employees. It has been demonstrated that they require their own PME subsystems, some of which will be confidential and many will be of a soft nature. These services are important in supporting employees and enhancing their morale and identity with and commitment to the leisure business concerned.

LEARNING POINTS

■ The Western world is undergoing massive economic change which is impacting on the leisure industry.

■ The impact is in the form of increased mechanisation, economies of scale and cutting costs in the form of downsizing and delayering.

■ Managers must be aware of the HRM issues when bringing about change in organisations.

■ The dimensions of HRM issues are demonstrated by F.W. Taylor, R. Likert and A. Maslow.

■ It is essential that managers fully understand the ethic, culture and structures of their organisations.

■ Appoint the right people to match the human resource needs of the organisation.

■ There are many techniques that can be used to commit and involve employees attaining an organisation's goals.

■ Performance related pay is a common way of influencing work patterns and might be used to increase productivity, reduce overtime or bring about the more efficient use of labour.

■ Performance related pay can be used at inappropriate times, for example, instead of capital investment or situations when there is considerable downtime.

■ Some of the performance related pay techniques are piecework, work measured payment by results (PBR), measured day work (MDW), bonus schemes (proportional, progressive, regressive, variable, banded, measured day and stepped), multi-factor and group profit and share schemes.

■ Appraisal schemes are important mechanisms for involving staff in their own development. There are two basic types: judgemental which lean towards an authoritative stance and developmental which is concerned with the development of the individual and represents the Human Relations Movement.

- Encouraging the commitment of employees to work towards organisational goals is extremely dependent on having full support from senior management. If it is attained, it represents Likert's System 4.

- Commitment and optimised output are primarily influenced by the structures, systems, culture of the organisation, employee–organisation relationships and job design.

- There are a number of techniques that can be attributed to gaining the commitment of the employee: attitude survey, team briefings, suggestion schemes.

- Quality is a term that has been introduced and given a high profile in the leisure business recently. It has been linked specifically with CCT and the publishing of the Citizen's Charter. Quality as a mechanism is only a half way stage; it needs to be the ethic of the business and have full support from senior management.

- A number of techniques are used to promote quality, many of which rely on PME. They are: BS 5750/ISO 9000, total quality management (TQM), quality circles.

- A business should pay attention to its hygiene factors if it wishes to minimise the fall-off of output.

- Welfare and health matters are part of the hygiene equation and can play an important role in maintaining output and committing staff to the ethic of the organisation. Such factors can come under the headings: well-being, welfare, health promotion, substance abuse, stress, counselling. Many of these factors require their own in-built PME subsystems.

- The range of techniques mentioned in this chapter can only be selected for use in support of a PME by individual managers in individual businesses surrounded by unique environments. There is no panacea arrangement that will answer a business's difficulties. Each situation is unique.

- Every business must have an effective PME system which will be unique. Without the employees to support it through the type of techniques illustrated, they will not succeed, nor will they succeed unless they have senior management's full support and belief.

REFERENCES AND FURTHER READING

1 Argyris, C. (1971) *Management and Organisational Development: the path from XA to XB*, McGraw Hill Book Company

2 Badmin, P. A. (1993) *Leisure Operational Management*, vol. 2, 2nd ed., Longman

3 Berg, L. and Manley, W. V. (1966) as quoted *Organisational Relations and Management Action*, McGraw Hill Book Company

4 CIRIA (1989) Report 109 BS5750, A Synopsis

5 Department of Health and Safety Executive (1991), *Aids in the Workplace*, booklet, HMSO

6 Goss, D. (1994) *Principles of Human Resource Management*, Routledge

7 Hertzberg, (1966) *Work and the Nature of Man*, World Publishing Company

8 Hill, S. 'Why Quality Circles failed but Total Quality Management might succeed' *British Journal of Industrial Relations*, 29(4) pp 541–68.

9 Income Data Services Ltd (1980) *Guide to Incentive Payment Schemes*, Income Data Services Ltd

10 Likert, R. (1967) *The Human Organisation*, McGraw Hill Book Company

11 McGregor, D. (1960) *The Human Side of Enterprise*, McGraw Hill Book Company

12 Nietiaus, R. J. and Price, F. K. (1989) *Human Resource Strategies for Organisations in Transition*, Phenix Press

13 Salancik, G. (1977) *New Directions in Organisational Behaviour*, St Clair Press

8

Implementing performance, monitoring and evaluation

Introduction

The previous chapter has firstly, set a conceptual framework within which leisure organisations operate and secondly outlined a number of human resource management (HRM) techniques which can be applied to reward, enthuse and control employees. Leisure managers need to refer back to the ethic of the organisation within which they work so that they can consider what actions might be possible and what will be a waste of effort. For example, with a highly structured and hierarchical organisation run on Tayloristic principles, it would be a waste of time attempting to introduce quality circles. The manager would be rewarded far better by designing an elaborate detailed performance monitoring system that implied tight control. Organisational structure, culture and ethic has a strong influence over what is possible.

Performance, monitoring and evaluation do not stand alone in the management of leisure businesses — rather they infiltrate the business and are a little part of everything. Every business has a PME system no matter how simplistic or crude. Just knowing the number of employees and providing them with wages is part of a PME system. The perspective that is being adopted in this text is that PME is an integral element of all parts of the business and that:

- it exists within the business enterprise as it operates at the present time

- if any part of the enterprise changes, the PME system will have to change relative to the alterations made

- any changes in an organisation requires a PME system to be established in order to monitor the change itself.

As this chapter is about the implementation of PME, it must reasonably be assumed that something has happened to create a PME system to be installed or an existing PME system has been altered and needs implementing. This leads to the notion that circumstances, for whatever reasons, are changing, and the context of PME implementation is within the sphere of managing change — the principles of which form much of this chapter.

Like PME, the principles of managing change permeate the organisation that is being changed. It might be that only partial or incremental change is to take place, in which case the PME system at least would have to change by a similar amount and additionally a PME system would be required to monitor and evaluate the progress of that change itself. The added value to the reader is that the change principles cannot only be applied to changing or implementing PME systems, but they will apply to all elements of an enterprise that might require and contemplate change.

Changing a leisure business or enterprise, or its PME system, is fraught with problems. It is not the technical side that causes the difficulty, it is the people dimension. Changes require people to design and bring variations about and it is the employees who are required to respond to the change. The sports hall, conference centre or equipment will not worry or react one jot to the change envisaged. People will. It is therefore essential that managers bringing about change in a leisure enterprise diagnose the need for change carefully, plan the change in detail and implement the change with the right amount of judgement and sensitivity. As stated previously, human resource management knowledge and skills are fundamental to effectively bringing about change. Some of these aspects have been considered earlier in Chapter 7 but further elements will be introduced as appropriate when considering the two main themes of change — system intervention strategies and organisational development.

This chapter will take rather a different approach and the reader will be cast in the role of a leisure enterprise manager. The text will talk to managers about their enterprise and what they might do now. It is not possible to cast the reader as the manager of any particular facility as it would not be possible to explore the different types of enterprise, commercial or local authority or size e.g., a single unit facility such as a hotel or leisure centre or a chain of facilities and interests. Further, leisure managers vary according to the stature of their enterprise. Some are relatively small and managers are required to manage a whole range of business functions of which PME would be one. Others within major organsation have a whole range of supportive specialists. Therefore each manager's support system varies. Here the broad view is taken on the assumption that even if you are not a manager who is required to do everything, you will at least have an understanding of what the specialists are doing and why. Never a bad thing.

Each changed situation is unique and has its own unique solutions. There is no prescriptive answer and that is why it has been necessary to give the reader a brief conceptual framework in Chapter 7 along with some techniques for motivating employees. Every problem and impact on PME requires the manager to make unique judgements and decisions. The following will allow him or her to take a rational approach to implementing change.

The changed operational climate

Massive changes have taken place in all parts of Britain's businesses and government life (downsizing, delayering, CCT, etc.) and this in turn has changed the manner in which people are managed. On the one hand there has been a hardening of attitudes towards unit costs, productivity and subsidy per head, which smacks of Taylorism and on the other is a softer approach towards employees in the form of increased welfare, flexitime, and competence and commitment from employees which is reflected by the 'Humanistic School' of thinking. There has been a distinct cultural shift in the management of human resources towards a softer manner from the harder, mechanistic and more fragmented perspective of the personnel and industrial relations manager. There is a more humanistic feel about managing people and a recognition through the more recent title of human resource management (HRM) of the asset value of people to a business. This is never more so than in the leisure business. HRM managers instead of being sidelined have a part to play in strategy formulation and implementation. The ethic is now much more towards:

- Competence of employees — having positive attitudes towards learning and development

- Commitment of employees — to be motivated, to hear, understand and respond to management communications with the development of mutual trust

- Cost effectiveness — the organisation's human resource costs (wages, indirect costs, turnover, grievances, etc.) are less than those of competitors

- High congruence — that there is a high level of common interest between the management, shareholders and workers which reduces adversarial relationships.

The themes of human resource management have changed and may be reflected as:

- The psychology of human relations with emphasis on motivation, group dynamics and commitment. There is a recognition that there is more to work motivation than renumeration schemes and managers are looking for employee contributions to decision making, identifying with the values and culture of the organisation, personal development and a degree of involvement.

- Involvement in the strategic management process. HRM managers now have a part to play in the allocation of human resources in a rational way relative to the working conditions in order to gain a competitive advantage.

- The seeking of flexibility and quality. There is a recognition that quality or fitness for purpose, is an important ingredient of successful business and in order to satisfy both external and internal swiftly changing customer requirements, a flexible workforce is necessary. This requires multi skilling and skill development through training. There is additionally the need to have an external workforce available through such mechanisms as contract and self employed staff, casual and part-time employees — not an unusual characteristic for certain parts of the leisure industry involving tourism and hotel management. Leisure centres have reduced core full time staff and contract in specialists for particular activities.

The difference between the old personnel IR approach and the new HRM ethic is important. It means a less adversarial atmosphere and a more flexible and pliable work environment. The operating HRM ethic has changed to a much more flexible one which is far more receptive to change. This will enable our manager to have a much less rigid enterprise into which changed goals, structures, operating systems or PME might be introduced.

Situational uniqueness

You as a manager introducing change will be in a unique position. Each change in circumstance will be different and as the change manager it will be your responsibility to make the right judgements and decisions as to what:

- is the current macro situation

- aspects need to be changed

- is the present micro situation

- is the solution, decision, change required and objectives to be reached

- might be the range of techniques and approaches required to implement the solution

- is the range of the PME systems required to judge success, changes or failures against the objectives

- further changes need to be made.

It can be seen that a process of steps emerge that can be applied to any change process. They take place over time with possible overlaps and loop backs depending on the situation. The change manager might be in a group owning a chain of hotels or holiday camps in the commercial sector or be a single facility manager in a local authority. Equally he/she might find him/herself in an operational department with a more specific function such as bars and catering or marketing. It is appropriate to examine what type of diverse problems might afflict the leisure industry and the implications for PME systems. There follows a number of possible scenarios in both the public and commercial sector that might upset your world of today.

Commercial sector scenarios

Firstly you have to tender for a second round contract specified by a local authority client department. No doubt the local authority will have learnt from its previous years of contract monitoring and will write new specifications which will reflect its needs more closely. Pressure currently, suggests there will be greater emphasis on sports development, reduction of costs and increases in income. How will that affect the contract you are currently running? What changes will you have to make and how will you set up a PME system?

Alternatively the chain of holiday camps that you work for takes over another group. What will the implications be — delayering, downsizing, selling off selected assets, restructuring, developing a new culture in the bought asset and aligning or creating a new PME system to measure progress of the whole enterprise?

Other scenarios could be the recession lengthens and deepens for your company, or your company deals with specialised holidays to Germany. The value of the pound sterling drops ten per cent against the value of the Deutschmark, etc, etc.

Public sector scenarios

You work for a leisure department that is to have its budget cut by ten per cent for the next two years. How are you going to clamp down on costs, tackle the knotty problem of redundancy, re-align all the budgets and set up a PME system that will monitor the change and form a long term system after the change?

Another possibility would be, you belong to a leisure department in a district, four of which form a county. The county is to be disbanded and each district to become a unitary authority. The leisure department in your new authority is going to encompass the libraries and dual use joint provision enterprises. How will such a change affect the department and the incoming units? — restructuring, changed budgets and cost centres, new strategies, goals, missions and policies, establishing new cultures and ethics and the impact on the PME system which would require reconstruction.

You could also consider the effects of delayering, so that client functions across the authority are centralised, or the changing of Government and the scrapping of CCT etc.

A scenario that may be common to both sectors might be the introduction of a 'Total Management Information System', which is very often reduced to the computerisation of the booking system for the uninitiated. Chapters 1 and 2 showed that management information systems are far more complicated than that. A PME system, depending on the width of interpretation could be classified as a management information system. This common example will act as a theme within which to explore the issues of change and implementation.

Before any progress is made, it is appropriate that as the change manager, a strategic stance is taken before proceeding.

What is change?

At this point, before jumping into managing a process of change, it may be a reasonable idea to examine what change is, its nature and how people respond to it.

Definition
Change is moving from an existing current state to some future desired state (this is shown diagramatically in Figure 8.1)

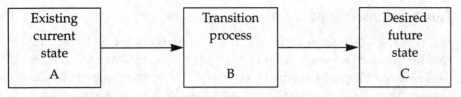

Figure 8.1 A diagramatical representation of change

Work through Figure 8.1. Your business is A, and at some time in the future you wish to move it to state C. In order to do this, the transition process B will have to be managed. It is interesting to note the reference to time. Change, in the context of this book does not refer to the dynamic routine that applies to all businesses all the time. For example, loops of programmes are being added to a mangement information system or PME on a daily or weekly basis. The changes with which you are concerned have a significant impact on the enterprise. Changes usually reflect a problem that requires addressing, the nature of which is illustrated in Figure 8.2. Pressure to change can be generated internally or externally but major changes are mainly motivated by the external environment or a strategic shift which reflects external pressures, e.g., CCT was imposed from without and initiated massive structural and operational change in local government leisure departments.

Externally driven —————— Source ————— Internally driven

Responding and reactive ——Control ————— Proactive directing
innovation

Difficult and messy ————— Complexity ——— Easy and
straightforward

Soft ————————————— Nature ——— Hard

Difficult to measure ————— Objectivity ——— Measurable and
quantifiable

Unquantifiable or ————— Time ————— Quick
partially slow

Figure 8.2 A diagram to illustrate the nature of change

Richard Branson is bidding to operate sections of the British Rail Network under the Government Privatisation policy because his business is in moving passengers/clients from A to B. He is strategically diversifying from one mode of transportation (aircraft) to another (railways). It is seen as a strategic market opportunity, the creation of which comes from the external environment. If he is successful, this will require change. Externally driven change provides the business with little control over the situation and the organisation can be little more than responsive. Internally generated change puts the organisation in control and gives greater ownership. A source of internal pressure for change can very often originate from problems of performance and is likely to arise directly from the PME system. For example, a study recently commissioned to examine attendance records at swimming pools discovered a four to six per cent fall off in attendance. In the commercial sector, this might be evidence of reduced staff morale or market share.

The complexity of problems has a direct effect on the way the transitional process of change should be managed. Broadly, there are two types of problem — the highly complicated 'soft' ones that are difficult to quantify and the straightforward quantifiable 'hard' problems. The first, invariably involves people and issues such as roles, morale and restructuring. The latter might involve introducing new machinery e.g., new disinfectant equipment for the leisure pool which has limited organisational impact, but the quality of service to clients/customers can be measured through reduced complaints, increased attendance and pH levels.

Time relates to the state you want the business to be in at some point in the future. This cannot always be selected. If the example of disinfectant equipment is taken, you will have some element of control; evaluating different types of equipment, designing specifications, requesting quotations etc., but it is probable that the purchase will be required within a particular financial year. At one extreme there are highly complicated soft problems that need rapid action e.g., receivers moving in on a bankrupt company. At the other end of the spectrum, there are complicated soft long term problems that have political dimensions relating to control and power. For example, prospective managing directors wishing to gain control over professional soccer clubs or changing the ethic of a run down organisation to that of high quality and client orientation.

Before moving to tackle your management of change problem, it might be best to consider the components of change. This will enable better understanding of the micro issues (plant, facility, organisation level). This may have an influence on where you decide to place your stance within the matrix of macro influence continuums, but this will be explained later.

D. A. Nadler (1993) has outlined a conceptual framework which enables a better understanding of the change process. It starts from the premiss that change will have driving forces and restraining forces, shown in Figure 8.3.

The driving and restraining forces should be appreciated in the context of the components involved in the transitional process from the current state to the

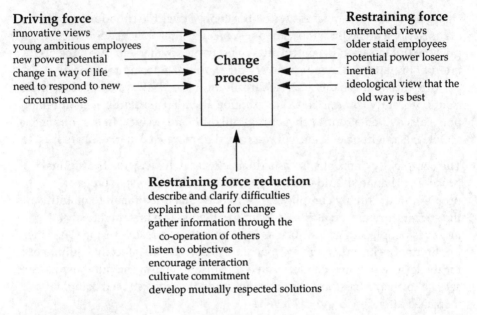

Driving force
innovative views
young ambitious employees
new power potential
change in way of life
need to respond to new
   circumstances

Change process

Restraining force
entrenched views
older staid employees
potential power losers
inertia
ideological view that the
   old way is best

Restraining force reduction
describe and clarify difficulties
explain the need for change
gather information through the
   co-operation of others
listen to objectives
encourage interaction
cultivate commitment
develop mutually respected solutions

Figure 8.3 A diagram to show the forces of change

future desired state e.g., the installation of a new management information system (MIS).

The people dimension behaves within the strategic direction and the inputs and outputs of the organisation. There are four distinct components that make up transitional process areas in an enterprise which are shown in Figure 8.4.

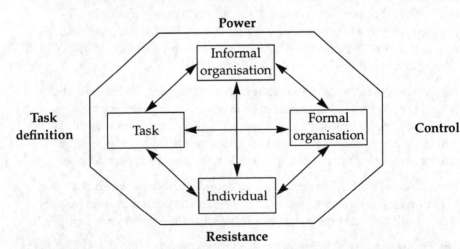

Power

Task definition

Control

Resistance

Informal organisation

Task

Formal organisation

Individual

Figure 8.4 A diagram to show the problems of change in relation to the components of an organisational model

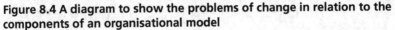

- Task represents the productive or service purposes of the organisation. If you were considering an MIS, it would be the collection, output and evaluation of data and resultant action. The crucial characteristics would be the hardware and software of such a system.

- The individual represents the employees who undertake the tasks. In the example, the designers of the system, collectors and inputers of data and the evaluators.

- The formal organisation represents the structures and process systems that motivate and facilitate individuals e.g., hierarchical staff structure, pay and bonuses, involvement, etc.

- Informal organisations are usually neither planned nor written and reflect through good practice and common usage such elements as communication and power. It influences values and norms and characterises how the organisation functions. There is always someone for example, who knows more about computer systems or programmes irrespective of their formal hierarchical position in the organisational structure.

The arrows in the diagram represents the relationships between the various components. It is necessary for these relationships to remain in balance. For example, does the task match the skills and abilities of the individuals for successful completion? Your business at present functions in a steady environment where the PME or MIS produces the appropriate outputs. If the new computer system is to be installed, individuals are unlikely to have the knowledge and skills to fulfil their new tasks. The relationship has got out of balance and needs rectifying — let's say training, to keep it simple.

Key points

- Change requires a managed transitional process.

- It is important to understand the source, control, complexity, nature and timing of the contemplated change.

- There is a need to appreciate the forces of change and how they might be optimised and minimised.

- The components of an organisation need equilibrium.

You now have an understanding of the conceptual issues involved in making change in your organisation and the components that require thought in moving the organisation from operating one PME or MIS to a new system in the future.

Stage 1 — Establishing a strategic stance

As change manager you find yourself in a complicated messy situation within which to manage. There will be, what can only be described as a series of continuums of influences which will have a marked effect on what you will perceive as possible and impossible change. This is illustrated in Figure 8.5.

Sitting at the top of the diagram is the power and political structure. It is not unusual, particularly in local government situations to set up a working party

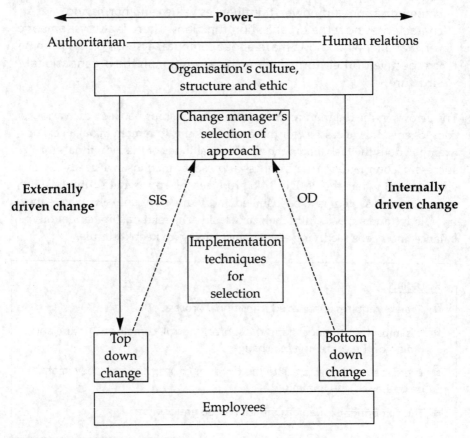

Note:
NB. SIS — Systems Intervention Strategies
OD — Organisational Development

Figure 8.5 Influences affecting a change manager's strategic stance

under the remit of a manager to investigate and propose a solution to a problem. If no one of influence sponsors or participates in the working party it is often probable that the outcomes/solutions will be academic and the real objective is to sideline or delay the issue. It is essential that the change manager has a sponsor who is influential in the power/political structure.

Beneath the power structure lies the culture, structure and ethic of the organisation which has a considerable bearing on what is possible to undertake. A highly authoritarian organisation faced by a problem that you consider requires a participative approach would be very difficult to instigate. Both management and employees would be distrustful. An organisation functioning at the other end of the spectrum, a human relations approach, would positively support a technique such as group problem solving as an entry to introducing change. Conversely an enterprise steeped in participation would take unkindly to a direct authoritarian instruction to change.

The very nature of the organisation e.g. Likert's Systems 1–4, imply the approach the change manager can take. System 4 can look to a 'bottom up' ethic where employees are using their full potential and they are involved, motivated and operating at Maslow's higher levels of need. System 1 will require a 'top down' change, and employees will resent being asked to participate. Negotiation on a confrontational basis will be underpinned by distrust. Enterprises operate between these two extremes but the change manager should select an approach that is compatible with the enterprise's position on the continuum.

Internally driven changes frequently have their origins in the business with a participative culture. This does not mean all change is driven from inside. In reality most change comes either from senior management or from the external environment. Senior management may have some control over what they initiate but they are predominantly responding to external issues like competitive pressures, recession, take over bid or legislation etc. which force some change one way or another. The most traumatic change circumstance is probably the take-over or bancruptcy.

The final dimension to the diagram is the base where a block represents the employees. Each set of employees will be different and are likely to reflect the structure, culture and ethic of the organisation. This might be represented by a strong unionised approach or as indicated in Likert's System 1 by an informal structure that does not accept and works against company goals in a subversive manner. The feel of the workforce will be dependent on other support mechanisms operated by the business such as welfare. To complicate matters still further, there are the motivations and personalities of the employees themselves as individuals. Any change to be implemented effectively requires employee support rather than resistance. Your selection of motivators and calculated encouragements to involve the workforce in a supportive manner is going to be crucial.

The change manager must evaluate this macro situation and come to some rational decision about the stance to be adopted within the framework illustrated in Figure 8.5. It needs to be practical and possible. Having adopted a position there are two broad approaches which can be used to bring about change. These are:

- Systems intervention strategies (SIS)
- Organisational development (OD)

illustrated in the diagram Figure 8.5 by the dotted lines.

Systems intervention tends to be linked with a 'top down' ethic whilst organisational development relates to a more participative approach. Both will be discussed later. Underpinning the SIS and OD are a whole range of techniques for diagnosing, planning and implementing the envisaged change. As change manager you will have the responsibility of selecting a battery of techniques to support the approach to bringing about the change. Further techniques will be introduced in the various stages of this chapter, most of which will be relegated for reference to the Appendix. Above all it must be recognised that change is both an intellectual and social exercise.

Key points

- Ensure you have senior influential support.
- Position yourself within the organisation's pattern of influences so that you have a reasonable chance to implement change.
- Employees have dimensions of their own.
- Change is an intellectual and social exercise.
- You have the responsibility of charting and implementing the change effectively.

Stage 1 has enabled you as the change manager to adopt a view and position among the organisational influences. This is unlikely to be a static position as the process of introducing a new PME/MIS scheme is progressed. There are two broad approaches you might take to solving your problem. The system intervention strategy or organisational development. We will not set out in detail either of the schemes here because there is sufficient common ground to construct a best model. The SIS as might suggest is based on Systems Theory developed in the 1970s and takes a holistic view where a number of parts of an organisation are arranged in such a way that they 'do something' (a production line produces goods, a series of data information gathering units provides an information system). The process of SIS is rather mechanistic and prescriptive in its philosophy and has a 'top down' feel to it. OD on the other hand is less prescriptive and views change as a more organic process in which people have a higher profile. OD makes the point that development is on-going and not just a single cycle of change. Both schemes have three distinctive phases which are shown in Figure 8.6.

Figure 8.6 The broad phases of managing change

The phases do not neatly stop and start as shown in Figure 8.6 . They overlap and are not as simplistic. It is therefore necessary to add other dimensions to better represent the process of change. Figure 8. 7 represents a truer model.

Stage 1 has already been examined and you have taken up a provisional strategic position in preparation for the remainder of the process. This is an additional stage to those shown in Figure 8.6. Stages 2, 4 and 5 remain the same except that overlapping is demonstrated with the dotted line. Stage 3 very much represents the OD dimension and is about involving the owners of the problem or change in the process of moving the organisation from the current state to some desired

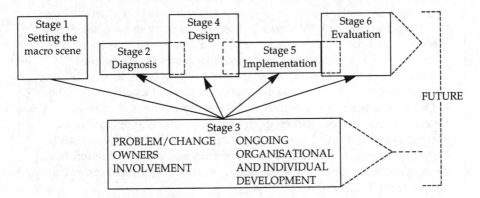

Figure 8.7 A SIS/OD model for change

213

state in the future. Apart from Stage1, which is down to your individual judgement, involvement and commitment should be encouraged throughout the process including Stage 6 which is an evaluation of the transition. It is unlikely that the change will be perfect, aspects will need improving, employees will be able to perform better and the whole process becomes circular and developmental. It will be necessary to consider each of the stages in turn.

Stage 2—Diagnosis

Diagnosis is very much about understanding what the situation surrounding the problem is. The nature of the investigation will depend on a number of aspects such as the size of the problem, its relationship within the business to other functions, the level, is it strategic or departmental and whether the problem is generated internally or externally.

Example

A rural local authority has a leisure department with four divisions. They are Sport and Recreation and its Development, Arts and Museums, Marketing and Client Function, and Tourism and Economic Development. Local government reorganisation has determined that 30 to 40 per cent of the authority is to be attached to the local urban centre which has a very strong tourism ethic. Approximately one third of the facilities will be transferred to the jurisdiction of the local urban area. The head of the division responsible for Arts and Museums is leaving for another post because of the unsettled situation. The head of Tourism and Economic Development wants to leave and the current policy is that no posts will be replaced. The new arrangements are to take effect in approximately one year.

It is clear that the problem is generated externally and that the local authority must respond. If it had a strategy, which it doesn't, it would have to be radically changed. Each division has a policy but two have no leadership and their sizes, with the remaining two, are to be reduced by a third. The problem is therefore going to impact considerably on the strategy, the policy and structure of the department, the nature of its tasks, its quantity of activity, its employees and the nature of its operations. The impact will be from top to bottom and throughout all elements and functions from finance, marketing, information gathering to monitoring and individual tasks etc. The change manager, which could be you in the diagnostic stage, would need to thoroughly understand the situation and all the potential impacts and implications. It is both a hard and soft problem — is comprehensive and very messy.

How are you going to get your thinking attuned to such a problem — because changing a PME or MIS is just as difficult. There are a number of techniques that could be used and illustrations are provided in Appendices 3 and 4. They are the use of diagrams which primarily come from SIS thinking and the Pugh Matrix which has its origins in OD thinking,

Diagnosis should be about:

- getting clear what people want

- establishing a boundary around the mess

- clarifying the relationships between the major subunits of the change

- establishing who has ownership and a stake in the change/problem

- understanding the structure of the mess

- developing the purpose and objectives that will be served by the change together with constraints

- consider the people and the organisational impact

- aim to bring about an ethic of involvement and willingness to change, by employees.

Appendix 3 outlines a number of different types of diagram that might be used in your diagnostic process. There are quite a variety, and selection of type can cause some problems but they will help you to:

- understand the present situation — a poor PME system

- clarify the desired situation — a good PME system

- and thirdly, how to plan and design the transformation from the existing to the desired over the specified time.

You should not be put off by the belief that you cannot draw, as the quality of diagrams is not important, it is the quality of understanding and ideas that tops the list. If quality is needed rough sketches can always be given to a graphic designer. There follows a number of principles concerning diagrams:

- If you are not used to the idea of diagrams they are not terribly difficult or easy. Their construction improves with practice and it's been said that if a situation cannot be presented diagramatically the situation is not clear in your own head.

- Diagrams are made up of pictures, words and symbols; the Ordnance Survey maps are the best example. Arrows are frequently used to indicate the flow of reasoning, materials or consequences. Diagrams should be used as the base for explanation and it is necessary that the reader, client or audience are taken through the diagram. Too often diagrams are flashed up on to the overhead to illustrate the flow of data or information and then whipped off again before the audience has gained any real understanding. Diagrams are tools of representation, understanding and explanation. Remember that a great deal of time and effort is taken in construction and time is needed to absorb them.

- There are roughly two types of diagrams: maps which show relationships in the dimensions of space and time and logical diagrams which show how things depend on one another. It is best not to mix the two types into a single map or diagram.

- Diagrams are holistic and if understood give a better feel for relationships and connections between components.

- As a diagram is formulated and constructed the understanding will grow. Diagrams can be incrementally increased as new aspects, relationships and processes are thought of. Where there are drawing/constructional difficulties there is usually a need for greater effort of understanding or more information As a complex diagram builds up over time, it might be necessary to divide it into units so that each element can be explained to an audience. For example, architect and the design of a leisure centre — services are shown separately from materials, finishes, etc.

- Diagrams can be used for the development and design of the solution to the problem that is the first stages of modelling.

- It is the logic of diagrams that is most important, not the artistry.

- It is not necessary to rigidly follow a particular type of diagramming. A combination of types and conventions may be used if it enables a better understanding of the problem.

- Diagrams can be an excellent form of communication.

Appendix 3 has brief notes on the following types of diagram and provides examples of those more frequently used. The types are:

- mind maps

- input–output diagrams

- flow-block, flow process and activity-sequence diagrams

- control loop diagrams

- relationship diagrams

- systems maps

- influence diagrams

- multiple cause diagrams.

You should now be in a good position to select a series of diagrammatical approaches which would enable you to develop a greater understanding of the present situation of your organisation in terms of the PME/MIS development.

Another approach to diagnosing the current situation is shown in Appendix 4 which examines the Pugh Matrix. In this approach, the impact of the people factors play a more dominant role. The method concentrates on four aspects of analysis i.e., the individual, group, inter- group and organisational. This forms one axis of the matrix. The columns are considered under the headings — behaviour, structure and content. You should read through Appendix 4 for an outline of the method and further reading is listed at the end of this chapter.

As the change manager, having selected a number of techniques to diagnose the situation with regards installing a new PME/MIS, and applied them, you have a good understanding of the problem and the types of changes that might be envisaged.

Checklist

- Really know the cause of the problem rather than just the symptoms which is often the case. Poor quality is a symptom rather than a cause.

- Be able to take a helicopter view of the situation.

- Be able to fully engage the problems/change

  — know what is the purpose of the change

  — be fully conversant with the arguments for the change and its importance.

- Be able to discuss the issues involved.

- Recognise the systems and sub-systems — represented diagramatically.

- Be developing angles on the solution to the problem.

- Re-check your ideas so far — iteration.
- Check back with your 'sponsor' and agree progress so far and any changes to your initial brief which are almost inevitable.
- Have involved problem/change owners in the process of change.
- Be developing outcomes like,
  - clear purpose
  - setting clear objectives both measurable and scalable
  - identifying constraining factors e.g., legislation, resources
  - devise measures to recognise achievement of objectives
  - give purposes and objectives priority ratings
  - develop criteria for making decisions later.

These factors should not be cast in stone but there should be a sufficiently clear direction for all to know where the project is going. Refinement can take place during the design stage. A process of iteration should be on-going i.e., going back over stages to develop improvements. If the checklist can be completed confidently one may progress to the design stage. If there are gaps, then more information gathering and analysis is required. Before progress is made to the design stage, there is a need to pause and consider the all important people factor.

Stage 3 — Involvement and on-going organisational development

The people dimensions are more important than the remaining parts of the staged process. It has already been stressed in Chapter 7 how important the ethic of the organisation is. This ethic will determine the approaches you will adopt to introducing the changes. For example, if you look at the completed Pugh Matrix in Appendix 4 you will see that there was a general discomfort at the introduction of new high technology computer systems. What would be your way to resolving this aspect of the problem if the ethic of the organisation was 'Scientific Management'? Would your approach be the same if there was a 'Human Relations' approach? The first would downgrade employees, move them sideways or pressurise them to leave. The second would develop and implement a comprehensive training package with a view to reinforcing career development with more able employees.

You should undoubtedly discuss such matters with your 'sponsor' and there is a good argument that a neutral third party should be on hand to act as a sounding board for much of your initial analysis. It might be deemed appropriate to delegate the whole of such a change process over to external consultants — this route will not be taken here — you feel that it's 'your change project' and there is a moderate 'Human Relations' ethic within the operation of business.

Chapter 7 outlined a whole range of techniques which might encourage employees to become involved in envisaged change. Further techniques are available in Appendix 3–11.

Involvement of employees in change and in the development of the organisation should be on-going and just because this change PME/MIS project has appeared should be no great cause for alarm. The involvement and commitment of employees should be automatic and commence from day one. There should be a policy of:

- education of employees to obtain an understanding for the need to change the PME/MIS

- understanding the implication for the organisation

- understanding and obtaining the 'felt' needs of participants

- open and effective communication

- Encouraging involvement and commitment from the workforce.

In order to develop involvement and commitment from employees, it will be necessary to devise mechanisms of encouragement. Quality circles were talked about in Chapter 7 and they could be an initial start position, but there will need to be work in groups. Ask yourself what you know about groups and enabling them to become involved in effectively progressing the introduction of a PME system to a 'best' desired position. Appendix 5 outlines a number of guidelines as to how you might constitute and operate working groups as an aid to your situation, viz:

- nature and formation

- composition

- context

- development — phases, practical action and process

- leadership

- ancillary factors — hidden agendas, consensus and stress.

It is probable that you would develop a series of groups that cascaded down the organisation when considering the design and implementation of the new PME/MIS. To be simplistic, let's suggest a control working group of representatives from each department/unit e.g., finance, personnel, performance etc. Each of the representatives would find themselves in the similar position to yourself of having a problem of change re PME/MIS, but on a departmental scale rather than on an organisation scale. They are connected to the organisational dimension through the working groups. The representatives would therefore find themselves having to understand the change envisaged and the resulting impacts. Like you, they would have to seek situational information. An effective way of gathering information in such circumstances is through information interviewing. The skills of such a technique will not only be essential to you but all those involved in the situational information gathering exercise. To help, Appendix 6 outlines 'interviewing for information' under the headings:

- introduction

- the need for interviewing

- preparation

- making contact

- recording

- interviewing in action

- controlling the interview

- dealing with the information.

Cascading information collection down the organisation has a triple advantage. It enables delegation by structuring the present situation: working groups encourage involvement through interest, understanding and the opportunity for individual development and the satisfaction of higher level needs: and it sets up a mechanism for the implementation and continuation of change at a later stages.

Key points

Working groups can:

- help in the establishment of the current situation

- enable involvement and commitment of problem/change owners

- establish a structure for implementation and continuation.

The direct way of encouraging involvement and commitment to change is through the reward and renumeration system. A number of techniques were examined in Chapter 7 with emphasis on renumeration. Additionally there is reward by recognition of competence and associated promotion. How this is handled will relate to the ethic of the organisation and where the focus might be, for example, the continuum of the Likert system 1–4. For those who are some distance from envisaged change an increase or change in the direct reward system is likely to encourage support, contribution and change more readily. Chapter 7 outlined a number of payment schemes from which a choice could be made according to circumstance e.g., typists changing to word processors (skill upgrade), multi-tasking (change in job content), or more accurate measure systems (performance/target related. Appendix 7 outlines some of the conditions that require consideration when changing the direct reward system. Recent examples of pay changes to accept new conditions of service have been seen in both further and higher education. Monetary reward can act as a great incentive.

Communication is another skill that need nurturing and encouraging. Communication must be both upwards and downwards and the cascaded work groups should be an important mechanism. It is necessary that communications is honest and above board if employee involvement and commitment are to materialise in the process of change. The following factors should be considered:

- there is a need to overcome suspicion, particularly in the areas of jobs and pay
- start to communicate early, outlining the implications and impacts
- explain why a new PME/MIS is to be introduced
- reassure re. redundancies, protection of earnings etc.
- describe and explain the process by which changes are to be brought about
- provide opportunities for employees to make inputs through the communication system.
- indicate how the changes will affect the long term
- encourage constructive discourse and interaction
- don't rush the process if it can be avoided but provide a time budget for the change.

Note: for the techniques associated with communications, see further reading.

Key points

Communication, like information, is the glue that brings an organisation together. Communication needs to be honest and open if it is to overcome the suspicions of the employee. It needs to start early before the rumours.

A further aspect that should be considered within the context of Stage 3 is training and development. This again should be within the very ethic and fabric of the organisation. It should be on-going and decisions reflecting its resourcing and importance should be made at a strategic level. Therefore your envisaged changes should be part of an on-going process which is accepted by all members of the organisation as normal. Special projects and the change impacts will need additional consideration. Introducing a new PME/MIS will have considerable impact on the operation of the organisation. You might like to consider what training and development may be required to retrain:

- data input staff

- output and analysis staff

- technical personnel

- persons devising the detail of the PME structure and data creation processes

- personnel involved with analysis and interpretation of data and information

- management on the new information, accessing it and the relationships to old and new types of decision that will be expected of them

- the impact on operational staff and changes in task structure etc.

As an important part of the design stage, it will be necessary for you and your working group to ascertain future training need. The resource implications will require presenting to management in investment/budget form for financial sanctioning. Training and development will become an important mechanism in your implementation package. It should then become an on-going process. Appendix 8 outlines a number of aspects that should be considered when devising and constructing a training and development plan.

At this particular point, an organisational development perspective has been adopted on the assumption that if any real involvement and commitment by employees is to be created, then a number of proactive approaches should be taken. These involve delegating information collection; involving and committing staff to work groups (teams) that cascade through the organisation; directly buying in commitment and involvement through direct renumeration deals; establishing a communication network that encourages interaction and participation: and supporting the whole change culture with a training and development package. The particular balance of these dimensions will be peculiar to your unique situation. The aspects that have been talked about during this stage infiltrate all parts of the process and fall back on many of the issues and techniques raised in the previous chapters. Further information concerning the application of techniques are provided in Appendix 4–8.

It is now time to move on to or back to the design stage.

Stage 4 — Design

The design stage to some extent was described in Chapters 1 to 6 where the various techniques of measurement were fully discussed together with what is meant by performance, monitoring and evaluation. Design, to a major extent, is about deciding which techniques are required for your particular PME/MIS. It may be that your performance measures are driven by a client's specifications in a CCT contract e.g., social objectives such as the number of single parent families using the facility. A profit orientated organisation will have an emphasis on issues like market share, payback periods, profit ratios and a measuring system. These will all feed back information sufficiently quickly so that decisions affecting operations will minimise problems and maximise benefits e.g., a drop in the pattern of bookings could lead to the decision to spend more funds on an immediate secondary promotional effort. There are a whole range of techniques from which to select.

Key point

Chapters 1–6 provide a range of techniques and information from which to select your PME/MIS design.

There is another aspect to design which is the planning of the implementation of change and the generation of possible solutions. There are a number of sub-phases that should be considered.

Setting objectives for the project

Objectives should include such matters as:

- time scale

- setting clear measurable objectives within appropriate time constraints. Where soft/qualitative measurement is required, use scales or indices

- prioritising purposes and objectives. It may be that there are several facilities that need new technology. Phase installation with a particular single site with a high priority and reduced priorities for lesser sites. It might be that one particular site will have a greater influence on persuading colleagues to the project's way of thinking

- clear criteria for making decisions e.g., Data Protection Act on structuring programmes and access policy.

- the hidden agendas which should by now be in open forum and can be accounted for in full.

The generation of options

This will have been an on-going process with perhaps strategic direction in the initial stages and further inputs from working groups in the diagnostic stage. Computer hardware costs in local authorities are very often driven by budgets and leave insufficient funding for changes or flexibility at a later stage. The Harrogate Conference Centre went from an initial budget of £9 million to £32 million. The commercial sector will be more flexible about the supply of capital, but more searching when evaluating the reasons for expenditure (rate of return, pay back, impact on sales etc.). There are a number of ways different options can be generated including:

- brainstorming

- modelling from diagramatically generated options

- discussions

- feasibility studies

- physical mock-ups

- information and data flow models

- cost benefit analysis, etc.

The selection of approach will often need adaption to the particular circumstance. For example, there is no point in spending large sums of money on modelling a PME/MIS when there is only limited capital for purchase.

Option — evaluation

The options should primarily be evaluated against the purpose and objectives of the project together with the constraining criteria which were identified earlier. The objective of a networked booking facility will be different from a set of options for an independent PC booking system. Having shortlisted the options against purpose and objectives, further rationalisation can take place against desirability and feasibility. It is necessary to be aware that the world does not stand still whilst design and planning is taking place. This is particularly so in the information technology industry. Some changes are predictable but others are unforeseen like withdrawal from the exchange rate mechanism would have meant an 11 per cent rise in price for systems purchased from Germany. There is therefore a need to assess risk in major changes and projects which should also includes the risk or cost of not going ahead.

When introducing such a system as a PME/MIS, a considerable amount of technical design will be undertaken. A specialised software package may need to be adapted or designed to meet your particular requirements. For this stage to be reached, it is necessary to know what outputs are required from the system. Appendix 9 provides an example of the initial thinking that might go towards identifying information needs for a single leisure centre. Appendix 10 outlines some of the particular difficulties that might be associated with installing a computer system into a facility or series of facilities.

Stage 5 — Implementation

Within the context of implementation, there is included the stage of planning, the implementation and the carrying through of the project. Broadly, there are three distinct types of implementation viz:

1. The 'big bang' approach. This was used by British Airways when they changed from the central site to Terminal 4 for their international flights. The whole changeover was accomplished in one weekend — successfully. The London Ambulance Service attempted to computerise their service using the 'big bang' approach and failed dismally.

2. The pilot study approach which was implied earlier for your project. If a number of centres are involved in developing a new PME/MIS, then it might be wise to run a pilot scheme in one centre, learn lessons and then incrementally extend the system to other facilities until the network is complete.

3. The parallel running approach involves running a new system next to the old for a period of time. The development of unitary authorities under the banner of local government reorganisation is an illustration of this method. This applies throughout the organisation not just as a PME/MIS.

It is perhaps appropriate to note here that some changes can hardly be planned and have to be the 'big bang' approach — like it or not. Where there is a takeover, or a receiver is installed in a bankruptcy case, there is little option but to make the necessary changes just to survive. Appendix 11 provides an outline of actions that are likely to be taken in the case of bankruptcy. It is hoped that the reader is not involved in such a traumatic event. This aspect is included as an appendix, mainly for interest, but also because it demonstrates that even where outside personnel come in to save a company, there is a planned approach and certain strategic actions taken. It is not ad hoc. What is omitted from the equation is participation by the employees.

The conclusion that can be drawn from the above is that careful planning is required if a project is to be implemented effectively. Figure 8.8 illustrates this. There is some similarity with the product life cycle graphical presentation.

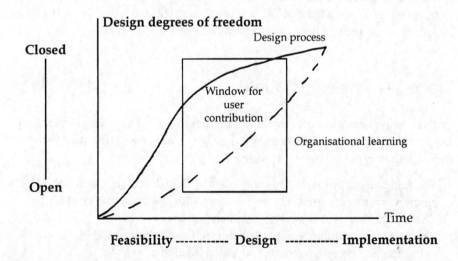

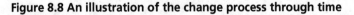

Figure 8.8 An illustration of the change process through time

It can be seen how the project design starts slowly, then makes rapid progress before settling on its planned course. The people element has an even slower start whilst involvement and commitment are enabled and resistance redirected or overcome. The box in the middle represents the opportunity for project/change owners to make inputs. It then becomes necessary to firm up on proposals before implementation.

Planning should be in detail. It will probably be necessary to use such planning and scheduling techniques as bar or gantt charts, critical path analysis (CPA) and/or programme evaluation review techniques (PERT). It should be remembered however, that planning methods are only as good as the assumptions and information provided and it is an unwise change manager that leaves no spare time. There are questions of error and people, as stated earlier who can become stressed under such change conditions. As change manager, be well advised to plan time to allow stability to form and energy to regenerate for the next phase.

Implementation is bound to raise resistance. Some resistance is good and generates creative discussion and a better solution, but there is a need to understand resistance a little more deeply. There are four factors to consider:

1. Organisations operate in a stable state with security and few threats. Change brings unknowns and anxiety. Those with power will resist because they have an investment in the status quo.

2. Change undermines the current system of organisational control. This particularly applies to formal organisations. As change takes place and structures and people shift, it becomes difficult to monitor performance and make adjustments as in normal times.

3. Because formal control systems assume a stable state, it is necessary to establish new controls to monitor the transitional state, even as in this case when a new control system (PME/MIS) is the centre of the change process

4. The organisation is a socio-political system and change upsets the balance of power. This sets off political activity which tries to influence the change for its own ends.

The actions to take in order to counter resistance, to some extent have been covered earlier, but in principle are:

- identify and surface any dissatisfaction
- establish participation in the change and transition process

- use the reward system

- give time for people to disengage from the present system. There is a need to mourn the old order.

Much of the structure, organisation and personnel should already be in place for your change/transition. You will have developed roles and tasks for individuals through the network of work groups so that transition will not be something that just starts today. Transition will have been managed in the following manner.

1. Communications:

   - Made clear the image and purpose of the future

   - Prevented misinformation, misconceptions and rumours

   - Handled resistance

   - Written to work groups and briefed the employees.

2. Tactics:

   - the use of consistent leverage points i.e., have balanced changes in all the component parts, informal and formal organisations, task redefinition and the individual job descriptions. Changes to only one component brings about dysfunctional outcomes

   - be consistent. e.g., training dovetails with new job descriptions, reward systems and tasks.

3. Organisational arrangements:

   - a transition manager — you in this case with the necessary power and authority

   - resources for the transition, personnel, funds and expertise

   - a transition plan with benchmarks and standards of performance

   - transitional management structure — maybe a task force, pilot project or experimental unit

   - develop feedback mechanisms — you need to know that the changes are progressing at the right pace and if there are any difficulties — surveys, sensing groups, consultation interviews, objective data, informal and formal communications — progress must be effective.

Implementation is the gap between the idea and reality. A recent USA study revealed those aspects of transition which were most likely to go wrong were:

- took more time than was planned

- major problems surfaced during transition

- poor co-ordination

- competing activities and resulting crisis

- employees did not have the necessary skills

- inadequate training was given

- uncontrollable external factors

- leadership and direction poor

- certain implementation tasks and activities, poorly defined.

As might be expected, the list mirrors all those areas of good practice recommended within this book. There is however, no right way to implement a change project such as installing a new PME/MIS. The change manager will always be faced by a unique situation in a unique circumstance. It is only possible for the change manager to apply best practice to every change situation. The change manager's thoroughness will establish the present circumstance and winkle out the best options for implementing. It is the manager's judgement and experience that will decide how effective the project will be on completion. Even the best of judgements can be nullified by unforeseen and uncontrollable circumstances.

Key points

For the successful implementation of a change project such as the introduction of a PME/MIS the following consideration list may help.

1. Principles of change

- organisations are organisms — require careful thinking and consideration

- organisations are occupational, political and rational and individuals operate similtaneously in all three areas

- allocation of clear responsibility and accountability for the successful outcome of the overall product/change

- limit the number of strategies for change at any one time

- decide on strategic change objectives and identify actions to be taken to achieve them
- identify progressive benchmarks
- establish clear measures to be monitored for the life of the change transition
- appoint a change manager with the necessary authority
- undertake a situational analysis and estimate the potential change to current traditional responsibility centres — budgets, revenue, costs, capital, marketing, operations and personnel, etc.
- The change manager to take up a strategic, realistic position within the ethic of the organisation.

2. Activities

- agree strategic objectives, resources and financial implications
- work hard at establishing the need for change and external reasons are often more acceptable that internal ones
- listen to resistance and use it to good efect — sometimes confrontation may be needed
- identify specific activities and allocate them through the network of work groups
- don't only think about change, think through it i.e., the impact
- be prepared to change yourself and include your own implementation objectives
- avoid 'big bang' changes — if possible
- it is preferable to initiate change through pilot or parallel running schemes if appropriate i.e., an incremental approach
- training and development are essential to effective change
- iterate
- continually monitor transition performance objectives/benchmarks
- resist pressure to speed up implementation in order to cut costs
- time budget change — balance the energy required for change against the capacity of personnel
- build in plateau of inactivity and stability

3. Message

- managing and implementing change is both an intellectual and social process

Stage 6 — Evaluation

Explained in Chapter 1, evaluation is about examining the data that has been collected, very often analysing it by comparing averages, percentages, ratios or subsidies etc against objectives or standards. In this way performance can be judged. If the preparatory work has not been done for introducing and establishing a PME/MIS, i.e., no benchmarks or objective measures have been set, any collected data will remain data. On the assumption that planning has been thorough it should be possible to evaluate the effectiveness of the change transition e.g. the installation of the hardware went into Leisure Centre No. 1 on time. The software worked well till 2p.m. when a power surge caused problems but it is a technical problem that is easily resolved, etc. Such monitoring will indicate the successful change mechanisms and the weaknesses. Weak areas will need attention.

When talking about monitoring, objectives and performance, it is easy to forget the main business asset of the leisure centre ie. the people that make things happen. They need monitoring as well — their morale, level of satisfaction, ideas etc. The business still needs their involvement and commitment and hopefully the change has brought about a new progressive ethic in employees.

Evaluation is, or should be continuous, and its effectiveness will rely on the PME system that has been installed. You may now like to get ready for the next element of change that will be thrust upon your enterprise from the external environment, be it political legislation or an upturn in the economic situation. You had better start a new situational analysis and ensure a powerful sponsor.

LEARNING POINTS

- PME infiltrates the whole business.
- If any change is made to an enterprise the PME system will have to change with it.
- A PME system will require establishment to evaluate the change.
- Implementing a PME system is unique to any situation and requires unique action by the change manager.
- Establishing a PME system requires the appointment of a manager with sole charge of the project.
- The manager should have committed support from the power base in the business in a sponsor.

- The change manager should evaluate the cultural ethic of the business in order to determine the possible. There is no point in developing a PME system which is impossible to implement.
- Externally driven change e.g., CCT is far more difficult to control than internally motivated change.
- There are two broad approaches to implementing a PME system. They are SIS and OD Probably a mixture of both approaches is best.
- Implementing a PME system requires six stages:
  1. <u>Setting the Macro Scene</u> — establishing a power/political/philosophical base.
  2. <u>Diagnosis</u> — evaluating the present position.
  3. <u>The People Dimension</u> — providing opportunities for involvement by employees and giving them ownership of the project.
  4. <u>Design</u> — considering the detail and process of implementation and establishing the PME system to determine progress.
  5. <u>Implementation</u> — Big Bang, incremental or pilot study — beware the Big Bang.
  6. <u>Evaluation</u> — how successful have the first five stages been and what alterations are required ?
- Projects have both driving and restraining forces. Restraining forces can be valuable but require careful management.
- Use the tools that are available to help diagnosis, employee involvement, design, implementation and evaluation.
- Make a special note of the aspects that are likely to go wrong when implementing any project such as a PME system.

REFERENCES AND FURTHER READING

Badmin, P. A. (1983) *Operational Management*, vol. 2, 2nd ed., chapter 2 Longman

Goss, D. (1994) *Principles of Human Resource Management*, Routledge

IDS Ltd. (1980) *Guide to Incentive Payment Schemes*, Income Data Services Ltd

Nadler, D. A. (1993) 'Concepts for the Management of Organisational Change', article in *Managing Change* eds. Maybe, C. and Mayon-White, B. OU Press, 2nd ed.

Pugh, D. S. et al (1983) *Writers on Organisations*, Penguin Books

Pugh, D. S. (1984) *Organisation Theory: selected readings*, Penguin Books

Taylor, P. and Kearney, J. (1995) *Demand for Swimming in UK Local Authority Pools*, Leisure Management Unit Sheffield Univ

Appendices

Appendix 1—Sample monitoring sheets

1 General observation sheet

This sheet should be used for the recording of any points relating to the centre which do not form part of a particular inspection. It is particularly useful for issues such as health and safety.

General observations			
Location	Data	Time	Weather
Area	Observation		Comments

Location manager's comment:

Action agreed and time scale

Monitored by ....

Location manager's signature ....

2 Activity monitoring sheet for outdoor pitches

Activity monitoring: Outdoor pitches LOCATION:				
	Date:		Time:	Weather:
Are the following in accordance with relevant clause	Y	N	Comments	Inspection
1. Information regarding activities				
2. Was facility available at specified time				
3. Is a current price list displayed at the location				
4. Has the correct price been charged				
5. Has the correct ticket been issued				
6. Is hire equipment available				
Are the following present and in good order				
1. Goal posts				
2. Goal nets				
3. Line markings				
Secondary services				
1. Are changing rooms available				
2. Are disclaimer notices displayed				
3. Are all facilities, showers and wash basins available				
Location manager's comments				
Action agreed and time scale				
Monitor's signature				
Location manager's signature				

3 Marketing inspection sheet

Activity monitoring: Outdoor pitches LOCATION:					
Area inspected	Date:		Time:	Week No:	Inspection
DOES ITEM COMPLY WITH CLAUSE	YES	NO	COMMENTS		1st 2nd or 3rd
1. Does the contractor maintain a list of facility charges?					
2. Has the contractor displayed a price list in a prominent position					
3. Has the contractor ensured that all relevant information advertising the activities has been displayed and made available to the location					
4. Has the contractor submitted all publicity material/sample leaflets to the authority for approval prior to publication					

5. Has the contractor complied with the authority's standard publicity and advertising requirements in respect of
 	
    use of media
    quality of paper
    artwork
    logos
    typesetting
    distribution					

6. Has any market research been undertaken					
7. Does a marketing plan exist					
Location manager's comments					
Action agreed and time scale					
Monitor's signature					
Location manager's signature					

Appendix 2—Exemplar questionnaire

The following questionnaire was used to carry out a user/audience survey for a multi-purpose arts venue. The questionnaire demonstrates a number of question formats as well as some points of good practice.

Whilst due to the varying nature and purpose of leisure facilities this questionnaire is unlikely to be readily transferable. It will give an insight into the form and construction of a user questionnaire and may act as a basis for adaptation to individual situations.

The list below highlights a number of good practices which can be found within the questionnaire.

- Paragraph 1   Purpose of questionnaire
-   Instruction as to what to do on completion
- Paragraph 2   Confirmation of confidentiality
-   Incentive for completion
-   General instruction
- Paragraph 3   Section/Topic instruction
- Question 1   Forced choice question, ten plus category ensures exhaustive choice
- Question2   Dichotomous response question
- Question 3   Clarification of context/time period
- Question 7   Open response question, list would be too long if made exhaustive
- Question 13   Answers not mutually exclusive therefore specific question instructions required, BA
- Question 20   Form of ranking question, what's important? and what is the most important P20
- Question 21   Semantic differential question
- Question 23   Open-ended question in case respondent wishes to make further statement or feels strongly about a particular issue raised in the questionnaire.
- Question 24   Use of the questionnaire to recruit to the mailing list.

- Question 25   Enrol people for further research if possible.
- Question 25   Always thank the respondent for his/her time.

Darlington Arts Centre Audience Survey

Hello, and welcome to the Arts Centre. This Autumn we're carrying out a survey to find out more about you, our audience. While you're in the Arts Centre it would be a great help if you could fill in this questionnaire, and then return it to a member of staff or post it into one of the boxes provided before you leave.

Pens are available in the foyer, and, if you need any help with filling the questionnaire in, do please ask a member of staff. Please be assured that all of the information you give will be treated as STRICTLY CONFIDENTIAL. To say 'thank you' for helping us with this, we have organised a PRIZE DRAW open to everyone who fills in the questionnaire. All you have to do to enter is fill in your name and address on the last page: **one lucky winner will received £25 in theatre tokens**.

Wishing you a very pleasant visit to the Arts Centre, and thanking you in advance for your help with this survey.

Please tick one box only [   ] unless otherwise asked.

Please write in today's date   / ...... and the event you are attending

. . . .

Firstly, some questions about theatres that you visit:

1. Have you ever been to an event at the Arts Centre before today?
   Yes [   ]1   No [   ]2
   If YES, how many events have you been to at the Arts Centre in the last 12 months (since October 1992)? *Please do not include today's event.*

None	[ ]	Once	[ ]	Twice	[ ]
3 times	[ ]	4 times	[ ]	5–6 times	[ ]
7–9 times	[ ]	10+ times	[ ]		

2. Have you ever visited this Theatre?   Yes [   ]   No [   ]
   If YES, how many times have you visited Darlington Civic Theatre within the last 12 months?   (Since October 1992).

None	[ ]	Once	[ ]	Twice	[ ]
3 times	[ ]	4 times	[ ]	5–6 times	[ ]
7–9 times	[ ]	10+ times	[ ]		

3. Which, if any, of these venues have you been to in the last 12 months? (Since October 1992) *Tick more than one box if appropriate.*

Billingham Forum	[ ]	Dovecote Arts Centre, Stockton	[ ]
Grand Theatre, Leeds	[ ]	Middlesborough Town Hall	[ ]
Newcastle Playhouse	[ ]	Newcastle Theatre Royal	[ ]
Queen's Hall Arts Centre, Hexham	[ ]	Sunderland Empire	[ ]
West Yorkshire Playhouse, Leeds	[ ]	York Theatre Royal	[ ]

Other [ ] *(Please write in which ones)*...

Now a few questions about you:

4. What is your age?

16–19	[ ]	20–24	[ ]	25–34	[ ]
35–44	[ ]	45–54	[ ]	55–64	[ ]
65+	[ ]				

5. Are you Female or Male?   Female [ ]   Male [ ]

6. Are you:

In employment	[ ]	Looking after the home/family	[ ]
Retired	[ ]	Not eligible for employment	[ ]
Unemployed	[ ]	Full-time student	[ ]

7. What is your occupation?

Please write in your occupation ....
If you are not in employment or are retired, please give your former occupation, if any:..

8. About how far you live from the Arts Centre? (*Students, please answer for your term-time address*)

0–3 miles	[ ]	4–6 miles	[ ]	7–12 miles	[ ]
13–24 miles	[ ]	Over 24 miles	[ ]		

9. What is your postcode? (*Please give your postcode below, e.g. DL3 7AX. If you can't remember it fully, please give as much as possible and add the name of the street, the city/town/village and county or district in which you live*)

Postcode .... Street ....

City/town/village .... County/District ....

Next, some questions about this event:

10. How many people are there in your group today (including yourself?

Myself only	[ ]	Two	[ ]	3–6	[ ]	
7–0	[ ]	11–15	[ ]	16–19	[ ]	
20 or more	[ ]					

11. If you are in an organised group of seven or more people, does it mainly consist of:

People from work [ ] *(If so, please write in what kind of work)* ....

People from school/college [ ] *(If so, please write in which)* ....

Members of a club/society [ ] *(If so, please write in which)* ....

12. When was your ticket for this event booked?

After 6.00 pm today	[ ]	Earlier today	[ ]
Between yesterday & a week ago	[ ]	Between 8 days & a month ago	[ ]
Between one and two months ago	[ ]	More than two months ago	[ ]
		Don't know	[ ]

13. How did you find out about this event? *(Tick as many boxes as you like)*

And what was your main source of information? *(Tick one box only)*

	I found out through: (Tick any box)	My main source of information was: (Tick only one box)
Arts Centre What's On brochure	[ ]	[ ]
Leaflets about this event	[ ]	[ ]
Posters at the theatre	[ ]	[ ]
Poster elsewhere	[ ]	[ ]
Newspaper news item/review	[ ]	[ ]
Newspaper advertisement	[ ]	[ ]
Radio	[ ]	[ ]
Television	[ ]	[ ]
Someone who is with me today	[ ]	[ ]
Told by someone else	[ ]	[ ]

Other [ ] (Please say what) ....

14. If you found out through a leaflet or theatre brochure, please say where you saw it or how you obtained it:

	By post	At this theatre	At another theatre	Elsewhere (*please state where*)
Season brochure	[ ]	[ ]	[ ]	[ ] ....

Now, some general questions:

15.   Are you on the Arts Centre's mailing list?

Yes [ ]   No [ ]   Don't know   [ ]

If you aren't, but would like to be, please tick here [ ] and make sure you give your name and address at the end of this questionnaire.

16. Which if any, national daily newspapers do you read regularly? (*i.e. on most days — tick as many boxes as apply*)

Daily Express	[ ]	Daily Mail	[ ]	Daily Mirror	[ ]
Daily Star	[ ]	Daily Telegraph	[ ]	Guardian	[ ]
Financial Times	[ ]	Independent	[ ]	The Sun	[ ]
The Times	[ ]	Today	[ ]		
Other	[ ]	*(please write in which)*			

17. Which, if any, national Sunday Newspapers do you read regularly? (*i.e. most issues—tick as many boxes as apply*)

Independent on Sunday	[ ]	Mail on Sunday	[ ]	Observer	[ ]
News of the World	[ ]	The People	[ ]	Sunday Express	[ ]
Sunday Mirror	[ ]	Sunday Times	[ ]	Sunday Telegraph	[ ]
Other	[ ]	(please write in which)			

18. Which, if any, of the following local newspapers do you read regularly? (*i.e. most issues — tick as many boxes as apply*)

Darlington Advertiser	[ ]	Darlington & Stockton Times	[ ]
Evening Gazette	[ ]	Northallerton & Bedale Times	[ ]
Herald and Post	[ ]	Teesdale Mercury	[ ]
Northern Echo	[ ]		
Other	[ ]	(please write in which)	

19. Which, if any, of the following local radio stations do you listens to regularly? (*i.e. on most days — tick as many boxes as apply*)

BBC Radio Cleveland	[ ]	Great North Radio	[ ]	TFM	[ ]

Other [ ] (please write in which)..

Finally, some questions about your visit to the Arts Centre:

20. Why did you choose to attend this event? (*Tick as many boxes as apply*) And what was your main reason? (*Tick one box only*)

	Reasons for attending (Tick any box)	Main reason for attending (Tick one box only)
Curiosity	[ ]	[ ]
Company's reputation	[ ]	[ ]
Seen the Company/artist before	[ ]	[ ]
Professional interest	[ ]	[ ]
Related to studies	[ ]	[ ]
Music	[ ]	[ ]
Story/themes	[ ]	[ ]
Good previews/reviews	[ ]	[ ]
Star performer	[ ]	[ ]
To celebrate a special occasion	[ ]	[ ]
Wanted an evening out	[ ]	[ ]
Someone else's choice	[ ]	[ ]

Other　[　] (please write in your reasons) ....

21. How would you rate the following aspects of the Arts Centre? (please tick one box only on each line)

	Very Good	Fairly Good	Average	Fairly Poor	Very Poor
Atmosphere	[ ]	[ ]	[ ]	[ ]	[ ]
Bar services	[ ]	[ ]	[ ]	[ ]	[ ]
Comfort of seats	[ ]	[ ]	[ ]	[ ]	[ ]
Ease of access for the disabled	[ ]	[ ]	[ ]	[ ]	[ ]
Ease of ticket-buying	[ ]	[ ]	[ ]	[ ]	[ ]
Ease of obtaining advance information	[ ]	[ ]	[ ]	[ ]	[ ]
Friendliness/helpfulness of staff	[ ]	[ ]	[ ]	[ ]	[ ]
Overall quality of events	[ ]	[ ]	[ ]	[ ]	[ ]
Value for money	[ ]	[ ]	[ ]	[ ]	[ ]
Choice and range of events	[ ]	[ ]	[ ]	[ ]	[ ]

22. Please tick any of the following which you have done, or intend to do, while you are in the Arts Centre today: (Tick as many activities as apply)

Use of cafeteria　[　] Use of bar [　] Visit the art gallery　　　　　　[　]
See a performance [　] See a film　[　] Take part in a class/workshop [　]

23. Any further comments regarding your visit

....
....
....
....

24. Arts Centre mailing list

   If you answered YES to Question 15, and would like to receive further information about the Arts Centre, **FREE OF CHARGE**, please tick this box [   ] and write your name and address below
   If you would like to enter our **PRIZE DRAW** please tick this box [   ] and write your name and address below.

   Name: ....
   Address: ....
   .... Postcode ....
   We may, from time to time, send information about other events that we think will be of interest to you. If you do **not** wish to receive such information, please tick here [   ].

25. Finally, if you'd be willing to take part in further research, please tick here [   ].
   Thank you very much indeed for your help. Now please hand this questionnaire in to a member of staff or post it in one of the boxes provided. Alternatively, you can post this to me **Free of Charge** to: McCann Matthews Millman Limited, FREEPOST, PO Box 281, Cardiff, CF1 1YX.

This questionnaire is reproduced by the kind permission of Darlington Arts, Contract Services, Darlington Borough Council.

Appendix 3—Situational analysis through diagrams

The three main reasons for using diagrams in a situational analysis are:

- to understand the present situation
- to help clarify the desired situation
- to show how transition can be made from one to the other.

Diagrams are used to:

- simplify complexity
- provide a mental map of relationships
- help communications and get over ideas
- if they follow convention they can clarify the way an ad hoc diagram cannot.

In the formation of diagrams a number of factors require consideration viz:

- they should follow the convention appropriate to that group of user, e.g. underground maps, ordnance survey maps or circuit diagrams
- the degree of detail
- the audience to whom they are targeted
- the purpose of the diagram.

The process of constructing a diagram helps to bring logic and rationale to the situation/problem that is being explored. Throughout the text there have been a number of diagrams which have been used by the authors (hopefully) to clarify processes or relationships. There are a number of different types of diagram that might be used in developing clarity of thought when diagnosing businesses problems such as devising a new PME system or MIS. The types of diagrams might be:

1. Mind mapping — used for putting ideas down rather more quickly than they can be written. See Diagram 3.1 which shows a mind map concerning PME and was drawn in about 15 minutes.

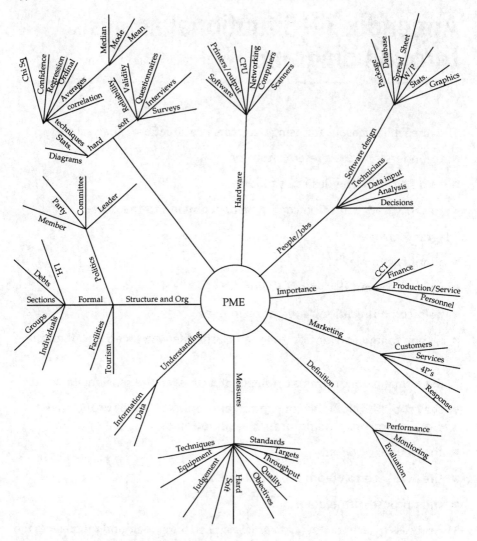

Diagram 3.1 Mindmap linked to PME

2. Input–output diagram. Diagram 3.2 is more formal and represents a
   process that, for example, provides a service or produces a product. The
   process is represented by the central block. The outputs, as tabulated
   arrows, show both desired and less desirable outputs. A holiday service
   may have both satisfied and dissatisfied holidaymakers. When
   constructing such an input–output diagram, it is best to consider
   process and what desired outputs are required. Then the inputs can be
   devised. The process contains all those elements of the system that are

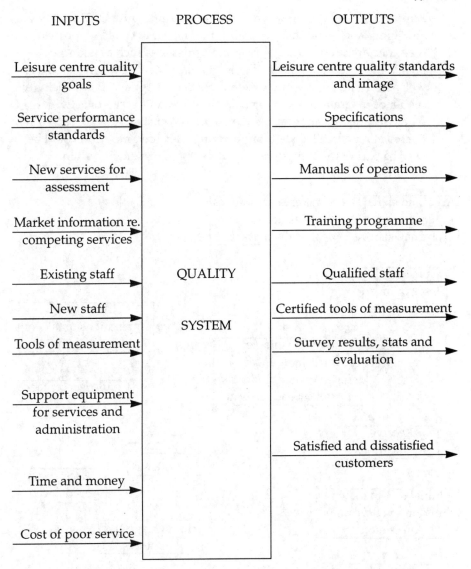

Diagram 3.2 Input–output diagram for a quality system for a leisure centre

not used up in the transitional process like the sport centre itself, equipment, add programmes and administrative equipment that are used over and over again. Diagram 3.2 shows a quality system which could well form part of your PME system.

3. Flow-block, flow-process and activity sequence diagrams. Flow-block diagrams are used to show flows of materials, information or energy. Such a diagram would be suitable for an information system or an

activity such as catering where there is an output product. The blocks are dominated by nouns such as computer, printer etc. Flow-process diagrams are similar but centre around processes such as taking a booking at reception. The blocks are therefore dominated by verbs e.g. welcome visitor, or enquire if help is needed. Diagram 3.3 is an activity sequence diagram. They are usually used to plot a series of activities where technological processes are not involved. The diagram represents the selection of skilled staff for operating a leisure centre and could be used as part of the PME system relative to the personnel system.

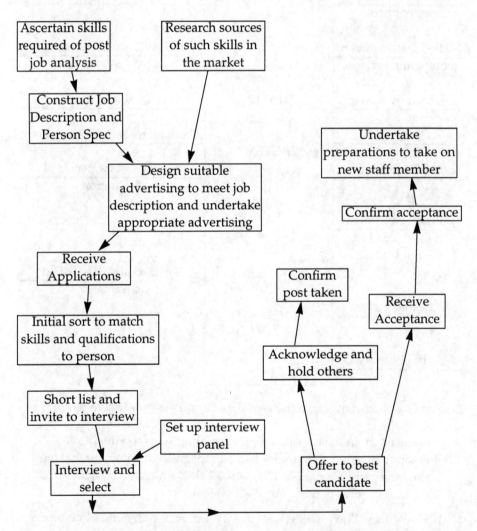

Diagram 3.3 Activity sequence diagram for recruiting skilled recreation personnel to a leisure centre

4. Control-loop diagrams. These are used as control mechanisms and have been illustrated earlier in the text (see Chapter 1, Figures 1.1 and 1.2, p. 5).

5. Relationship diagrams are used where there is no straightforward input–output process and there are different strengths of relationship between parts of an enterprise. Such a diagram helps appreciation of the different components and influences on a problem. Diagram 3.4 shows the beginnings of an information system looked at from the perspective of relationships. Another degree of sophistication might be to code the lines (dotted, width, etc.) to show the strength of the relationships.

6. Systems maps are a step on from relationship diagrams. To develop a systems map from a relationship diagram would require:-
   — the removal of diagram boxes which contain items other than components for example in Diagram 3.4 financial policy.
   — removing the lines which show relationships.
   — inserting boundaries around groups of related components to indicate systems or subsystems. Again looking at Diagram 3.4, the client department and local authority committees would form a subsystem in the provision of the leisure services system.

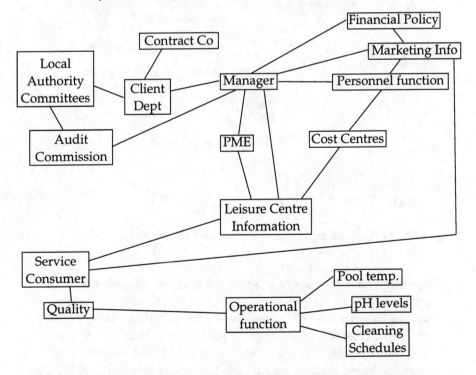

Diagram 3.4 A diagram to show information relationships in a leisure centre

7. Influence diagrams are a development from relationship diagrams and system maps. They seek to clarify the influences that components have on each other. An example can be seen in Diagram 3.5.

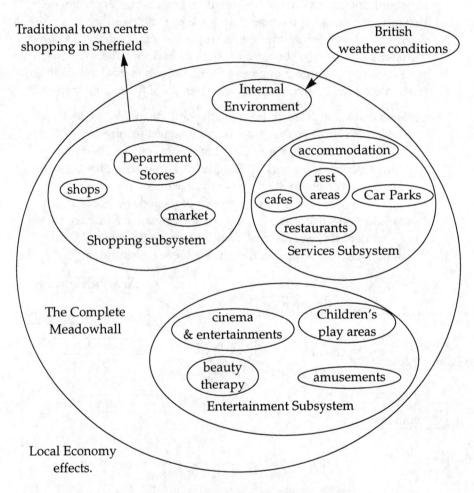

Diagram 3.5 Influence diagram for the Meadowhall Complex

8. Multiple cause diagrams are developed influence diagrams with the addition of words and phrases linked by arrows. Such an example is seen in Diagram 3.6 which is centred around a leisure centre. It may be the case that as part of a change programme of a PME system it is neccessary to look at energy costs with a view to reducing them. It might be found that the finished multiple cause sketch is as in Diagram 3.6.

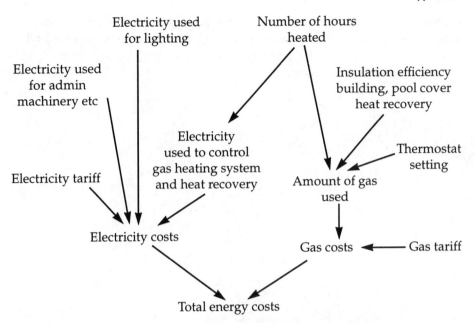

Diagram 3.6 Multiple-Cause diagram for a leisure centre's energy costs

When constructing multiple cause diagrams, the start should be at the outcome i.e. energy costs, and work backwards through the causal factors. Initially it might be considered that the total simply reflects total use, which of course it does, but on consideration it will be seen that electricity and gas consumption are not independent. Electricity is used to control part of gas use. The two subsystems are interdependent and the causes bringing about the total bill are more complicated than initially thought. Such a process could well contribute to the design of a PME subsystem just linked to energy consumption.

A situational commentary

A recent phenomenon in the UK has been the development of multiple retail and outlet complexes such as Meadowhall near Sheffield and the Metro Centre in Gateshead. They have regional significance on the pattern of shoppers and provide a controlled pleasant environment and many support services. Currently the controversy is the impact on town centres because such complexes are land hungry and have resulted in the use of extensive tracts of land, often derelict, on the outskirts of towns. Centres such as Meadowhall are very attractive to customers because there is a wide variety of choice, good quality products, a range of activities which will satisfy the whole range of the family and above all such a visit defeats the vagaries of the British weather. Diagram 3.5 is an initial attempt at showing how the complex has been influenced by conditions.

Appendix 4—The Pugh OD matrix

The Pugh OD matrix has two dimensions, the first is the analytical focus level and the second is the amount of intervention required (*see* Diagram 4.1). The vertical axis is represented by analysis at the levels of:

- individual

- group

- inter-group and

- organisation.

Note that these groupings are not at a level within the organisation but at an analytical focus level. There could therefore be a fear of new technology at all organisational levels from the receptionist right through to the managing director.

The horizontal axis (the columns) indicate the type and degree of intervention that might be required to bring about a necessary change. Moving from left to right the degree of intervention and therefore the impact and resource requirement increase. Changes in the left-hand column may require a training exercise to make employees more comfortable with new technology which might smooth over operational difficulties. A new MIS will relate to the right-hand column and will require major intervention.

Diagram 4.2 is an example of how such a matrix might be completed. The completion of the blocks helps the change manager understand the situation surrounding proposed changes much more fully. There is in addition some consideration of what activities might be undertaken in order to bring about the change effectively.

Degree of required intervention

ANALYTICAL FOCUS LEVEL	BEHAVIOUR What is happening now	STRUCTURE What is the required system	CONTEXT What is the setting
ORGANISATIONAL LEVEL			
possible approaches to solution			
INTER GROUP LEVEL			
possible approaches to solution			
GROUP LEVEL			
possible approaches to solution			
INDIVIDUAL LEVEL			
possible approaches to solution			

Diagram 4.1 The Pugh OD matrix

Degree of required intervention

ANALYTICAL FOCUS LEVEL	BEHAVIOUR What is happening now	STRUCTURE What is the required system	CONTEXT What is the setting
ORGANISATIONAL LEVEL	Uninformed, anxious and suspicious of new MIS. Unaware of internal situation in time to change stance. Never hit targets/ budgets/performance	Poor target & information requirements. Poor equipment. Importance of data not understood. Structure of organisation department and divisions not standardised. Poor external information.	Local authority wide. Series of facilities limited sources of technical expertise and equipment
	Performance evidence survey. *Group discussions*	*Re-configure and define all information needs*	*Re-define information sources at each facility and network.* *Buy in technology and expertise*
INTER GROUP LEVEL	Poor movement of information between departments, accusation of holding on to information; failure to keep to budgets and targets	Divisions independent and not linked by policy or strategy. Facility functions splintered eg. catering, events, programme. Resistant to interaction	Physical distance different centre/ facility ethics
	Inter group confrontation with a third party. *Working group to clarify information shortages.*	*Re-define responsibilities and roles. Change targets to facility wide, develop liaison.*	*Reduce psychological and physical distance, exchange staff and roles, change divisional relationships develop social interaction.*
GROUP LEVEL	Little group feeling relative to information. Unknown targets. Poor understanding for need of performance measures and the need to monitor and evaluate. Poor leadership?	Targets and functions between shifts poorly defined. Poor inter-staff relationships. Poor group supervisory structure. Manager/leader overload.	Poor technical information and equipment. Poor group composition for team spirit. Poor physical set up for data. Personality difficulties
	Training re. PME and importance. *Group development training.*	*Re-design shift patterns and job rotation. Re-define roles and targets. Change targets to reflect whole performance Develop groups*	*Change technology, layout and set up. Re-jig shifts and relationships.*

Diagram 4.2 The Pugh OD matrix as might be applied to installing a new PME/MIS

ANALYTICAL FOCUS LEVEL	**BEHAVIOUR** What is happening now	**STRUCTURE** What is the required system	**CONTEXT** What is the setting
	Training re. PME and importance. Group development training.	*Re-design shift patterns and job rotation. Re-define roles and targets. Change targets to reflect whole performance Develop groups*	*Change technology, layout and set up. Re-jig shifts and relationships.*
INDIVIDUAL LEVEL	Frustration. Little job satisfaction. Resistant to change. Little chance for development. Fear of new technology.	Poor job descriptions. Little job satisfaction. Few targets to attain. Tasks too easy or too difficult.	Poor match of individual with information/data tasks/job. Training. Recognition and reward variance with the few objectives defined.
	Training new technology Career planning Counselling.	*Job and task restructuring/ modification/redesign. Job enrichment/motivator factors.*	*Redeploy existing staff and recruit according to new technology needs. Improve training. Renumeration in line with ability, motivation and targets.*

Diagram 4.2 The Pugh OD matrix as might be applied to installing a new PME/MIS — *continued*

Appendix 5—Working in groups

The nature of groups

Groups are useful mechanisms for developing individuals, gaining their commitment and involvement and solving problems or issues. Primary groups are small with six to eight members whilst secondary groups are larger and may be formed by two or more primary groups. There are formal and informal groups both of which can have power. Formal groups are of the secondary type and demonstrate characteristics such as goals and objectives, criteria for membership, leadership and identified responsibilities for individuals. Informal groups have an unwritten understanding within the group, have informal working arrangements for making decisions or handling disputes. They often become united in the resistance to change. Through membership of a group, the individual can satisfy higher needs as expressed by Maslow in the area of self actualisation, personal development, being proud of the department/unit and esteem through recognition. When change is brought about, the individual may be affected in two main ways:

- the group or organisation is abolished, e.g. dept.

- individuals are made redundant or put on short time.

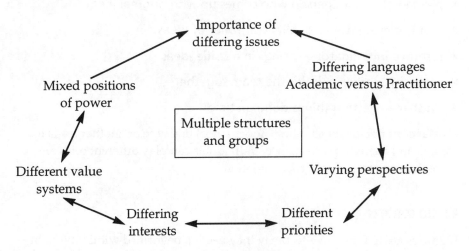

Diagram 5.1 Differences that can bring about group conflict

255

There is a lowering of needs satisfaction and employees withdraw back to safety needs and become defensive. Groups are a tool which can enhance satisfaction of needs and encourage employees to become commited and involved. The composition of groups and the manner in which they are managed can increase the amount of conflict (see Diagram 5.1).

How can the benefits of groups be optimised and the liabilities minimised? There are a number of understandings and processes that can improve group performance. These are briefly listed below.

Group composition

- members need to have the ability to do the job — selection
- there needs to be a leader
- balanced attitudes and values give stability but there is evidence that variety increases productivity
- suspiciousness and aggresiveness should be avoided
- radicalism, adventure and character can increase output.

C. H. Belbin detected eight types of individual role that shaped group performance.

- chairperson — who acts as a co-ordinator
- shaper — motivates people into action
- plant — the quiet person who comes up with original ideas
- monitor/evaluator — quality controller of ideas
- resource investigator — brings in outside ideas
- company worker — holds the team together
- finisher — getting things done on time.

A balance of personalities is best. Too many of one type or another leads to conflict and reduced performance. Individuals can play different roles or more than one role in the group situation.

Group context

If groups are to function effectively they need to be formed within the right context and so the following factors need to be recognised:

- the task or objectives of the group need to be agreed and preferably generated internally — objectives should be realistic and practical

- members of the group with multiple tasks often reflect conflicting roles within the group — wearing more than one hat

- the resources required need to be made available for the groups to perform properly

- the mission for the group needs to be worth accomplishing

- groups need to be the right size for the task and operating as group (6–8 best, 10–12 maximum). Large groups reduce participant interaction and communications become difficult. Best to keep the group smaller and bring in interested parties as neccessary.

Group development

Group development phases

In 1965 Tuckman identified four phases of group development.

1. **Forming** — Establishing formal and informal contracts, agreeing the purpose, group title, composition and life span of the group, establishment of individual identity, leadership patterns emerge.

2. **Storming** — initial consensus challenged by storming/a form of conflict, more realistic agenda, personal agendas are revealed, the situation needs managing and if done well will develop trust between members and informal contracts.

3. **Norming** — the establishment of group norms i.e. fixed notions of work patterns, how decisions are taken, setting ideas of commitment, degrees of openness and trust.

4. **Performing** — if forming, storming and norming are successfully achieved, then the group is able to function meaningfully and sustain a peak of activity. If tasks are changed or new members introduced to the group then the first three stages of the process are repeated.

The first three stages can be quite quick and depends on how the group is set up. If storming is suppressed it is unlikely that the group will ever perform in a mature way and it will often splinter.

Practical action

There are a number of practical steps that can be taken to improve the manner in which groups function including:

- select commited staff
- meet frequently or/and regularly
- share projects and tasks
- have monthly lunches
- identify joint training needs
- train together either through a facilitator or workshops
- develop a common knowledge base.
- undertake periodic group maintenance work.

The above lists are what might be called maintenance activities that surround the problem/change and the working of the group.

There are some other factors that can contribute to group effectiveness which form a closer part of the task, viz:

- reach a consensus on the mission/purpose
- develop priorities
- define objectives to which the group are committed
- role clarification
- periodic reviews and evaluations
- use appropriate problem solving techniques and use external specialist knowledge if neccessary
- exercise leadership
- monitor the power/relations.

Improving group processes

The actual operation of the group and the manner in which individuals can be developed to be more effective require attention. Because the observer in this case will be directly developing individuals, it is particularly important that a sensitive approach be adopted. It is neccessary to observe the group in operation. This can be done in three phases.

Classifying behaviour

- proposing seeking information, summarising/building — actions to meet the need of the group

- encouraging, realignment — action to support the needs of others

- defending/attacking — action to support own needs

- overtalking — action to support own needs

- chatter — action to support own needs.

Observing the flow of information

Have approximately 10 copies of seating positions and arrow in direction of communication, if it is to all, the arrow to the centre of diagram. Change to a clear sheet every two to three minutes.

Observing the satisfaction of personal needs

- how does the group meet problems like fatigue, hunger, discomfort, smoke, seating arrangements, etc?

- how does the group deal with people who are left out or are unsure of themselves, feelings such as anger, socio-emotional support roles, etc?

- are physical and emotional needs dealt with and how; efficiently and unobtrusively or issues of inference made into big issues?

- how does the group react to non-verbal signals — tapping, yawning, looking out of windows, etc?

Such observations give considerable insight into how efficient and effective a group can be in handling its business. The question is, how can its operations become more effective? Nobody has the right to give feedback and everything that is said should be tactful, sensitive and acceptable. Good points should be emphasised and perhaps the suggestion of discussion about collected observations. The observer needs to earn the right to give feedback through the sensitive approach and respect for the contribution. A useful start is to gently suggest, sitting in a single circle, using a flip chart and recording action notes.

As mutual confidence and respect is gained the suggestions might be stronger e.g. wouldn't it be a good idea to have a special time slot for important agenda items, or prepare a meeting time budget. At a later stage there could be formal discussion about the process of meetings and how they could be improved. The information observed could be formally recorded and feedback based on the records of observation and description. Judgements by the observer should be avoided and the context and evidence the basis for discussion and change.

It is interesting to note that this form of increasing the effectiveness of group operations has devised its own performance, monitoring and evaluation system. Group members if they have gone through the four phases of development should have 'grown' as individuals and be more able to make valuable contributions to group problem solving.

Leadership

Leadership may not be designated and might pass from member to member at an appropriate juncture or point in time. Formal groups are much more likely to have a leader in an official sense like a change manager. The role of the leader is crucial to the effective functioning of the group and this is irrespective of style, e.g. authoritative to parcipitative. The role of the leader should seek to integrate the group around the task, looking for creative ways to give satisfaction through goal achievement.

The role of leadership may differ according to the group. Inexperienced groups will need a gentler, paternal approach whilst an experienced group will need a formal leadership role. Leaders should undertake the following tasks:

- direct subordinates to devise group goals and establish action plans to attain their goals
- look for feedback from outside the group to find out how good their performance is
- ensure that the group remains sufficiently satisfied to carry on their work
- defend the group from outside attack
- review better ways of achieving goals
- develop the group — team comradeship, worthwhileness, pride, etc.
- encourage approval and support from sponsor/senior management.

In order to perform these activities it is necessary that leaders of groups develop certain skills viz:

- when to suggest the use of particular techniques either to improve the development of the group's effectiveness or in search of attaining goals

- when to abandon the formal framework and become informal
- when to use or stop using well known in-house methods known to group members
- when to suppress discussion and move a debate forward
- when to introduce pauses and rests
- to manage the leadership role effectively as chairperson.

Ancillary factors

Hidden agendas

It is not unusual for individuals within groups to have their own agendas which run contrary to group goals. These can be of a macro or micro nature. There may be some political aim, for example, influencing the type of hardware to be purchased for a PME system or at a minor level to impress the boss or embarrass a colleague. Hidden agendas can be avoided by establishing strong contracts of trust and common tasks and these may need renegotiating if hidden agendas are exposed. Recruitment of the right committed employees is another way of avoiding hidden agendas.

Too much consensus

This can lead to complacency and an illusion of invulnerability. A number of symptoms may arise in the behaviour of the group such as efforts to rationalise and avoid warnings, direct pressure on those taking an opposite view, self censorship or protecting the group from adverse information.

Stress

Stress can be associated with groups and personnel introducing change. Group members tend to be working at the leading edge where risk and uncertainty is greater than in the routine of the business. The dynamics of change can over-motivate and involve group members. The leader should be aware of this danger and ensure settling down phases between changes so that activity is not too intense. Stress is also discussed in Chapter 9 under Welfare.

Appendix 6—Interviewing for information

Introduction

There are many types of interviewing, for a job, counselling, disciplinary, etc. Each has its own approach. Interviewing for informtion is usually conducted on a one-to-one basis where the interviewer wishes to explore situations and questions are asked in response to what the interviewee says — not the structured questionnaire approach.

The need for interviews

When diagnosing a situation ready for change or solving a problem start by gathering information in the form of job descriptions, past data and information files, hardware details, diagrams, etc. There is a need to find out about the softer, qualitative factors e.g. relationships, informal networks, morale and opinions on data collection. Interviews of this nature are closer to qualitative market research or counselling interviewing. The approach requires less formality, a comfortable approach to asking personal questions, and being encouraging and sympathetic. The interviewer should be neutral.

Preparations

Early preparation is required and should cover the following:

- decide on the information required to study the problem
- identify and locate written information
- decide on what information can be gained from interviews either to supplement written material or altogether new
- identify the people who should be interviewed
- prepare the background material for the interview e.g. background to the person

- focus on the topics that you really want information about. There may be too broad a remit and prioritisation will be necessary.

Making contact

This stage involves

- identify interviewee
- get agreement to take part
  - explain about the investigation
  - what information is required and
  - how the interviewee can help,
- get the agreement of interviewee's superior and trade union if necessary.
- agree a time and place to hold the interview which should be in private.

Recording

There are two broad approaches:

- tape recording
- note taking.

Tape recorders record everything, which is a great advantage, but can inhibit respondents and might have a fault and fail to record. The other disadvantage is that they take additional time to transcribe and organise into useful blocks of information. Note taking is not so complete but it is possible to categorise information under key headings with key words and comments during the interview. It takes less time to write up the notes in a useful format. It is unethical to tape record someone without their agreement. Always check that you have the right equipment for each interview:

- name of interviewee and time and place
- key discussion items
- note pad for notes

- pen/pencil
- tape recorder and spare batteries and tapes
- wristwatch.

Interview in action

In depth interviews are complicated and the interviewer has the difficult balance of making the interviewee comfortable and willing, yet covering the interview content and in a reasonable time. The interview should go through certain stages.

1. Opening the interview — summary of purpose, make them feel at home, issues of confidentiality, gaining trust.
2. Opening the way — start with straightforward requests for information — gives you clues about the interviewee e.g. how they respond or do they keep to the topic. Try to use something the interviewee says as a 'hook' to introduce the next question.
3. Interview development — interviews are unlikely to stay in checklist order and the interviewer will have to keep a record of topics covered and side issues that are raised. Interviews tend to develop a logical progression of their own. When the interviewer wishes to move the topic should be summarised so far and then factual questions asked about the next topic on the agenda. Questions concerning the interviewee's feelings can be uncomfortable and a sensitive approach is necessary like 'What sort of words would you use to describe your feelings?'
4. Completing interviews — it is best to signal the end of an interview by 'and lastly would you. . .'. It is also a good idea to give the interviewee the opportunity to add any comments if they wish. The interviewee should feel good at the end of the interview.

Controlling the interview

Control relies very much on the skill and experience of the interviewer. Particular attention needs to be paid to the following:

- wording the questions properly — this relates to good preparation of topics and practice. Key words are who, why, when, where, what and how

- using silence — don't be frightened of time when nothing is said. Thinking time is valuable.
- Probing and prompting — don't ask leading or biased questions, rephrase questions if necessary.
- Body language — nodding, looking interested.
- Keeping track of the time.
- Arrange a second interview if necessary.

Dealing with the information

In reality there are two packets of information. The first and primary one is the recording or notes gathered from the interview. The other, if taped, is your own performance which can be analysed in terms of personal development. The analysis of the information gathered from the interview should be on the basis of the check list of topic that was constructed in preparing for the interview. These might have been based on Systems Intervention Strategy approach, in which case the topics will approximate to the process. An organisational development approach would more likely use the Pugh Matrix content. If a series of interviews are to be carried out with a common checklist of topics, a matrix of opinions can be established with topics down the left hand axis and interviewee responses along the horizontal axis. This makes it possible to assess strength of opinion which can be most helpful when constructing a solution to the change/solution implementation.

Appendix 7—Factors affecting selection of pay and reward system

There are three broad initial factors to consider:

- structure and organisation of the business
- managerial style and philosophy
- industrial relations climate.

1. Structure and organisation and style of business:

   - Is company policy centralised or decentralised ie. local bargaining?
   - Geographical location and resultant custom and practice
   - Highly structured business v the fluid flexible business
   - Is the business: authoritarian, paternalistic, consultative or participative?
   - Business objectives — fulfil market requirements rather than keep down costs or/and recruit and retain workers or contracted workers.

2. Industrial relations factors:

   - What are general trade union views?
   - Historical perspective e.g. tradition, length of agreements etc
   - Effectiveness of current system/scheme
   - Degree of management control.

3. Technical factors
   In terms of technical factors, each scheme is unique because of the particular situation and the local needs. It is more to do with management than the application of theoretical process. It is important to consider the amount of worker effort and the accountability required.

   Effect and accountability:
   - Type of effort — competence, energy, standards , time, pay per hour.
   - Limit of accountability — individual, group (fewer than 20) or unit where individual or group inputs cannot be differentiated (e.g. a sports centre).

One should also consider the technical dimensions — length of job/task cycles, numbers of job/task modifications, degree of automation, changes of service, task stoppages (shortage of materials, components, machinery, weather, absence, instruction etc), wastage, travel.

4. Labour market dimensions.

   - Time required to fill vacancies.

   - Labour stability and employee retention.

   - Labour turnover — number of leavers as a percentage of average number employed.

   - Knowledge skill requirements.

   - Local, regional or national recruitment.

5. Disputes and procedures.

   - Disputes about pay — frequency

   - Duration of disputes.

6. Employee characteristics and dimensions.

   - Percentage of pay determined outside work unit rate and so not negotiated.

   - Number of trade unions — whole company, several, none.

   - Occupational structure — number of grades etc.

   - Absenteeism — numbers, reasons, lateness, lay offs etc.

   - Average age of workforce 15–29, 30–44, 45+.

   - Direct labour costs i.e. costs per unit of service of product.

   - Percentage of male and female employees.

7. Factors affecting measured day work (MDW) (*see* Chapter 10).

   - Don't want large fluctuations in output.

   - Consistent output required (quantity and quality).

   - Output largely machine or process driven.

   - Operations closely linked to teamwork requiring labour flexibility.

   - Low material wastage.

   - Management wishes to control output flow.

   - Management wishes to control earnings.

8. Factors affecting payment by results (PBR) (*see* Chapter 10).

   - A steady output does not matter.

   - Short task cycles and controlled by individual or small groups.

   - High manual content.

   - Measurable work.

   - Management should be capable of effective control of work flow.

   - Method of work not subject to frequent change — materials, processes etc.

   - When working in groups individuals should have similar tasks.

9. Pay scheme failure systems.
   It is senior management's responsibility to operate and monitor pay schemes and ensure they are appropriate for the situation. To this end they should carry out regular audits. Formal pay reviews should be held at least every three years. There are three main factors that might bring about a requirement for pay structure change:

   - changes in technology

   - employee learning and improvement curves

   - setting new standards.

There are a number of symptoms that might become apparent to indicate that a payment/reward system was running into difficulty. These might be:

   - proliferation of special allowances

   - disparity of earnings between employees

   - supervisors are reluctant to take any action that might upset earnings or bonuses

   - inconsistency in the measurement systems

   - fiddles — slack time, hiding products, incorrect time records, cross bookings, etc.

   - loss of managerial control of work allocation

   - managerial relaxation of standards

   - limiting output below a reasonable potential

   - individuals setting their own earning goals.

Appendix 8—Training and development

Training and development may be defined as:

'forms of activity aimed at the improvement of the human capital within an organisation'

Is training and development a cost, an investment and in who's view — employer, employee or government?

- employer — improve the performance of the workforce
- employee — increase pay for better skills.

The main advantages of Training and Development are seen to be:

- helps employees learn jobs more quickly and effectively
- improves work performance of existing employees and keeps them up to date in specialist skills
- leads to greater volume of work resulting from fewer mistakes — and greater rapidity
- frees management time, less of which is spent rectifying errors: also reduces wastage
- can help to reduce labour turnover among new and established staff
- can help to reduce redundancy and recruitment costs, through retraining
- incorporating safety training can help reduce accidents
- can help attract good workers
- is a precondition for flexible working
- creates an attitude more receptive to coping with change.

A report in 1989 by the CBI which examined 40 businesses implied that failure to adopt a training and development perspective reflected:

- a failure to recognise or implement management practices designed to meet, not only existing, but future skills needs

- an unrealistic reliance by managers upon national and local labour markets to satisfy company skills needs at whatever level

- a willingness to regard the practice of poaching the skilled labour of others as the chief response to skill pressures, regardless of the consequences at company level and in pay inflation terms.

Training in an organisation is vital because:

- it needs to be an integral part of the business core strategy

- historically, UK had a poor record of training (see Handy, Constable and McCormick, 1987).

- UK Ltd is not clear where the responsibility for training lies. In Japan, education is general and vocational (job/career) training is focused on the business. In UK, the businesses see training as a cost rather than an investment and would prefer to see the education system take up the costs. Currently the responsibilities are still unclear with the NVQ system being driven by both education and industry. Degree courses were being driven by vocational sector interests

- there is a continuing debate about training and education

- training should not only be instrumental but should also be an employee motivator

- training should be part of the culture of an organisation i.e., it should not be reactive but proactive; it should not be triggered by external competence factors

- pay should be related to the acquisition of skills and the successful completion of training linked to progression through the business

- all personnel should have access to training

- training should be interlinked with the appraisal and development system

- current training is fragmented because of the hierarchical structure from shop floor to management. The context that is missing from UK training is, corporate culture, working environmental climate, organisational structure, management styles, career patterns and individual learning abilities

- appropriate resources and funding should be made available for training

- training should be incorporated into a TQM system.

Training and development

Broadly, there are two main approaches neither of which are mutually exclusive:

- The individual's personal career which focuses on monitoring by management of job support and self development initiatives

- development of the employee within social groups which focus on such activities as action learning and outdoor training.

The training process

Like any other business activity, training has to be managed and operated. In a strategic sense it is necessary to:

- outline the strategic organisational objectives

- identify the organisation's major activities

- set the standards for individual tasks

- set training objectives relative to organisational objectives, activities and tasks.

Regular training needs' audits should take place. One of the ways of approaching a training needs analysis might be to use the accompanying evaluation grid in Diagram 8.1.

REFERENCES AND FURTHER READING

Badmin P. A. (1993) *Leisure Operational Management: People*, vol. 2, 2nd ed, Longman

Goss, D. *Principles of Human Resource Management*, Routledge

Handy, Constable and McCormick (1987) *The Making of the British Managers*, BIM/CBI 1987

Priorities for evaluation	Data information sources	Methodology of data/information collection	Concepts	Timescale
Awareness of Corporate change in strategy, e.g. introduction TMQ	Line managing of all facilities	Telephone survey Agenda item Regular visits	Awareness measures	Within four weeks of activating the strategy
Evidence of as a result of Management training course	Trainees and line managers	Self administered rating scale Line managers reports	Behaviourally anchored rating scale (BAR) dimensions and items	One month after course completion
Effects of HASAW training	Personal records	Statistical analysis of records	Performance measures	Four to six weeks after event
Cost benefit analysis for facility of customer care training for receptionists	Cost data Benefit data	Secondary analysis of data. Performance observation	C/B measures customer satisfaction. Secondary sales, repeat bookings, etc.	One month after training

Diagram 8.1 Training/development evaluation table

Appendix 9—MIS manager of an operational unit

Source	Decision area	Reason	Information	Speed	
				Commercial	L.Govt.
Meters (H)			Routine collection from:	Next a.m.	Daily
Pay slips (H)			— services		
Job slips/invoices (H)	FINANCIAL	Targets — income	— staff	Weekly	Weekly
Tills (H)	BY COST CENTRES	Targets — expenditure	— maintenance	Monthly	Monthly
Booking sheets (H)	AND GLOBAL		— catering, bars,	Annual	Annual
Stock control (H)			— product sales		
Receipt shop special events (H)			— supportive products		
			— costs by centre		
Perhaps specialised					
counts and routines (H)	SOCIAL OBJECTIVES	Political justification	Routine or special	Long term	Geared to
e.g. count mid activity (H)		e.g. no unemployed,	counts	although can	Committee
Reception desk records (H)		deprived, handicapped,	Users by activity type/	happen quickly	Meetings say
Surveys & Research (SH)		OAP etc.	time etc		bi-monthly
Note: Very little done in this			Income by cost centre		
area, neglected		Commercial image			
ILAM Indicators		specifications			
Interviews (SH)					
Complaints book (H)	STAFFING	Scarce/Expensive	Staff satisfaction	Annual	As above
Customer discussions (S)		Resource	Customer satisfaction	Constant	
Pay slips (H)					
Staff turnover (H)			Budgets	Monthly	

contd . . .

Main Purpose: Efficient operation of facility
H = Hard data/information
S = Soft data/information

Appendix 9 contd.

Source	Decision area	Reason	Information	Speed	Speed
Interviews (S) Surveys (SH) Complaints book (H) Informal discussions (S) Scanning local information New fashion trends competitors etc. (S) Suggestion box (SH) Attendances — classes, beds, special events Bookings etc. (H)	CUSTOMER SATISFACTION	Defining new products / Experiences / target markets / opportunities Support of present customer loyalty Specifications	Attendance Verbal and written evidence		on going with periodic revues
Safety records (H) Accident book (H) Facility routine Report procedure (H) Material expenditure budget (H)	MAINTENANCE/SAFETY	Attraction and standard of facility Safety and efficiency Specifications	Routine recorded procedures e.g. — safety checks e.g. — fire drills e.g. — inspections Use of materials	Immediate Weekly Monthly Annual Rapid and long term	Immediate Weekly Monthly Annual Rapid and long term
Reports and routine procedures both written / automated and verbal Longer term analysis of data One off monitoring systems	OPERATIONAL EFFICIENCY	Standards/Specifications	Information system both verbal and written	Rapid and long term	Rapid and long term

H = Hard data/information
S = Soft data/information

Appendix 10—Introducing new technology

Enid Mumford of the Management Business School wrote about 'Effective Technical and Human Implementation of Computer Based Systems' (ETHICS). If this is matched (see Diagram 10.1 below) against the SIS approach, there is little difference.

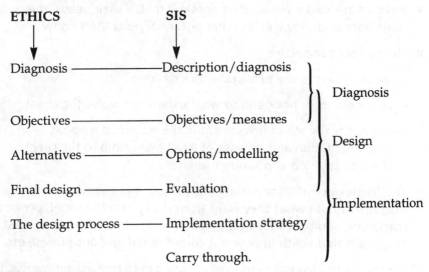

Diagram 10.1

Mumford recommends a highly participative approach by purchasing organisations which reflects the organisational development focus, but it is probably recommended as a good marketing tool.

Recommending an approach

Early identification of user needs and of the potential for the product (computer system) to fulfil those needs is required. The following will help:

- Clarify in detail the requirements of the client — do they want a booking system, an integrated system, a network or a management information system? The needs of each are very different and the less sophisticated clients will be confused.

275

- Clarify the types of users e.g.,

  — Top managers will want managerial information upon which to make decisions; for instance rate of return, pay back, effect on the bottom line, ratios etc.

  — High tech users need to develop ownership of the system especially its capacity and shortcomings and how existing applications can be transferred and enhanced to the new. It will be hardware and software driven.

- Consider what clients may wish in the future from the system.

- If clients are sold a system that does not match their needs, they won't come back and they will let other potential purchasers know.

- The market perspective.

  — involve users in the product/service design

  — consider when, how, and to what extent to involve the client

  — it is not really about investment in the system, it is about implementation and transfer of 'real' ownership to the client through training and support services.

- The framework of information. The project manager must talk to all managers about what they want from the system (financial, personnel, marketing and operations etc.) what information, who has it, what do they want to do with it, how is it co-ordinated and out-putted, etc.

The user organisation will need to be prepared to receive the innovation. This can be achieved through a pilot study and involve the users. Maybe a division or a single facility. The advantages are:

- it can be done as an experiment and can add considerable background information

- it tests the technical feasibility

- it provides a credible demonstration for the more sceptical.

Points to watch:

- are you clear about the purpose of the experiment?

- select the site/department very carefully, it does not want to be too difficult and success or failure will influence decisions later

- are you omitting those most resisting change?

- involve the leaders and decision makers
- demystify technology
- avoid extremes of view/commitment.

Ownership has to move from supplier to user:

- implementation team must have a powerful sponsor who has the necessary authority to make decisions
- there should be only one co-ordinator
- there should be only one responsible client manager to link the innovation/project i.e., single communications authority
- the criteria for success needs to be matched if the innovation is to remain credible
- be a diplomat, problem solver, give the right signals and credible messages
- phase the innovation to develop a new working behaviour, don't overstress the client and enable and encourage feedback
- service the customer until they have ownership

An agency providing advice and services to a number of tourist outlets, introduced computerised systems to their county wide offices to help operate the business, provide a data base and support their outworkers. The comments for and against the change before, during and after were:

For:

- improve credibility of the business
- accuracy of data for clients
- accuracy of data about clients
- more elaborate and detailed information
- facilitated easier record keeping
- all sources of information available in one place (workstation)
- could prepare standard reports and forms
- clerical staff word processing
- know what information is available
- staff performance more effective

- mail shots
- the spread sheet facilities for budgets and cashflows etc.
- required less space than the previous manual systems
- can aggregate and disaggregate data, budgets, mail shots etc.

Against:

- very apprehensive about new technology
- difficulty of getting the information from the outworkers and in-putting data
- the pressure to keep files/data bank up to date
- little flexibility in the system — standardisation
- the need by outworkers for access to workstations which are always all in use.

Appendix 11—Turnarounds

Turnarounds are a 'Big Bang' approach to change and used for speedy actions associated with bankruptcies and financial collapses. Speed is of the essence. Expected progression would be as follows.

1. Gain financial management control — e.g. external turnaround manager legalised.

    (i) Develop cash flow forecasts — cash control very important.
    (ii) Centralise cash control — very important.
    (iii) Expenditure controls over capital and revenue — important; has an attitude impact as well as control factors.
    (iv) Inventory control — especially high value items.
    (v) Debtor control — age analysis, review of credit policy, short term cash flow.
    (vi) Improve security where control is lax — losses of materials, assets etc.

2. Establish and communicate credibility with stakeholders — public relations exercise with banks, suppliers, customers and employees.

3. Assess existing managers and replace if necessary (often quick at senior level). The management structure will need to implement a new start. At British Leyland, Michael Edwards reduced the directors from 30 to six in the first afternoon.

4. Evaluate the business and identify issues essential to survival — a quick exercise.

5. Decide action plan — focus on the small number of issues that give the greatest benefit.

6. Implement organisational change if necessary — where there are structural changes e.g. divisionalisation or decentralisation, communicate the benefits to the employees.

7. Motivate managers and employees for change — communicate at all levels to facilitate a new culture/ethic, if necessary.

8. Installation or improvement of a new budgetary system with simple straight forward budgets and variances — there is not full control until it is in place.

It is essential that there is swift implementation of control strategies required for turnaround. Simultaneously there should be cost reductions , asset reductions and revenue generation. After the immediate emergency action more time can be taken in planning and actioning a more rational approach.

Index

Index